Lecture Notes in Computer Science 1251

Edited by G. Goos, J. Hartmanis and J. van Leeuwen

Advisory Board: W. Brauer   D. Gries   J. Stoer

Springer

Berlin
Heidelberg
New York
Barcelona
Budapest
Hong Kong
London
Milan
Paris
Santa Clara
Singapore
Tokyo

Keith Hardy   Jim Briggs   (Eds.)

Reliable
Software Technologies –
Ada-Europe '97

1997 Ada-Europe International Conference
on Reliable Software Technologies
London, UK, June 2-6, 1997
Proceedings

 Springer

Series Editors

Gerhard Goos, Karlsruhe University, Germany

Juris Hartmanis, Cornell University, NY, USA

Jan van Leeuwen, Utrecht University, The Netherlands

Volume Editors

Keith Hardy
Ultra Electronics Command & Control Systems Knaves Beech Business Centre
Loudwater, High Wycombe, Buckinghamshire HP10 9UT, U.K.
E-mail: khardy@ueccs.co.uk

Jim Briggs
University of Portsmouth, Department of Information Science
Locksway Road, Southsea, Honts. PO4 8JF, UK
E-mail: briggsjs@sis.port.ac.uk

Cataloging-in-Publication data applied for

Die Deutsche Bibliothek - CIP-Einheitsaufnahme

Reliable software technologies : proceedings / Ada Europe '97, 1997 Ada Europe
International Conference on Reliable Software Technologies, London, UK, June 2
- 6, 1997. Keith Hardy ; Jim Briggs (ed.). - Berlin ; Heidelberg ; New York ;
Barcelona ; Budapest ; Hong Kong ; London ; Milan ; Paris ; Santa Clara ;
Singapore ; Tokyo : Springer, 1997
  (Lecture notes in computer science ; Vol. 1251)
  ISBN 3-540-63114-3

CR Subject Classification (1991): D.2, D.1.2-5, D.3, D.4, C.2.4, C.3, K.6

ISSN 0302-9743
ISBN 3-540-63114-3 Springer-Verlag Berlin Heidelberg New York

© Springer-Verlag Berlin Heidelberg 1997
Printed in Germany

Typesetting: Camera-ready by author
SPIN 10549909   06/3142 – 5 4 3 2 1 0   Printed on acid-free paper

Preface

Reliable software is a topic which now embraces not just safety-critical applications, but also those that are mission-critical or environment-critical. As the processing power of microprocessors continues to increase relative to price, the opportunities also increase to use software in situations where it was previously not financially viable. As a result, the impact and risk to the community through software technology rises at an alarming rate. Software developers have a duty therefore to ensure that every reasonable effort is made to provide reliable solutions for the community and surrounding environment.

The papers presented at Ada-Europe'97 offer different, but valuable, approaches to the development of reliable software. At the top end of the criticality scale, the need for specialist tools for safety-critical software is discussed in a number of papers, such as Thornley's paper on experiences with the use of SPARK and Dobbing's paper on the task-safe minimal Ada real-time toolset. These are supported by papers addressing the analysis of such systems, such as one on performance requirements by Pierce et al. For those interested in other approaches to verification there are a number of contributions discussing the special needs of testing reliable systems in a quantifiable manner, such as Wegener's paper on systematic unit testing, and Bell's on an analysis toolset - one of three papers from the Hughes Canadian Automatic Air Traffic Control System (CAATS) project.

It is a difficult time for the Ada community. Although the language definition has completed its transition to the new standard for Ada 95, industry compilers and toolsets for this standard are only just starting to become available. These new tools, although not as immature as the early Ada 83 tools, cannot be expected to be stable and many only contain a limited subset of the Ada 95 language features, with fully-featured compilers not expected until next year when the new validation suite is available. This has not stopped a number of projects exploring the new features of the language, particularly through the GNAT compiler, to gain early exposure and much needed experience with the new features of the language. These projects include the SPIF project described by Dupouy et al, the sort race construction set from Feldman, and using Ada 95 as a basis for the architecture of systems by Ögren. Additionally, work has already been carried out on some of the new features of the language that may present new problems, as demonstrated by the papers from Wellings, Burns & Pazy on task termination, Holzmüller & Plödereder on finite unions, and Gellerich and Plödereder on parameter-induced aliasing.

Ada 95 offers the opportunity to take advantage of more of the object-oriented concepts, however. English highlights some of the potential pitfalls of using inheritance. Two papers discuss other OO aspects, such as the integration of syntactic constructs and structural features for formalised object-oriented methods (Cheung, Chow & Cheung) and the use of Jackson System Design for high integrity Ada software by Yeung. Waterman discusses some of the techniques required for testing some of the new features of the language.

Another new feature of Ada 95 is the way it addresses performance and scheduling constraints. These aspects have been picked up by papers from Gonzalez Harbour, Gutierrez Garcia & Palencia Gutierrez on implementing application-level sporadic server schedulers and Romanovsky, Mitchell & Wellings on programming atomic actions.

Although there may not be many Ada 95 projects available to discuss at this stage, there are some interesting Ada 83 projects, none more so than the CCO MARS 96 project. Pichon describes how it integrated HOOD, Ada and XInAda technologies. Two more contributions, on code-data consistency (Célier) and developing scripting capabilities for simulators (Jovanovic, Sotirovski & Van Aswegen), refer to the CAATS project.

Although it has not been possible to mention all the papers, we have given a flavour of the content of these proceedings. These are exciting times for the reliable software community as we continue to encounter and rise to new challenges - not just from the arrival of Ada 95, but from a constant change in the technology available in terms of tools, methods and techniques, and in the increased complexity and scope of the real world problems we are required to solve. We hope you agree that this conference has gone some way to addressing these.

Jim Briggs & Keith Hardy
May 1997

Table of Contents

Finite Unions for Ada 95

Bernd Holzmüller, Erhard Plödereder

Department of Computer Science
University of Stuttgart,
D-70565 Stuttgart, Germany
email: {holzmuel,ploedere}@informatik.uni-stuttgart.de
phone: +49 (711) 7816.375 - fax: +49 (711) 7816.380

Abstract: In a recent project the Ada language turned out to be not as flexible as we expected it to be. This forced us to model our application in a way that was less elegant, less maintainable and less efficient. In this paper we propose to add a language construct to the language that would enable us to do what we were missing. The extension is based on finite unions with dispatching and can quite easily be integrated into the language and efficiently implemented.

Keywords: Language Extension, Polymorphism, Finite Unions, Dispatching, Multi-Methods

1 Introduction

In a recent project of our department we adapted a compiler generation toolkit that produced Ada 83 code to the new Ada 95 standard. Because abstract syntax trees are a really good candidate to use object-oriented mechanisms like inheritance, polymorphism, and dispatch, we chose to rewrite the tools to take advantage of these new features of Ada. During the process of adaptation, we recognized that the Ada language would not allow us to do several things we would have liked to do and forced us to do things we did not want to do. One main problem was that we had not been able to define dispatching operations externally, that is, within a different package as the package the controlling type is defined in. A second, minor problem was the lack of a general mechanism to enable polymorphism over access types in Ada which necessitates many extra conversions in assignments. This paper investigates solutions to these problems and proposes an extension to Ada based on finite unions with dispatching that is very flexible, easy to understand, and efficiently implementable.

The contents of this paper are as follows: the next section will briefly discuss the problems we encountered when adapting the toolkit to produce Ada 95 code and present some possible solutions. Then, in section 3, we will propose a language extension based on finite unions that will be shown to not have the problems as class-wide polymorphism has and additionally allows some other flexibilities like multi-methods. An implementation model for finite unions is also given in that section. Finally, we compare finite unions with the concept of final classes as adopted by, e.g., the Java language, before we summarize in section 4.

2 Problems with Adapting a Compiler Generation Toolkit to Ada 95

The compiler generation toolkit *Cocktail* [10] developed by the "Gesellschaft für Mathematik und Datenverarbeitung (GMD)" consists of several tools supporting the generation of scanners, parsers, abstract syntax trees, tree evaluators and transformers. For each of these tasks, one or more separate high level specifications may be given. The tools are designed such that each specification of new tree attributes is integrated into one single tree description (the package `Tree`) but each evaluator specification results in a separate package. Further, tree transformers and evaluators may be specified using the *puma* tool, which is based on pattern matching on tree nodes. Each puma file also generates a new Ada package. For a more detailed description of this project and the tools, refer to [3].

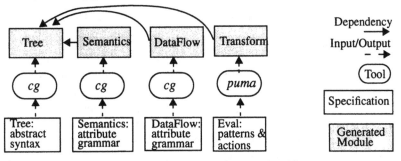

Fig. 1. Overview over the Cocktail-generated architecture

The approach followed by these tools has one important drawback when Ada 95 is used as target language: even though dispatching seems to be the appropriate solution to implement tree evaluator or transformer operations, this is not possible for the architecture given because Ada requires such operations to be declared in the same package as the controlling type. For example, an `Eval` routine in the package `Semantics`, generated from an attribute evaluator specification, is forced to explicitly discriminate over the type (tag) of the current argument via nested if-statements—case-statements cannot be used because 'Tag' is not a discrete type—which is clearly less efficient than using dispatching and less maintainable in case of hand-written code additions. If dispatching is to be used, Ada requires the `Eval` subprogram to be defined within the `Tree` package. There are three general approaches to this problem. First, we could adopt a different kind of architecture for the system. Second, we could try to work around this problem using the rich typing facilities of the Ada language. Third, a language extension could be proposed. We will consider each of these possibilities in the following subsections.

2.1 Approach 1: Architectural Changes

From the above considerations, the most obvious solution to the problem is to rewrite the toolkit such that for each given attribute and evaluation specification the tool would integrate these specifications in a way that appropriate operations are defined in the generated `Tree` package and thus would be made dispatching operations. The revised architecture is shown in figure 2.

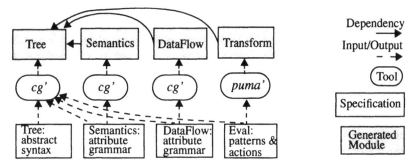

Fig. 2. Alternative architecture to support 'external' dispatching operations

There are two main problems with this approach. Firstly, the `Tree` package is getting quite large, needing a huge amount of recompilation time for `Tree` in case of each small change in one of the specifications. This problem could be somewhat moderated in placing the 'real' implementations in the packages corresponding to the specifications, i.e., `Semantics`, `DataFlow`, etc., and letting the implementation within `Tree` just call this implementation. The second, more important problem is that each addition of a dispatching operation in one of the specifications results in global recompilation. Generating one package per node type could avoid some dependencies and thus part of the recompilation. However, this approach has the problem of circular dependencies between package specifications and still seems to be too inefficient.

2.2 Approach 2: Using Ada's Rich Typing Facilities

The original variant record approach to model abstract syntax trees had the problem of name collisions which required for each kind of node to a) define a corresponding type and b) declare one component in the variant record of that type. This approach needs a twofold indirection for each component access and is a maintenance nightmare regarding hand-written code. We could follow a hybrid model using discriminated tagged types which would allow us to define a partition of the (leaves of the) syntax tree, each part represented by a discriminated tagged type that is itself derived from a more abstract type. A straightforward partitioning of the syntax tree would, for example, define one part for each of the major syntactic categories like expressions, statements, and declarations. Then—following the alternative architecture from the previous section—dispatching is only over these major categories, further reducing the size of the `Tree` package. However, the use of variant records still has the problems of name collisions and hard to maintain case-statements, and additions of dispatching subprograms still require global recompilation.

Nothing has been gained concerning our initial problem: to be able to add a dispatching operation to an existing set of types. Essentially, the problem is due to the open nature of polymorphism together with the requirement of local type checking in Ada. Both are mutually excluding properties that obviously cannot be achieved together.

Because of this discrepancy between openness and locality, no other possibility to solve this problem seems to exist within the current language definition than to use finite polymorphism through variant records and forgo dispatching altogether. Thus, we start to take language extensions into consideration.

2.3 Approach 3: Language Extension

A quite obvious modification of the language semantics would be to allow the definition of dispatching subprograms in packages other than the type of the controlling parameter. This generalization would have to face at least two severe problems:

1. The set of dispatching operations is no longer locally determined. Thus, the size and content of the dispatch vector cannot be determined at compile time but has to be determined at link time.

2. There are additional requirements concerning visibility between packages that have to be checked at link time to enable local (compile-time) checking of dispatching subprogram calls.

These requirements and their implementation are discussed in detail in [14] for object-oriented languages in general. The implications for the language are rather heavy, so that we refrain from considering this extension for the Ada language. The next section shows how a much simpler language extension will be sufficient to handle our problem as well as several others.

3 Finite Unions

The idea of finite unions goes back to Algol 68: a variable may be declared to be of a union type, i.e., it may denote any value from the discriminated union of all types contained in the union. Such variables are polymorphic in a more restricted form as the open form of polymorphism supported by today's object-oriented languages. Nevertheless, this form of polymorphism can be quite useful for a number of reasons:

1. to gain flexibility as will be shown in the following discussions,
2. to improve program understandability because flow of control is limited to a finite number of branches [17],
3. to prevent that the set of types (and thus the set of dispatching subprograms) is being extended later, as might be desired for security reasons, and
4. to enable more polymorphic calls to be statically bound without global program analysis and thus to improve efficiency.

The definition of finite unions allows a trade-off between extensibility on one side and the software qualities for an application given by points 1-4 on the other side. However, there are applications where the set of types over which polymorphism is desired is already known at compile-time, so that extensibility is not needed. An important category thereof is the use of program generators as is the case in our project. The generated code defines a set of types according to some definitions in an underlying set of more abstract specifications. However, this set of types is not intended to be extended directly, i.e., without changes in the specifications and regeneration of the code, and thus can be modeled using finite polymorphism.

3.1 Finite Unions with Dispatching

A problem with the finite union approach in Algol 68 is the requirement to explicitly query the type or 'tag' of the current object in a (type-)case-statement and accordingly branch the computation. Although the *definition* of 'variants' is more extensible and maintainable than in the variant record approach, the *use* of a polymorphic variable is equally error-prone and hard to maintain. For that reason, modern languages always couple polymorphism with dispatching to remedy this problem. However, no language is known to the authors that enables dispatching connected with finite polymorphism. To do so, however, would enhance flexibility in the following ways:

1. The abstract relation between types can be expressed by enumeration in a union definition after the types have been defined. This may be compared with the specification of a supertype to an existing set of types, which is possible in languages like Sather [18] or Cecil [6]. Furthermore, this relation may be defined differently for different applications, supporting application-specific classification [11, 12].

2. Because the set of possible types is closed at union definition time, the legality for dispatching calls can be based on (direct) visibility rather than on a set of implicit subprogram "parameters" associated with the object (the dispatch vector). As a consequence, dispatching subprograms may be defined externally (i.e., in different packages) to the types they operate on, without any additional language rules.

3. Dispatching calls with more than one 'controlling' argument are easily achievable without relaxing strong typing. The compiler would locally assert that, for each possible combination of argument objects, a corresponding subprogram definition is visible to handle those arguments ("completeness"). The different controlling arguments could even be of different types. This form of dispatching, known as *multi-methods* or multiple dispatching [1,4,5,6,8], has quite strong implications on the module system of the language if open polymorphism is involved [7,14].

4. A mixture of polymorphically defined operations and specifically defined operations to implement a subprogram for a union type would be possible. Ambiguities in the sense that more than one definition matches a possible argument tuple could be checked locally. For that reason, anonymous union type arguments in parameter profiles (i.e., arguments that are declared using a union type definition rather than the name of a subtype) seem to be a good idea because they enable to specify the behavior of that subprogram for a subset of a corresponding union type.

This model is proposed with some concrete syntax for Ada in the following subsections, providing usage examples and implementation considerations. Note that finite unions are not intended to replace the usual, open form of polymorphism in Ada, but to coexist with it.

3.2 Finite Unions for Ada 95

We will denote union types by the following concrete syntax:

```
type T is union (T1, T2, T3);
```

stating that T denotes the union of three types, T1, T2, and T3. T is said to *cover* T1, T2, and T3. Variables of type T may then be legally assigned values of either T1, T2, or T3. Subprogram calls with arguments of type T have the semantics that from the set of visible subprograms at the point of the call a subprogram is chosen to handle the actual arguments and result expectation. Although this set of subprograms is known at compile-time, the resolution process will generally take place not before run-time, i.e., the call is dispatching. To achieve deterministic behavior, however, the compiler has to perform a "completeness" and a "non-ambiguity" check—comparable to what happens in connection with overloading resolution—to guarantee that for each possible combination of argument types one single appropriate subprogram to choose exists.

External Definition of Dispatching Subprograms. Consider the modeling of abstract syntax trees again. If the set of tree nodes is defined as a union type, adding another dispatching operation, e.g., a tree evaluation routine Eval, in a different package is not a problem anymore. For each type within the union the compiler can statically check that exactly one subprogram is visible to handle arguments of the appropriate type, illustrated in figure 3 (note the union over access types).

```
package Tree is
   type Plus_Ptr; -- dto. for other nodes
   type Expr_Ptr;

   type Expr_Node is abstract
      tagged record
         Val: Integer;
      end record;

   type Plus_Node is new Expr_Node
      with record
         Left, Right: Expr_Ptr;
      end record;

   -- dto. for other nodes

   type Plus_Ptr is access Plus_Node;
   type Expr_Ptr is union (Plus_Ptr, Minus_Ptr, Const_Ptr);

   type Node_Ptr is union (Plus_Ptr, Minus_Ptr, Const_Ptr, ...);
end Tree;
```

```
with Tree; use Tree;
package Semantics is
   procedure Eval(E: Plus_Ptr);
   procedure Eval(E: Minus_Ptr);
   procedure Eval(E: Const_Ptr);
   ...
end Semantics;

package body Semantics is
   procedure Eval(E: Plus_Ptr) is
   begin
      Eval(E.Left);         -- dispatching call
      Eval(E.Right);        -- dispatching call
      E.Val := E.Left.Val + E.Right.Val;
   end Eval;
   ...                      -- dto. for other Nodes
end Semantics;
```

```
with Tree, Semantics;
procedure Main is
   N: Tree.Node_Ptr := ...;
   ...
   Semantics.Eval(N);    -- dispatching call
end Main;
```

Fig. 3. External dispatching operation Eval

Abstract Subprograms on Union Types. Assume that we want to define a subprogram with union type arguments, and that the set of corresponding subprogram implementations is to be specified within one single package. We may then want to provide an abstract interface to this subprogram rather than letting visibility determine the set of available subprograms for a given call. To achieve that, we introduce abstract subprogram declarations for subprograms working on union types. We are then able, for example, to declare Eval as follows:

```
package Semantics is
   procedure Eval(Tree.Node_Ptr) is abstract;
   ...      -- declarations of Eval for each type in Node_Ptr here or in the package body
end Semantics;
```

Note that abstract subprograms based on union types do not necessarily have to be given in the same package the union types are defined in, as can be seen in the Eval example. Further, abstract subprograms allow the hiding of implementing subprograms for the various cases within the body of a package while exporting the abstract subprogram declaration. And it allows a more efficient implementation of dispatching subprogram calls (see section 3.4). In case an abstract signature is given, checks for completeness and non-ambiguity have to be performed only once, when the package body is compiled, whereas in the non-abstract case the checks have to take place for each call in a context of different visibility.

With these few mechanisms introduced so far, we are already able to solve our problem: dispatching subprograms can be easily and conveniently defined in packages other than the corresponding union type. In the following section, we regard some more detailed semantics of the model and provide some further extensions.

3.3 Details and Further Extensions of the Model

This section shows how finite unions with dispatching easily provide for multiple dispatching, how they may be combined with class-wide programming, and how inheritance and a specialization relation between union types may be defined.

Multi-Methods. Multiple dispatching via union types is easily modeled. Multiply dispatching calls are checked for completeness and non-ambiguity statically, exactly like singly dispatching calls are. Consider the following example where graphical objects are to be put onto different kinds of screens:

```
... -- assume type definitions for the various screen and object types
type Screen_Type is union (BW_Screen, Greyscale_Screen, Color_Screen);
type Object is union (Rectangle, Square, Circle, Polygon);
procedure Put(O: Object; S: Screen_Type) is abstract;

O: Object;
S: Screen_Type;
...
Put(O, S);      -- dispatch to appropriate implementation of Put for current argument types
```

If the set of graphical object types is likely to be extended later, we would define these types by an extensible tagged type hierarchy rather than using closed polymorphism (note the combined use of union and tagged types):

```
...  -- Screen_Type as above
type Object is abstract tagged ...;   -- root of object hierarchy
procedure Put(O: Object; S: BW_Screen) is abstract;
procedure Put(O: Object; S: Greyscale_Screen) is abstract;
procedure Put(O: Object; S: Color_Screen) is abstract;

type Rectangle is new Object with ...;
-- inherits and redefines Put(O: Rectangle; S: BW_Screen); etc.
```

Each tagged type has to provide primitive operations to "put" itself on all kinds of screen types to make calls like Put(O,S) above legal.

Inheritance and Compatibility Between Union Types. Inheritance between union types may be introduced to enable a convenient form of union type definitions based on the definitions of other union types. For example:

```
type Expr_Ptr is union (...);
type Node_Ptr is new Expr_Ptr with union (...);
```

At this point it is arguable whether union types should be compatible by name or by (the subset relation of) their covered sets. And—if compatibility is by name—whether convertibility should be based on the relations of the covered sets or on inheritance. We believe union types to be in an inherent semantic relationship as soon as their covered type sets are in a subset relation. Therefore, we propose compatibility to be based on the types covered rather than the names of the union types. For example:

```
E: Expr_Ptr;        -- no initialization required
N: Node_Ptr := E;   -- legal because Covered(Expr_Ptr) ⊆ Covered(Node_Ptr)
```

This approach may be compared with compatibility between class-wide variables, one being declared of a subclass of the other. And it makes it easier to define anonymous union types as in the following section.

Anonymous Union Types in Signatures. It is often possible to define a subprogram such that it may handle arguments of different kinds uniformly. Such subprograms are called *polymorphic* and have either class-wide or union type arguments or both. To enable the convenient definition of polymorphic subprograms over a subset of the covered set for some union types, anonymous union types are introduced. We may then define a polymorphic Put operation as follows:

```
procedure Put(O: union (Rectangle, Square); S: BW_Screen);
```

which would be a legal candidate for a call with an Object and a Screen argument.

Specificity of Subprograms. Anonymous union types in signatures allow the introduction of overriding. A subprogram S *overrides* another subprogram S' if each (anonymous) union type parameter of S is covered by the corresponding parameter type of S'. A single type T is considered equivalent to **union**(T). A call with union type arguments then selects the "most specific" implementation with regard to the argument object tags. That is, an overriding subprogram is preferred over an overridden subprogram. This enables to specify together default implementations and implementations for more special cases. Example:

```
procedure Put(O: union (Rectangle, Square); S: BW_Screen);
procedure Put(O: Square; S: BW_Screen); -- do Put more efficiently
```

Specificity requires a more elaborate check for non-ambiguity by the compiler taking the specificity relation into account to resolve potential conflicts. Note the difference between class-wide and union polymorphism in this regard: class-wide subprograms in Ada are not related with other class-wide or specific subprograms in a way that would allow preferred selection of more specific definitions.

3.4 Implementation of Finite Unions

In order to implement finite polymorphism, we need to maintain the information at run-time, which type the actual object belongs to. In Ada, this information is bound to each object of a tagged type. This implementation model, however, is no longer possible if we may use any type for polymorphism and thus do not know at object creation time whether a tag should be associated with the object or not. Our implementation model therefore associates the tag with the object *view* rather than the object itself, i.e., tags are associated with variables and formal parameters, for example. This implementation model of tags is discussed in detail in [13] and could be efficiently applied to implement finite polymorphism in Ada.

A second obstacle to implement finite polymorphism stems from the fact that we want to allow dispatching operations to be defined externally. We cannot easily use one dispatch vector for each (union) type because the size of these vectors would not be determinable locally. Thus, we propose a different implementation scheme that uses dispatch vectors based on subprograms instead of types. For each dispatching call of a subprogram F with one union type argument, a dispatch vector as shown in figure 4a is created by the compiler (actually, one vector per package is often sufficient, as shown below). To allow more than one, say n, union type arguments, the data structure to control dispatching has the form of a n-dimensional matrix. An efficient representation of such matrices is proposed in [2]. To perform the call, the address of the dispatch vector

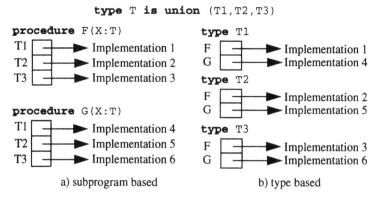

Fig. 4. Two approaches to model dispatch vectors

is used together with the offset determined by the tag to access the corresponding subprogram implementation.

Coexistence of Finite Unions, Multiple Dispatching, and Tagged Types. Allowing combined union-type arguments together with one class-wide controlling argument in dispatching calls, our implementation strategy could look like the following: the n-dimensional data structures for the n union type arguments would be used to find the offset to the dispatch vector of the (tagged) type that is itself found using the tag of the class-wide argument. Thus, we need one instruction more than with the previously considered forms of dispatching where only union types are involved. Consider the following definitions and their corresponding dispatch data structures shown in figure 5.

```
type U is union (U1,U2,U3);
type T is union (T1,T2,T3);

type V is tagged ...;
procedure F(X1: union (T1,T2); X2: U1; X3: V)              -- F1
procedure F(X1: union (T1,T2); X2: union (U2,U3); X3: V) -- F2
procedure F(X1: T3; X2: U; X3: V)                          -- F3
```

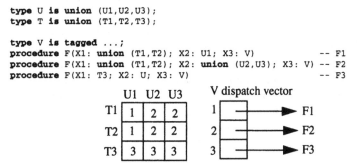

Fig. 5. Data structures for a combination of two union types and one tagged type

Space consumption of this implementation is higher than the type based dispatch vector approach (figure 4b) because visibility determines which subprograms are to be used for a given dispatching call and thus dispatch vectors may look different for calls in contexts where different declarations are visible. We can, however, reuse a dispatch vector for different calls with arguments of the same static types within the same package (though name hiding inside a package may prevent reuse), thus often needing only one data structure per dispatching operation and package rather than per dispatching call. This overhead can be further reduced by allowing abstract subprogram definitions on union types as described above. Only subprograms defined within the same package as the abstract subprogram contribute to this declaration, and each call of the abstract subprogram will select from this contributing set. Thus, in this approach, only one dispatch vector for the abstract operation is required.

To summarize, the implementation of dispatching for finite unions can be made equally efficient in both time and space as the usual class-wide polymorphism approach if only abstract subprograms are used. The use of multi-methods requires additional overhead for checking completeness as part of overloading resolution and the introduction of subprogram specificity requires additional checks for non-ambiguity. In case of abstract subprogram declarations, these checks have to be done only once, else they are required for each call with changed visibility.

Note that the implementation of multiple dispatching as described above will generally be more efficient than simulating it through double dispatching as proposed by Ingalls in [15] or using conditional statements!

3.5 Finite Unions Versus Final Classes

The notion of final classes originates from the Java language [9] and means that such classes may not be subclassed. This concept is also known from Dylan [8] as 'sealed classes' or as 'final bindings' from the Beta language [16], though in Beta it is not available at the top-level. At first glance, final classes seem to enable to limit the degree of polymorphism as finite unions can do. But this actually does not hold: There is no way to declare variables other than to hold objects of exactly one (final) class or to hold objects of arbitrary many classes, namely all subclasses of the declared (non-final) class. The fact that some branches of the class hierarchy may be fixed does not prevent from adding new classes to build other branches. What would actually be needed is a construct to state that the given subclasses of a class may not be extended for a given view. This property, however, cannot be associated with any single class but only with an explicitly given set of classes, or, implicitly, by naming a programming unit (e.g. package) that contains all possible classes. The 'sealed' mechanism in Dylan is nearer to this requirement because sealed classes may still be subclassed, but only within the same library (which is a collection of modules determined by the programming environment). However, Dylan seems to not prevent modules to be added to a library a posteriori with the effect that a polymorphic use of such a class is again unbounded.

From these observations, an alternative model to union types could be considered that allows a tagged type to be annotated such that it may only be derived from within the same package. Then, external dispatching operations and even multi-methods defined on such closed classes could be allowed and implemented as described above. However, the property of being final would have to be defined once and for all, thus hindering reuse. Union types, in contrast, allow existing types to be collected freely, independently of their declaration (derived or not), and enable a closed *view* on these types to be established.

4 Summary and Future Work

We identified some inflexibilities within the Ada language and proposed a minor language extension based on finite unions and dispatching that can cope with the problems encountered by easy provision for externally adding dispatching subprograms. It has been shown that this extension enables further flexibilities like application-specific classification and multi-methods. We investigated some interactions with other language features like tagged types and provided an efficient implementation model for finite unions that is based on view-based tagging and subprogram based dispatch vectors. Finally, we have contrasted finite unions with the concept of final classes and found that none of the currently known languages integrating final classes is able to model the effects of finite polymorphism.

We have restricted our discussion to 'In' parameters only because of space restrictions. However, it should be straightforward to generalize the proposed model for 'Out' and

'In Out' parameters as well, referring to what has been said in [13]. We are planning to implement a prototype of finite unions for Ada by modifying the GNAT compiler.

5 References

[1]   Rakesh Agrawal, Linda G. DeMichiel, and Bruce G. Lindsay. Static Type Checking of Multi-Methods. In *Proceedings of the ACM Conference on Object-Oriented Programming, Systems and Languages*, pages 113-128, 1991.

[2]   Eric Amiel, Olivier Gruber, and Eric Simon. Optimizing Multi-Method Dispatch Using Compressed Dispatch Tables. In *Proceedings of the ACM Conference on Object-Oriented Programming, Systems and Languages*, pages 244-258, 1994.

[3]   Hiltrud Betz, Bernd Holzmüller, and Rainer Koschke. Experiences in Adjusting a Compiler Toolkit to Generate Ada 95 Code. Ada User Journal, March 1997.

[4]   Daniel G. Bobrow, Linda G. DeMichiel, Richard P. Gabriel, Sonya Keene, Gregor Kiczales, and David A. Moon. Common Lisp Object System Specification. *SIGPLAN Notices*, 23, September 1988.

[5]   Giuseppe Castagna, Giorgio Ghelli, and Giuseppe Longo. A Calculus for Overloaded Functions with Subtyping. Information and Computation, 117(1):115-135, February 1995.

[6]   Craig Chambers. The Cecil Language. Specification and Rationale. Technical Report 93-03-05, Department of Computer Science and Engineering, University of Washington, March 1993.

[7]   Craig Chambers and Gary T. Leavens. Typechecking and Modules for Multi-Methods. In *Proceedings of the ACM Conference on Object-Oriented Programming, Systems and Languages*, appeared as ACM SIGPLAN Notices, 29(10):1-15, October 1994.

[8]   Dylan Interim Reference Manual, Apple, June 1994

[9]   James Gosling, Bill Joy, and Guy Steele. The Java Language Specification. Addison-Wesley, 1996.

[10]   J. Grosch and H. Emmelmann. *A Tool Box for Compiler Construction*. Compiler Generation Report No. 20, GMD Forschungsstelle an der Universität Karlsruhe, Jan. 1990.

[11]   William Harrison and Harold Ossher. Subject-Oriented Programming. In *Proceedings of the ACM Conference on Object-Oriented Programming, Systems and Languages*, pages 411–428, 1993.

[12]   Urs Hölzle. Integrating Independently-Developed Components in Object-Oriented Languages. In *Proceedings of the 7th European Conference on Object-Oriented Programming*, pages 36–56, Springer, 1993.

[13]   Bernd Holzmüller. Extending the Object-Orientedness of Ada 95. In *Proceedings of the 1996 Ada-Europe International Conference on Reliable Software Technologies*, Montreux, Switzerland, pages 357-369, Springer LNCS 1088, 1996.

[14]   Bernd Holzmüller. On Designing Extensible Object-Oriented Languages with Dispatching and Modules. Unpublished, 1996.

[15]   Daniel H.H. Ingalls. A Simple Technique for Handling Multiple Polymorphism. In *Proceedings of the ACM Conference on Object-Oriented Programming, Systems and Languages*, pages 347–349, 1986.

[16]   Ole Lehrmann Madsen, Birger Møller-Pedersen and Kristen Nygaard. Object-Oriented Programming in the Beta Programming Language. Addison-Wesley, 1993.

[17]   Carl Ponder and Bill Bush. Polymorphism Considered Harmful. Software Engineering Notes, 19(2):35-37, April 1994.

[18]   David Stoutamire and Stephen Omohundro. The Sather 1.1 Specification. Unpublished, August 18, 1996.

Ada Bindings for C Interfaces: Lessons Learned from the Florist Implementation

T.P. Baker, Dong-Ik Oh

Department of Computer Science, Florida State University
Tallahassee FL, USA 32306-4019, Internet: baker@cs.fsu.edu

Abstract. There is an acknowledged need for wider availability of Ada application program interfaces to commercial off-the-shelf software components. One instance of work that is being done to address this need is Florist, the most recent in a series of implementations of the standard POSIX Ada bindings. Experiences with Florist and its predecessors illustrate the strengths and weaknesses of some of the available techniques for implementing an Ada binding based on an existing C-language API.

1 Introduction

Florist is a free implementation of the POSIX Ada bindings packages for use with the GNAT compiler. It provides application program interfaces for both the basic system services (POSIX.5, also known as ISO/IEC 14519-1:1995) and the real-time and threads extensions (POSIX.5b, also known as IEEE Std 1003.5b-1996).

Florist is a second-generation implementation of the POSIX Ada bindings, which draw on experiences with several earlier implementations. One immediate predecessor is Forest, a free implementation done by Kenneth Almquist of AT&T, which has been distributed with GNAT for several years. The other immediate precursor of Florist is a prototype implementation done at the Florida State University by Wan-Hua Lin[4] and Yi-Gang Li [3].

All these POSIX Ada bindings consist of "glue" code that accesses the functionality of an underlying operating system using the OS vendor's C-language application program interface (API). This is not the only way the POSIX.5 standards can be implemented. It is possible that an operating system could be written in Ada, and support only the Ada interfaces. The U.S. Navy has sponsored prototyping of some of the POSIX Ada interfaces in that form. It is also possible to implement the POSIX Ada bindings by direct operating system calls using the assembly language (trap) interface to the local operating system. However, the quickest and cheapest way of obtaining a POSIX.5 implementation is to construct it as a layer over the standard POSIX C-language API.

Timeliness and low cost are important considerations in the development of Ada bindings. Most large software systems today make use of several commercial off-the-shelf (COTS) components, including at least an operating system, a database engine, and a graphical user interface. COTS software components typically include a C-language API. A recent report of the U.S. National Research

Council[2] points out that the additional cost and lag-time in development of Ada API's are obstacles to wider use of the Ada language. The problem of producing an implementation of POSIX.5 is therefore an instance of an important general problem– how to efficiently produce a good Ada binding for an existing C API.

In this paper, we report some of what we have learned from the Florist implementation and its predecessors, about the design, implementation, and maintenance of Ada bindings for COTS C-language API's.

2 Automatic Generation

One of the methods that has been used to accelerate the generation of Ada bindings for C-language API's is automatic translation. There are several tools that will translate C-language header files into equivalent Ada packages. Silicon Graphics, Inc. has used such a tool to provide Ada interfaces that correspond to the C-language header files supported by their operating system. Intermetrics has successfully used another toolset, called c2ada, to produce Ada 95 bindings to X Windows, Microsoft Windows, and GCCS.

The essential character of such translations is that they mirror the C-language header files. This is both a strength and a limitation. It is a strength because no separate documentation is required; the documentation of the C-language header files should generally be sufficient to use the corresponding Ada packages. It is also a strength because the Ada packages can be easily updated to match changes in the C header files. It is a limitation because there is no information hiding. The Ada package interfaces must mutate over time to follow mutations in the C headers. Even minor differences in the C headers that would not require modification of a C application may result in visible changes to the Ada package specifications. This is not good for a long-lived Ada application, where stability of the Ada API is important.

Automatic translation techniques are also limited by the nature of the C language. There is considerable "noise" in C header files. Even among operating systems that support standards like POSIX, the standards permit gross variations between header files with the same names. This makes direct translation of C header files impractical for standardized open interfaces, such as the X/Open and POSIX OS API's. These variations include such things as extra declarations, conditional "includes" of other header files, selection between alternate versions of declarations based on user-definable flags (such as _POSIX_C_SOURCE and _XOpen_Source), variations in order and number of struct type components, variations in representation of opaque types, and replacements by macros of apparent names of functions, types, and structure component names. (See Figure 3 for an example of some of these features.)

For example, consider changes in the header file signal.h between releases 2.4 and 2.5.1 of SunSoft's Solaris(TM) operating system (not a very major revision, by OS standards). The differences in the two versions of the file itself amount to 230 lines of code (ignoring changes in comments and whitespace).

This includes 14 new constants, and both removal and addition of entire type and subprogram declarations. The code includes conditional compilation commands, which support different C views of the system API (e.g. traditional, POSIX, X/Open). Thus, to produce an Ada package specfication one would need to run it through the C preprocessor first. Unfortunately, this has the side-effect of pulling in various other header files. The differences in header files pulled in by `signal.h` are shown in Figure 1. Expansion of some such embedded headers could be avoided by explicitly pre-expanding them, under the assumption that they are shared by several C header files, and so should be mapped to separate Ada packages. However, that leads to further difficulties, since the exact set of these auxiliary packages will change from one version of the OS to another.

Solaris 2.4	Solaris 2.5.1
	`time.h`
	`sys/time.h`
	`sys/select.h`
	`sys/procset.h`
`sys/stdtypes.h`	
`sys/signal.h`	`sys/signal.h`
`sys/types.h`	`sys/types.h`
`sys/isa_defs.h`	`sys/isa_defs.h`
`sys/siginfo.h`	`sys/siginfo.h`

Fig. 1. Differences in other header files included by `signal.h`.

Some constructs in C header files simply cannot be translated automatically, and so must be worked around using techniques such as pre-editing of the C sources, hand-written glue code, or specification of special-case translation rules to the tool. This hand work needs to be redone each time there is a new release of the COTS product to which the API applies.

Automatic translation tools themselves require porting and maintenance. The maintainer of a binding that is implemented with such a tool relies on the tool's continued availability. For example, the **c2ada** tool has been successfully ported to several systems, but porting it to a new system is the user's responsibility. Moreover it depends on the programming language Python, so a long-term user depends on the the continued availability, portability, and maintenance of Python. For example, when we attempted to install c2ada on our system, we found and corrected OS-dependent C header files conflicts, then linker conflicts, then direct dependences on the code and directory tree structure of the Python 1.3 source distribution (we had Python 1.4); it is not clear how long it would have taken to get it to work if we had persisted.

Finally, direct Ada translations of proprietary C header files are subject to the copyright of the original files. In the case of commercial products, this can limit the value of the Ada binding.

In summary, automatic translation is a valuable time-saver for constructing Ada interfaces to COTS products, where copyright can be obtained, some hand-tailoring is acceptable, and there is no requirement to preserve a stable Ada package interface across different vendors' products or across different releases of a single vendors' product. Thus, the technique makes very good sense for a COTS vendor who wants to provide Ada bindings for the vendors' own products. Automatic translation is not so well suited for direct implementation of a portable Ada binding such as POSIX, that must provide a stable Ada package interface across different implementations. Automatically generated package specifications may be useful indirectly, as a lower layer, with hand-written glue code to project the desired Ada interface. However, such an implementation falls short of the ideal of automatic translation, as it is likely to require hand re-work to port it to each version of the product to which it interfaces.

Because Florist is an implementation of a standardized set of Ada package specifications, to which we wanted to avoid adding unnecessary glue code, and which we wanted to make automatically portable to any POSIX-compliant operating system, we did not attempt to automatically translate the C headers to Ada package specifications.

3 Translation of Fragments

An alternative to translation of the full C header files is to translate just small fragments, which are embedded within hand-written Ada code. This technique is used by Almquist's Forest implementation of the POSIX.5 packages, which includes a program called ctoada[1] and several scripts. The ctoada program makes use of the front end of the Gnu C compiler (gcc) to read in C header files, parse them, and translate them into semantic trees. It also reads in a file describing the intended correspondences of names of type and function declarations expected to be in the C header files with names and forms of Ada declarations. It puts out a file containing a macro definition for each pair of C and Ada names, which when processed and expanded by the m4 macro processor will produce the text of an Ada declaration that is equivalent to the C declaration in the header files. There is another program that produces similar m4 macro definitions that produce Ada expressions corresponding to the values of C preprocessor constants. The Forest package specifications and bodies contain m4 macro calls for declarations of interface types, functions, and constants. They also use m4 macro calls for conditional compilation of target-dependent bits of glue code.

For example, the POSIX Ada bindings define an implementation-dependent subtype, Child_Processes_Maxima, which specifies what is known at compile time about the maximum number of simultaneous processes that may have the same user ID. Forest defines this via a call to a macro, CHILD_PROCESSES_RANGE, and the macro definition is generated by the tools.

For another example, the C-language signal interfaces use a system-dependent data type called *struct sigaction*. Forest needs a corresponding Ada type declaration to implement the body of the package POSIX_Signals. This is done by a call to the macro DECLARE_signal_action, whose definition is generated by the program ctoada. Figure 2 shows the input scheme provided to ctoada, the m4 macro definition produced by ctoada from this scheme under the Solaris 2.5.1 operating system, and the expansion of the macro call into Ada code.

```
define DECLARE_signal_action indent 0
    type signal_action is struct sigaction
end define
```

The macro definition scheme for DECLARE_signal_action.

```
define([DECLARE_signal_action], [type array_type_9 is array (integer
range 0 .. 1) of Interfaces.C.int;
type signal_action is record
    sa_flags:     Interfaces.C.int;
    X_funcptr:    Bad tree;
    sa_mask:      POSIX_Private_1.signal_mask;
    sa_resv:      array_type_9;
end record;
pragma convention(C, signal_action);])
```

The macro definition generated by ctoada.

```
type array_type_9 is array (integer range 0 .. 1) of Interfaces.C.int;
type signal_action is record
    sa_flags:     Interfaces.C.int;
    X_funcptr:    Bad tree;
    sa_mask:      POSIX_Private_1.signal_mask;
    sa_resv:      array_type_9;
end record;
pragma convention(C, signal_action);
```

The expansion of the macro call.

Fig. 2. Forest treatment of *struct sigaction.*

Note that this is a case where the tools fail. The immediate reason is clear if one examines the corresponding C delcarations, which are shown in Figure 3. There is a C union type declaration, which the program could not handle. This is minor problem, which could be solved by expanding the capabilities of the ctoada program. However, there is a more difficult problem that is not so easily solved. The C structure declaration does not comply with the POSIX specifiations. The component names *sa_handler* and *sa_sigaction* are not present. Instead, they are given as macros, that refer to subcomponents in a nested structure.

This technique does not eliminate the need for hand work, but it greatly simplifies the job of porting an Ada binding to new versions of the underlying C-language API. It has the benefit that one can ignore much of the content of the C-language header files and just focus on bits that are of interest. The combi-

```
struct sigaction {
        int sa_flags;
        union {
#ifdef   __cplusplus
                void (*_handler)(int);
#else
                void (*_handler)();
#endif
#if defined(__EXTENSIONS__) || ((__STDC__ - 0 == 0) && \
        !defined(_POSIX_C_SOURCE) && !defined(_XOPEN_SOURCE)) || \
        (_POSIX_C_SOURCE > 2)
                void (*_sigaction)(int, siginfo_t *, void *);
#endif
        }       _funcptr;
        sigset_t sa_mask;
        int sa_resv[2];
};
#define sa_handler      _funcptr._handler
#define sa_sigaction    _funcptr._sigaction
```

Fig. 3. Solaris 2.5.1 declaration of *struct sigaction*.

nation of automatically translated pieces, conditional compilation, hand-written code permits the implementation to be thin. A disadvantage is that porting the binding to a new environment means porting the tools and maintaining the binding means maintaining the tools, through changes in the operating system, gcc compiler, and m4 macro processor.

At an early stage, we intended to use m4 with ctoada and the other Forest tools to implement Florist. As a warm-up for this project, we used the Forest mechanisms to reimplement the package interfaces that the the GNAT Ada runtime system (GNARL) uses to obtain services operating systems that have a POSIX-like C-language API. This was successful in reducing the amount of glue code as compared to the original implementation, and in allowing one to more easily port the GNARL to new OS's and new OS versions[5].

However, we ran into several problems. When we tried the ctoada program on new operating systems, we found that it died on some of the more complicated type definitions in the header files, such as the *struct sigaction* example described above. By patching the tool, we enabled it to get through the header files, but there was still a need for some hand editing. This was needed for some type declarations that the tool could not translate, and for the cases where the C header used macros to stand in for functions and record component selectors. Then, when we went to a new version of the gcc compiler, we found that ctoada would no longer compile, due to dependences on gcc installation configuration information that had changed since the gcc version from which ctoada was derived. We also found problems with some identifiers in the Ada sources being incorrectly interpreted as calls to m4 macros. This was correctable by using different names for the m4 macros. We also needed to use features that varied across implementations of m4, and so relied on a particular version of m4 being portable to each system.

Our goal for Florist was that it should automatically configure itself to new operating system versions, and that users could be easily port is to a new operating system without our help. We judged that maintaining and porting Almquist's Forest tools would require more effort than we wanted to ask of Florist users.

4 Binding-specific Generators

The current Florist implementation is mostly hand coded, with a few automatically generated packages. It uses a combination of two mechanisms to configure itself to a new system. The first phase is execution of a configuration script, similar to that used by all the Gnu software products. We generate the script using our own derivative of the Gnu autoconf m4 macro set, but the user does not need m4 to run the script. The shell script that the Gnu tools produce is executable on virtually all UNIX-like systems. The configuration script searches for the POSIX C header files, specific object libraries, and for specific names within the header files. For each POSIX function, it attempts to compile and link a dummy program that calls the function. The result is a set of C preprocessor #include directives and macro definitions that specify which POSIX features are supported by the underlying C-language interface of the underlying OS. The second phase is compilation and execution of a portable POSIX C program, which we call c-posix. That program generates the complete Ada source code of a few Ada package specifications, principally the one called POSIX.C.

The POSIX.C package provides a complete direct Ada binding for all of the standard POSIX C-language interface. For features that are not supported by the local operating system, it provides dummy declarations to permit compilation of code that refers to the interface. This is to support a special requirement of POSIX.5, that lack of OS support for any feature does not cause failure of a compilation, but only causes an exception to be raised at run time. There are also Ada constants that can be interrogated to determine whether a given feature group is supported, and for C interface functions that are not supported by the OS, a dummy body is provided that returns a failed status value with the appropriate error code. The POSIX.C package is almost entirely interface declarations. The only code in the body is for a few type conversion functions, and that code is completely portable.

POSIX.C is self-contained. It does not use the standard Interfaces.C package, but instead provides its own Ada declarations for all the C types that are needed. Very few of the C-language types that are used by the POSIX C interfaces are covered by Interfaces.C, so we were forced to define Ada version many C types ourselves. We also found that the Interfaces.C.Strings package was not suitable for our purposes. The POSIX.5 implementation packages need direct visibility of the Ada equivalent of C's char * and char [ ] types. The Ada type chars_ptr_array is not equivalent to char [ ], since its representation includes dope. We originally used the types from Interfaces.C.Strings, with unchecked conversions and various constrained subtypes of chars_ptr_array. The code was very hard to read. We also had trouble remembering which package contained which type declaration, among all the C interface types. We tried adding our own declarations for the few interface types we had been using from **Interfaces.C** and **Interfaces.C.Strings**, to **POSIX.C**. This simplified our code and made it much more readable.

The **c-posix** program also generates the specifications of the packages **POSIX**, **POSIX.Limits**, and **POSIX.Options**. The rest of the 40 package specifications, and all of the 37 package bodies of Florist are pure portable Ada code.

For example, in Florist the declaration of the subtype **Child_Processes_-Maxima** in Florist is directly generated by **c-posix**. There is no Forest-style macro-call in the source code. The Florist treatment of the C-language*struct sigaction* is shown in Figure 4. This and all other system-dependent declarations are contained in the single implementation package **POSIX.C**, whose specification is generated by **c-posix**.

```
type struct_sigaction is record
    sa_handler : System.Address;
    sa_mask : sigset_t;
    sa_flags : int;
end record;
for struct_sigaction use record
    sa_handler at 4 range 0 .. 31;
    sa_mask at 8 range 0 .. 127;
    sa_flags at 0 range 0 .. 31;
end record;
for struct_sigaction'Alignment use ALIGNMENT;
```

Fig. 4. Florist treatment of *sigaction*.

Note how the difficulties with **ctoada** have been solved. Nonstandard parts of the C structure definition, that are not specified by the POSIX standard, are simply left out of the Ada declaration. Nested structure definitions are not visible; the field-names that are implemented as macros in C appear as normal Ada component names. The Ada representation clause does this, using information extracted by **c-posix** using the standard C-language operations to discover the sizes and addresses of component objects. The code of the program **c-posix** that deals with such declarations is very repetitive. We have made it simple to modify, by appropriate use of C macros. For example, the code that generates the declaration above is shown in Figure 5. The macro **GT2** provides all the information needed to generate a single *struct* component. The **#ifdefs** allow us to provide a dummy delcaration for systems that do not support the POSIX standard.

At the time of this writing, Florist has been compiled and tested on Solaris2.4, Solaris2.5.1, and a Linux-based Gnu system with kernel version 2.12. The configure script and the **c-posix** program have been tested on versions of the IRIX, AIX, OSF/1, and HPUX operating systems. We have not yet been able to get access installations of GNAT on the latter systems to compile and test the Ada code. We are hoping that by the time of the conference we will have more to report.

```
/* generate the declaration of subprogram g_sigaction
 */
#ifdef HAVE_struct_sigaction
  GT1(sigaction,1)
#else
struct sigaction {
    void (*)() sa_handler;
    sigset_t sa_mask;
    int sa_flags;
    void (*)(int,siginfo_t *, void *) sa_sigaction;
  };
  GT1(sigaction,0)
#endif
  GT2(sa_handler, void (*)())
  GT2(sa_mask, sigset_t)
  GT2(sa_flags, int)
#ifdef HAVE_sa_sigaction
  GT2(sa_sigaction, void (*)(int,siginfo_t *, void *))
#else
#endif
  GT3
  ...
/* call the subprogram, to generate the Ada type declaration
 */
g_struct_sigaction();
```

Fig. 5. Source code from *c-posix* for *sigaction*.

.

5 Conclusions

Our experience leads us to believe that one must approach the design and implementation of Ada bindings in more than one way. There are at least two distinguishable cases, that will benefit from different treatments.

For a vendor of a COTS product, automatic translation of C headers provides a cost-effective method of providing Ada bindings for the vendor's customers. Copyright and maintenance considerations make it more cost-effective for this work to be done by the vendor, rather than by a third party. Therefore, in this case Ada users will be better served if they can persuade the COTS vendor to take on the responsibility of providing an Ada binding.

The second case is that of a standard Ada binding, such as POSIX.5. The overhead of developing and maintaining such standards does not make sense unless they are for an interface that will be supported by multiple COTS products, and will be used by many applications. If there is an underlying portable C-language interface, the implementation of the Ada binding should use this, providing its own tools to perform any local configuration that may be needed. For this case it might be practical for the implementation of the Ada binding to be provided by a third party.

This leaves cases where a specific application needs an interface to a particular COTS product, for which there is no standard interface and for which the vendor does not provide an Ada binding. Automatic translation of C header files may make sense if the system is not expected to be maintained across many upgrades of the COTS component. However, if it is expected to be maintained over a term that is long enough to encounter a series of COTS component versions or require porting to a completely different COTS product, it may make more sense to develop an application-specific package, that hides the specifics of the COTS API. By isolating an limiting the visibility of COTS-dependent interfaces, such a package is likely to pay for the cost of rewriting its internal glue code. Moreover, since most applications do not use more than a small subset of the typical COTS component interface, writing an application-specific binding may be less hand work than is required to make up for the limitations of the automatic tools if one attempts to translate a full set of C header files.

Florist Availability

The Florist 1.1 implementation is available in source-code form via anonymous from the Florida State University Computer Science Department (via URL ftp://ftp.cs.fsu.edu/pub/PART/FLORIST). There are plans to improve and extend this implementation, at least to support the draft POSIX.5c socket interfaces. We welcome electronic mail correspondence, including defect reports, suggestions for improvements, and offers of help porting Florist to other systems.

Acknowledgments

This work is part of the FSU POSIX/Ada Real-Time (PART) Project. PART has been funded by the Ada Joint Program Office, through the HQ U.S. Army CECOM, Software Engineering Directorate.

References

1. Almquist, Kenneth: The Forest Software Library. available from New York University via URL ftp://ftp.cs.nyu.edu/pub/gnat/contrib/forest.
2. Boehm Barry et al.: Ada and Beyond: Software Policies for the Department of Defense. U.S. National Research Council Report. (1996)
3. Li Yi-Gang: A Prototype Implementation of the POSIX/Ada Realtime Extension. Technical report, Computer Science Department, Florida State University. (1995) available from the Florida State University via URL ftp://ftp.cs.fsu.edu/pub/PART/publications/lireport.ps.gz.
4. Lin Wan-Hua: A Prototype Implementation of the POSIX Ada Interface. Technical report, Computer Science Department, Florida State University. (1995) available from the Florida State University via URL ftp://ftp.cs.fsu.edu/pub/PART/-publications/linreport.ps.gz.
5. Moon Seung-Jin, Baker T.P., Oh Dong-Ik: Low-level Ada tasking Support for GNAT – Performance and Portability Improvements. in Proceedings of the Washington Ada Symposium, also available via URL ftp://ftp.cs.fsu.edu/pub/PART/-publications/wadas96.ps.gz. (1996)

An Ada 95 Sort Race Construction Set

Michael B. Feldman

Department of Electrical Engineering and Computer Science
The George Washington University, Washington, DC 20052
(202) 994-5919 (voice)
(202) 994-0227 (fax)
mfeldman@seas.gwu.edu (e-mail)
http://www.seas.gwu.edu/faculty/mfeldman

Abstract. A "sort race" is a set of sort algorithms, executing concurrently and using some kind of visualization scheme to display the state of the various sorts as they proceed. The sort race is often used in algorithms and data structures courses to illustrate the disparate behavior and time performance of different sort algorithms; it has also served software engineering education, as an interesting, even exciting, example of concurrent programming and separation of concerns.

This paper describes a set of Ada 95 packages providing a "sort race construction set," which allows users to create sort races on various platforms using various techniques for rendering the race display. We have used the construction set with GNAT to implement sort races using the Macintosh user interface and graphics libraries, VGA graphical displays on MS-DOS computers, and standard 24 x 80 character displays.

Keywords. Ada 95, Concurrent Programming, Algorithm Animation.

1 Sort Races

The video *Sorting Out Sorting* was produced about fifteen years ago by the University of Toronto Dynamic Graphics Project. This famous video was a pioneering effort in using animation in teaching and understanding algorithms and data structures; it is still shown widely to undergraduates in data structures and algorithms courses.

One of the techniques used in the video is to represent an array of N numerical values by a bar graph, with the height of each of the N vertical bars proportional to the magnitude of the corresponding array element. The array is sorted by some sorting algorithm, typically one of the many that uses exchanges to interchange values in the array. The algorithm is animated by interchanging the bars of the bar graph, to correspond with an interchange of values. Thus can the sorting process be observed visually.

What makes the video so interesting is the simultaneous portrayal of several different algorithms, with each bar chart in its own area of the screen. This creates a "sort race," with each algorithm moving at its own pace. Watching the race gives the observer a very striking comparison among the sorting algorithms.

Figure 1 shows the basic animation, as it might appear in the video. The three sorts were all initialized with the same array of randomly-chosen integers. Quick Sort has already completed its work and Shell Sort is making decent progress, while Bubble Sort is still crawling along.

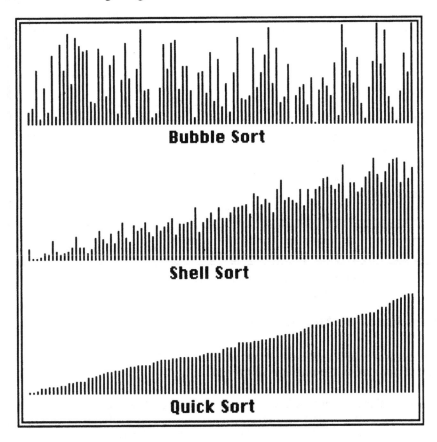

Figure 1. A sort race

Aside from their obvious use for teaching sort algorithms, sort races are an interesting, "fun," exercise in concurrent programming. Indeed, at The George Washington University, we have used sort races for many years in both data structures and concurrent programming courses [Feldman 86, Feldman 90]. Our students have coded these in the teaching language PFC (Pascal for Concurrency) [Burns 93] as well as the "real" languages Ada, Modula-2, and Occam.

In these class projects we have tended toward simple character-based animations. Though simple, they are instructive to run and to code, and can be written quite portably. Figure 2 shows a "screen shot" of a race run on an ordinary ANSI-compatible 24 by 80 character terminal. In this case, the three sorts were all initialized with the same array of randomly-chosen uppercase letters. Quick Sort and Shell Sort are finished, while Bubble Sort is, as usual, taking its time.

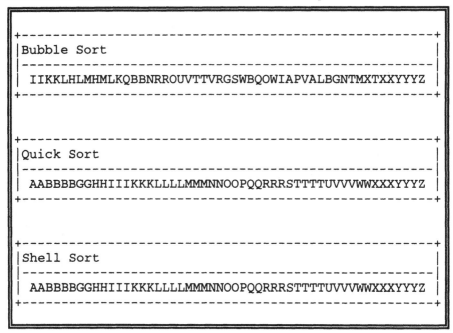

Figure 2. A sort race on an ordinary character terminal

2 Sort Races in Ada 95

A sort race is a perfect application for Ada 95, as Ada 95 provides objects of task and protected types, as well as packages and generic units.

We have developed a set of Ada 95 packages providing a "sort race construction set", which allows users to create their own sort races on various platforms using various techniques for rendering the race display. This suite is an interesting application of Ada 95 concurrency, including tasks with discriminants, selective abort, and other features, as well as protected types.

In addition to providing an instructive visualization, the sort race has interesting software engineering aspects here, specifically in the area of separation of concerns in software construction. The job of a sort is to put elements in order. Therefore, each of these sorts is an ordinary procedure, which carries out its sort algorithm in a state of blissful ignorance about how its state is being displayed, and about its status as a contestant in a race. The sorts themselves contain no code related either to the visualization or to the concurrency. All visualization-specific information is encapsulated within a small generic visualization package exporting a procedure that is imported by the (otherwise ordinary) exchange procedure.

An Ada 95 implementation of the ANSI-terminal sort race from Figure 2 will thus have the structure given in Figure 3.

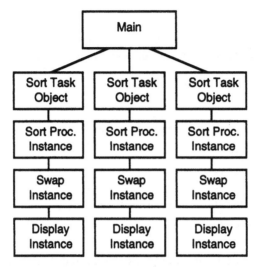

Figure 3. Structure of a simple sort race program

The sorts themselves are adapted from published generic sort procedures [Feldman 96], and have in common that they are all *in situ* procedures relying on simple exchanges. The generic interface of a typical sort (we choose Quick Sort here) is

```
generic

    type KeyType is private;
    type ElementType is private;
    type IndexType is range <>;    -- integer subscripts
    type ListType is array (IndexType range <>) of ElementType;
    with function KeyOf   (Element: ElementType) return KeyType is <>;
    with function "<"(Left, Right: KeyType) return Boolean is <>;
    with procedure Exchange (List: in out ListType; Index1, Index2: IndexType) is <>;

procedure Sort_Quick_Generic(List: in out ListType);
```

The interface of the swap procedure is

```
generic

    type ElementType is private;
    type IndexType is range <>;    -- integer subscripts
    type ListType is array (IndexType range <>) of ElementType;
    with procedure Display (List: in ListType; Index: IndexType);

procedure Swap_Generic(List: in out ListType; Index1, Index2: IndexType);
```

and its implementation is

```
procedure Swap_Generic(List: in out ListType; Index1, Index2: IndexType) is

    TempValue:ElementType;

begin -- Swap_Generic

    TempValue    := List(Index1);
    List(Index1) := List(Index2);
```

```
    Display(List, Index1);
    List(Index2) := TempValue;
    Display(List, Index2);

end Swap_Generic;
```

Each sort instance is executed by a task object initialized by a pointer to a record which, in turn, contains pointers to the sort and display instances.

```
    type SortPointer is
      access procedure (List: in out Our_Types.ListType);

    type DisplayPointer is
      access procedure (List:  in Our_Types.ListType;
                        Index: in Our_Types.IndexType);

    type SortInfo is record
      MySort: SortPointer;
      MyDisplay: DisplayPointer;
    end record;

    task type Sort_Task (MyInfo: access SortInfo) is
      entry Start;
      entry Go(V: Our_Types.ListType);
    end Sort_Task;
```

Activating these tasks concurrently gives the desired "race" behavior; the main program computes an initial array (generally filled with randomly-generated values), passes a copy of this array to each task via the Go entry, and off they go.

We note that the Display procedure must be "tasking-safe," because otherwise there is no guarantee that a display operation will complete before the task calling it loses control to another. For example, displaying a character in a given row/column position of an ANSI screen requires an 8-character cursor-move instruction to be sent to the terminal before the character is sent. Breaking this 9-character sequence by "swapping out" the calling task results in a very chaotic-looking screen! We therefore implement the Display operation as an Ada 95 protected procedure.

3 Making an Interactive Sort Race

The design above results in a very simple sort race, which is be activated from the command line and runs the race once. The program design gets much more interesting and complex when we allow the user to interact with it, via keyboard entries or even mouse-selected menu items.

Consider a program designed to run in a graphical user interface (GUI) environment such as the Apple Macintosh or Windows 95 systems. Figure 4 gives a "screen shot" of a 4-sort race executing on a Mac. This program has four top-level menus:

- the Apple menu, from which the user can display an "about box" describing the program, crediting the authors, and so on;
- the File menu, from which the user can select "start sorting" (if no sort race is running) or "stop sorting" (if a race is in progress);

- the Initial menu, from which the user can select an initial array state of "upward," "downward," or "random" (the default);
- the Speed menu, letting the user slow down or speed up the action.

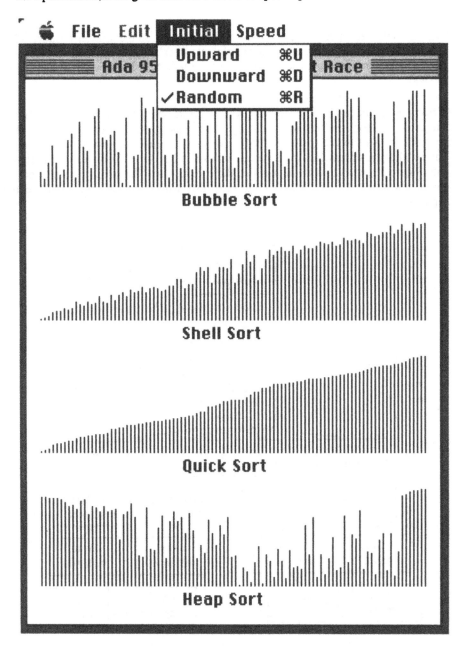

Figure 4. GUI-based interactive sort race on Apple Macintosh

The program must be able to handle such menu events in mid-race without freezing, crashing, "hung" tasks, or other unpleasantly surprising behavior. Also, in GUI environments the user can do other actions like drag the window to another spot on the screen, click in a window from a different program, and so on.

Even a much simpler interactive program—one running on a character terminal with keyboard input—has many of the same aspects. Because the user can, in mid-race, press any key at any time, the program must be able to respond without surprising behavior.

Writing a robust and well-behaved Ada 95 concurrent program, running in an interactive environment that was not designed for Ada-style concurrency, has therefore proven to be an interesting design study involving a number of new Ada 95 features. The resulting program has the structure shown in Figure 5. Comparing this figure with Figure 3 reveals that we have added three tasks: one to handle user events, one to control the sort tasks, and a third "interface" task whose purpose will soon become apparent.

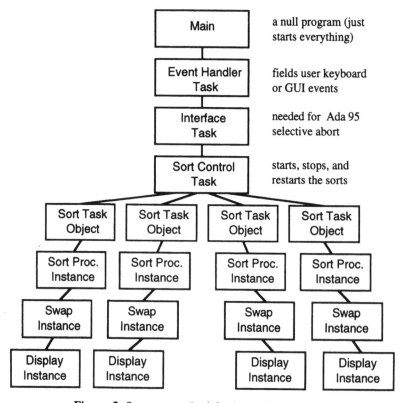

Figure 5. Sort race revised for interactive operation

4 The sort task objects

Let us work from the sort task object out to the user interface. We want the sort race to run continuously until it is interrupted. Assuming no interrupts occur, the controller must start the racing tasks with an initial array, then wait until all sorts are completed, then restart them with a new initial array. The sort task's main loop must therefore respond to the following commands:

- start sorting the array; when sorting is completed, "check in" with the controller and wait for a new start command;
- stop sorting the array and wait for a new start command;
- quit and terminate.

This leads us to a revised interface for the sort task:

```
task type Sort_Task (MyInfo: access SortInfo) is
  entry Start;
  entry Go(V: Our_Types.ListType);
  entry Quit;
end Sort_Task;
```

How does the task allow itself to be interrupted in mid-sort? This is just what the Ada 95 selective abort, or asynchronous transfer of control (ATC) was designed for. Here is the task body:

```
task body Sort_Task is

  MyArray : Our_Types.IntVector(Our_Types.IndexType'Range);

  InterruptFlag: InterruptAction;  -- (None, Quit, Reset)

begin
  select
    accept Start; -- wait for "start button"
  or
    terminate;
  end select;

  loop
    InterruptFlag := None;

    -- initialize our copy of the unsorted array

    select
      accept Go(V: Our_Types.ListType) do
        MyArray := V;
      end Go;
    or
      terminate;
    end select;

    -- here is where we do the sort
    -- set an asynchronous call to interrupt the sort
    -- if user selects "Stop" or "Quit"

    select
      Controller.Quit_or_Reset (TellMe => InterruptFlag); -- selective abort
    then abort

      MyInfo.MyTitle.all;
```

```
        for count in MyArray'Range loop
          MyInfo.MyDisplay.all(MyArray, Count);
        end loop;

        delay 2.0;                    -- freeze action before starting

        MyInfo.MySort.all(MyArray);   -- do the actual sort here
        DoneCounter.OneSortDone;      -- check in only if sort complete

        delay 0.1;                    -- just to yield

      end select;

      exit when InterruptFlag = Quit; -- sort again if Reset or None

    end loop;

  end Sort_Task;
```

The selective-abort syntax requires a triggering statement to be a delay or entry call, hence the call

```
Controller.Quit_or_Reset (TellMe => InterruptFlag);
```

If the trigger occurs in mid-sort, the controller will have passed back a flag indicating whether the task is to abandon only the current sort, or its entire existence. If the sort cycle runs to completion, it must check in:

```
DoneCounter.OneSortDone;
```

so the controller can keep track of the number of completed sorts, in order to start another cycle.

5 The controller task

The task body is as follows:

```
  task body Controller is

    InterruptFlag:  InterruptAction;

  begin

    select
      accept Start;
    or
      terminate;
    end select;

    ValueRandom.Reset(G); -- seed random number generator

    Main_Loop:
    loop

      DoneCounter.Zero;    -- reset counter
      InterruptFlag := None;

      select                  -- start, or restart after a stop
        accept StartSorting;
      or
        terminate;
      end select;
```

```
Sort_Cycle:          -- keep cycling till "interrupted" from UI
loop

   -- set asynchronous call to grab "interrupt" from UI
   select
     Interface.Quit_or_Reset(TellMe => InterruptFlag);
     exit Sort_Cycle;

   then abort

     -- complete this unless we're interrupted

     for Count in V1'Range loop
       V1(Count) := ValueRandom.Random(G);
     end loop;

     for WhichSort in SortRange loop
       Race(WhichSort).all.Go(V1); -- push all "Go" buttons
     end loop;

     DoneCounter.AnotherCycle; -- wait till all 4 sorts check in

     delay 2.0;

   end select;
end loop Sort_Cycle;

-- we get here only if interrupted by Stop or Quit
-- accept up to 4 calls from sort tasks' asynchronous select;
-- since we don't know how many tasks are still sorting,
-- we may not actually get 4 calls; that's OK.
for WhichTask in 1..4 loop
   select
     accept Quit_or_Reset(TellMe: out InterruptAction) do
       TellMe := InterruptFlag;
     end Quit_or_Reset;
   else
     null;
   end select;
end loop;

exit Main_Loop when InterruptFlag = Quit;

end loop Main_Loop;

end Controller;
```

The controller is also using ATC to wait for a possible interrupt from the user interface.

6 The interface task

Finally, because the controller's triggering alternative must be an entry *call*, and the event handling task must execute an entry *call* to signal the controller, we need an interface task to "couple" the other two tasks. Its body is:

```
task body Interface is
begin
  select
    accept Start;
  or
    terminate;
```

```
    end select;

    loop
      select
        accept ResetSort; -- from UI
        -- wait for this call from controller
        accept Quit_or_Reset(TellMe: out InterruptAction) do
          TellMe := Reset;
        end Quit_or_Reset;
      or
        accept Quit;        -- from UI
        -- wait for this call from controller
        accept Quit_or_Reset(TellMe: out InterruptAction) do
          TellMe := Quit;
        end Quit_or_Reset;
        exit;
      or
        terminate;
      end select;
    end loop;

  end Interface;
```

7 Discussion

We have developed several implementations of the sort race kit using the respective GNAT versions:

- platform-independent Ada 95, requiring only an ANSI-compatible terminal;
- Apple Macintosh, using the recently released MachTen CodeBuilder, which includes GNAT bindings to the Macintosh GUI Toolbox and permits linking of stand-alone Mac applications [Tenon 97];
- DOS compatible computers using VGA graphics via the VGA and console packages developed by Jerry van Dijk [van Dijk 97]

Source code, released under the GNU General Public License, is available by anonymous ftp from `ftp://ftp.seas.gwu.edu/pub/ada/sortrace`.

8 Conclusion

Developing a well-behaved sort race program in which Ada 95 concurrency lives harmoniously with the Apple Macintosh GUI presented us the opportunity to develop an approach to concurrent programs in which the concerns are nicely separarated into platform-independent (sorting, concurrency) and platform-dependent (user interface) parts. The concurrency concerns, in particular, are quite similar from platform to platform. Having completed the program for the Macintosh case, we found that the focus on separation was vindicated: porting to other models of user interaction was relatively straightforward.

Algorithm animation is a useful pedagogical tool; we can certainly say from experience that it attracts and holds the interest of the students, especially when they can develop their own animations instead of just watching those developed by the instructor. The sort race construction set not only gives students and other users the wherewithal to construct their own sort races, but also provides, in its own right, a very interesting program artifact illustrating the power of Ada 95 in concurrency and encapsulation.

9 References

[Burns 93] Burns, A., and G. Davies. *Concurrent Programming*, Reading, MA, Addison-Wesley Publishing Co., 1993.

[Feldman 96] Feldman, M.B. *Software Construction and Data Structures with Ada 95*, Reading, MA: Addison Wesley Publishing Co., 1996.

[Feldman 90] Feldman, M.B. *Language and System Support for Concurrent Programming (Curriculum Module CM-25)* Pittsburgh, PA: Software Engineering Institute, April 1990.

[Feldman 86] Feldman, M.B. "Modula-2 Projects for an Operating Systems Course," *Proc. 17th ACM-SIGCSE Technical Symposium on Computer Science Education*, Cincinnati, OH, February 1986.

[Tenon 97] Tenon Intersystems, *MachTen CodeBuilder*, information available at http://www.tenon.com/products/codebuilder

[van Dijk 97] van Dijk, J., VGA and Console IO Packages for GNAT/DOS, available from van Dijk's site at http://home.pi.net/~dijklibo/ as well as the many familiar GNAT/DOS sites, e.g., ftp://ftp.seas.gwu.edu/pub/ada/ez2load

Computer Aided Teaching of Programming Languages
An Ada-specific Development

J.E.Cooling[1], N.Duff[1] and J.Cooling[2]

1 Dept. of Electronic and Electrical Engineering, Loughborough University, Loughborough, Leics. LE11 3TU; email: J.E.Cooling@lboro.ac.uk; Phone: 01509 222816;   Fax: 01509 222854

2 Feabhas Ltd. PO Box 7611, Hungerford, Berks, RG17 0FA; email: Jo@Feabhas.co.uk; Phone: 01488 686432;   Fax: 01488 686435

Abstract:. This paper is concerned with the application of computer-based techniques for the teaching of programming languages. Here the concepts and ideas of computer-aided teaching are discussed within the context of an Ada-specific role. Issues covered include the psychology of teaching and learning, the perception of teaching material by students, and the use of animation to enhance learning.   The essential features of a specially developed Ada computer-based teaching package are described within the paper.

Keywords. Computer aided teaching, animation and simulation, programming languages, Ada.

1 Introduction - Fundamental Issues

1.1 Teaching - a role for computers?

Educators generally agree that passive listening is an ineffective method of learning. This method yields only 10% retention rate, although good visual aids double this [1].   Much greater improvement in retention rates can be achieved through interactive dialogue between teacher and student. Such interaction can be carried out in many ways, though in modern computer-based techniques, three distinct strands predominate.

The first, Computer Aided Learning (CAL), is a student-centred learning process, where the 'teacher' is a computer program.   The second, distance learning, is primarily student-centred, but with significant support from a remote teacher/mentor. This modern version of the correspondence course is here called Computer Based Teaching (CBT). Both CAL and CBT are intrinsic to distance learning via the world wide web. And, from the recipients point of view, both are low-cost training techniques.

Computers, however, even though they are a powerful instructional medium, are no substitute for a good human teacher. This is why there is a significant role for Computer Aided Teaching (CAT), where the computer is basically a *support tool* for the teacher/lecturer. What CAT does is support traditional teaching methods and enhance student appreciation of concepts and theories. Thus it is an augmentation, not a replacement technique. The combination of man and machine can deliver quality teaching and training.

Programmed instruction made an appearance in Britain in the 1960's. Its innovators claimed that it helped to overcome some of the deficiencies of classical classroom teaching techniques. It was from this background that Computer Aided Teaching emerged. Results have shown [1, 2] that learning is more successful when traditional lectures are supplemented by such methods. Moreover students seem to enjoy being taught via this medium, finding it a much more interesting approach. It is clear that good CAT techniques provide:

- An initiating learning stimulus
- A stimulating environment over a period of time.

The operative word is *good*. Such methods support:

- Active participation of students.
- Feedback and reinforcement.
- Individualization.
- Controllable teaching pace.

However, to produce an effective CAT package, it isn't sufficient to understand teaching requirements; learning processes are equally important.

1.2 Teaching and learning - a psychological detour

For any teaching technique to work it must:

- Attract the students' attention.
- Hold their attention for the duration of the course.
- Make the learning process easy.

Everyone is born with a certain capacity to learn. By 'learn' we here use a restricted definition: 'to gain knowledge or skill by study or being taught'. It is essentially a process of storing a sequence of neural events in memory. This memorising of information depends on the process of *attention*. Usually it is not the entire 'picture' of information that is recorded in memory, but particular patterns which build the picture. Such selective perception depends on the ability of the learner to *attend* to certain features whilst ignoring others. Teaching is composed of several kinds of stimulation which influences the processes of learning. It is imperative that such stimulations are identified and incorporated into the CAT sessions.

This, of course, goes only part-way in delivering effective course material. We also need to take into account the skills by which learners think, remember and retrieve information - their *cognitive* strategies. The natural instinct when learning is to make use of our existing knowledge and experience[3]. But learners, by definition, are newcomers to the subject; at this point they often have little knowledge of the topic being studied. As a result they frequently develop mental models which are wrong. Thus it is *essential* that CAT material has a positive effect on the cognitive processes.

1.3 Learning to program

How people learn to program is an excellent example of the acquisition of cognitive skills. It is globally recognized that programming languages are difficult to learn. The Ada language is no less so, considering its advanced topics of packages, exception handling, generics and tasking. Preece et al [3] observed the tendency for students to 'organize new knowledge according to natural language associations rather than in terms meaningful to the programming language'. This is typical of the novice programmer, and is a well-known problem area. Thus it is imperative that students are provided with methods to bridge the gap between current and future knowledge.

Previous work supports the use of structural analogy as a bridging mechanism. Moreover, it is considered that teaching packages would benefit by using analogies within the subject domain. This means that when describing Ada programming techniques, Ada-specific examples should be used.

2 Animation in the Learning Process

It is well known that cognitive aids, such as icons and mnemonics are useful in helping people remember things. Moreover, by animating the underlying function of icons, complex and abstract processes can be more effectively portrayed [3]. Animation helps to create an external visualization of internal (often hidden) behaviour. Animated sequences can readily depict movement, spatial elements, event dependencies and time-related operations, for instance. Studies have shown such presentations to be much more effective than static visuals.

Animation for the sake of animation is not recommended. It should be task specific, and not so 'busy' as to become counterproductive. Furthermore, to be effective, animations should be designed to focus on the key aspects of the function. Otherwise they may prove to be distracting, and result in a display of a confusing set of moving pictures.

Our own experience [4, 5, 6, 7] has generated the following guidelines:

- Use simple animations.
- Focus on important objectives.
- Keep sequences short and simple.
- Include reinforcement.
- Provide interactive opportunities.
- Avoid overuse of animation.
- Allow for variable speed control.
- Allow for replay.
- Organize into separate pages.
- Provide facilities to tailor a 'lecture' set.
- Provide index.
- Provide preview of indexed items.
- Use cueing devices such as sound and colour to emphasize the meaningful aspects of the presentation.
- Finally, reserve animation for the important features of a lesson.

3 CAT and Ada

3.1 Software visualization and the design of CAT packages

Software visualization is a graphical method of representing the different aspects of programming. By providing visual aids, it helps students to understand the concepts and structure of programming languages. It works as an *animation* of a program - it *simulates* the inner execution process. Additionally, by the elimination of continually switching between conceptual levels, simulation modelling can greatly reduce the cognitive load, thus minimizing confusion.

Any CAT package designed to support software visualization must take the following issues into account:

- Subject matter - *Ada programming language.*
- Techniques used - *animation and simulation.*
- Design schemes - *colour, graphics, text and layout of slides.*
- Navigational methods - *includes use of hotwords, hyperlinks and transition to and from pages.*
- Cueing devices - *aids to emphasize important features of the presentation.*

- Portability features- *runtime version of the package which can easily be distributed and installed on other machines.*

Development of CAT material is, by its very nature, a relatively expensive process. Thus development tools need to be effective, efficient and productive. Presentation packages *can* be used, but these have limited functionality. In general, computer-based teaching and learning material should be generated using an authoring tool. These provide, at the very least, two basic features: a drawing tool to create objects and a scripting language to program object behaviour. Moreover, modern tools enable authors to quickly and simply develop interactive multi-media applications.

3.2 A CAT package for the teaching of Ada

A basic CAT package has been developed for use in Ada language courses. It has been produced using Asymetrix Toolbook [8], a Windows-based authoring package. Its overall structure and presentation was based on the following criteria:

- Choice of course material.
- Simplicity of presentation.
- Specificity of display.
- Visualization techniques.

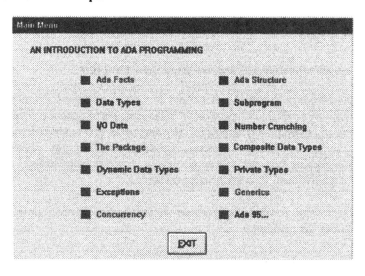

Figure 1

(a) Choice of course material.
The overall content is based on that given in the textbook 'Introduction to Ada' [9]. It is organized on a chapter by chapter basis, chapters being further subdivided into

sections. The presentation material for each chapter is organized as a set of individual pages. This, however, is not a fixed structure; it is left to the presenter to define the *actual* set of pages to be used.

(b) Simplicity of presentation.
The main menu layout is similar to that of book headings, easing the viewer into the presentation medium (fig.1). At this level of use what we have is an electronic equivalent of the overhead projector.

Wherever possible a specific set of basic colours are used - a grey background with black and blue text. Blue text represent 'hotwords'. Such words are hyperlinked to specified sections using the in-built features of ToolBook. They diversify the structure of a book, and make it possible to reference related aspects of a subject without losing the original position.

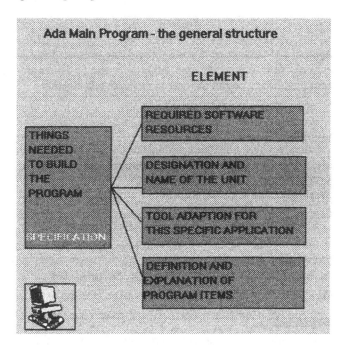

Figure 2

'Show-and-hide' techniques are used where appropriate. Consider, for example, figures 2 and 3, The first to be displayed is fig. 2, this showing the basics of the topic under discussion. However, on pointing to a screen item, further information is then displayed, fig.3. This is a simple but effective method of attracting attention to both words and their meanings. It also has a touch of minimalism - not displaying too much information too soon. Such features, of course, can be implemented using electronic slide presentation packages such as PowerPoint. However, authoring tools provide much greater flexibility in the design of screen displays.

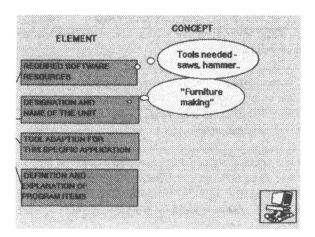

Figure 3

Aids are also included to support navigation through the presentation. Two 'running computer' graphical icons direct the user either forward or backward as chosen. Facilities are also included to permit the user to navigate non-linearly.

(c) Specificity of display.
It is a basic requirement that examples within the CAT package should be highly subject specific. This produces focused teaching sessions, ensures maximum attention by the learner and minimizes confusion.

This is used to good effect in illustrating the syntax rules and basic format of Ada programs. For example, a step-by-step progression from pseudo-code (fig.4) to Ada code (fig.5) is made by the clicking of hotwords to replace them with their Ada equivalent. Elaboration of the diagrams can be further pursued to bring in new features, as in fig.6. Thus complex issues can be presented in a controlled, incremental and organized fashion.

(d) Visualization techniques.
Visualization techniques are particularly appropriate for use in the programming language environment. Attention, though, must also be given to colour, text and cueing features.

In terms of attention-grabbing techniques, colour is very important. Used correctly it can:

- Reinforce the meaning of the slide content.
- Aid memory and understanding.
- Ensure that text is legible.

The Basic Format

with THINGS_THAT_ARE_NEEDED ;

procedure PROCEDURE_NAME is

ADAPTION REQUIREMENTS,
DEFINITION AND EXPLANATION OF
PROGRAM OBJECTS

begin

STATEMENTS FOR EXECUTION BY
THE PROGRAM ARE INSERTED HERE

end PROCEDURE_NAME ;

Figure 4

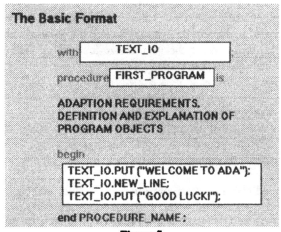

Figure 5

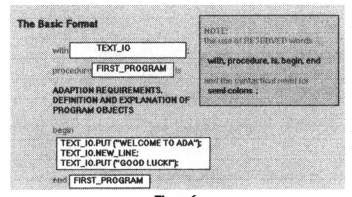

Figure 6

For text, the issues of concern are those of format, typeface, position and colour.

Cueing devices are used to draw the attention of the viewer to particular aspects of a slide. They can, for example, be used to indicate that an animation slide has been entered (in this CAT package, the cursor changes from a pointer to a question mark when it enters a field that activates animation). Note that other forms of cueing devices are available, such as sound and video clips.

Figures 7, 8 and 9 give examples of visualization - path animation - techniques to illustrate tasking features (unfortunately, as they rely on both colour and movement, most of their impact is lost here).

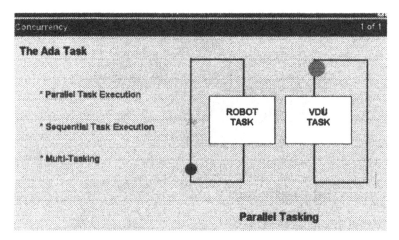

Figure 7

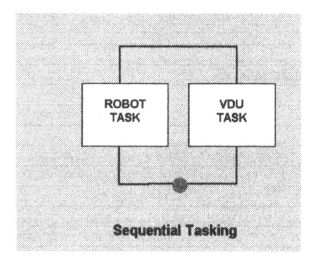

Figure 8

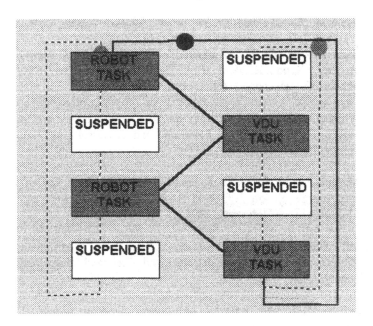

Figure 9

4 Comments and Conclusions

For the student to acquire knowledge, the teaching process should be structured, with emphasis on interaction, individualization, correct pacing and reinforcement. These ends can be more easily attained through the use of computers. CAL, CBT, CAT: all have a part to play in this process. Of these, Computer Aided Teaching is (in our opinion) the most effective training and teaching technique. This approach has been used by us in a variety of courses on software engineering; the results have been excellent. These experiences have convinced us that the development of an Ada teaching package is a worthwhile task.

5 References

[1] J.A.Kulik, C.C.Kulik, and P.A.Cohen. *Effectiveness of computer based college teaching: a meta-analysis of findings*, Review of Educational Research, 50(4), pp525-544, 1980.

[2] S.W.Tsai and N.F.Pohl. *Student achievement in computer programming: lecture vs. computer aided instruction*, Journal of Experimental Education, 46(2), pp66-70, 1977.

[3]   J.Preece et al. *Human Computer Interaction*, Addison-Wesley, 1994.

[4]   M.Elliott. *The use of computer assisted learning in the development of software engineering*, Report JEC/94/IT/ELL, Dept. of Electronic and Electrical Eng. Loughborough University, 1994.

[5]   A.J.Whinray. *Computer aided tools for structured software methods*, Report JEC/96/ELXD/WHI, Dept. of Electronic and Electrical Eng. Loughborough University, 1996.

[6]   C.Barrington. *The development of a computer aided teaching package for object-oriented design*, Report JEC/96/IT/BAR, Dept. of Electronic and Electrical Eng. Loughborough University, 1996.

[7]   N.Duff. *Animation and simulation for teaching programming*, Report JEC/96/IT/DUF, Dept. of Electronic and Electrical Eng. Loughborough University, 1996.

[8]   Asymetrix, *Multimedia ToolBook, Multimedia authoring system for Windows*, Bellvue, WA 98004-5840, USA.

[9]   J.E.Cooling, N.Cooling and J.Cooling. *Introduction to Ada*, Chapman and Hall, 1993.

The SPIF Project

Bertrand DUPOUY, Olivier HAINQUE, Laurent PAUTET, Samuel TARDIEU

Ecole Nationale Supérieure des Télécommunications
Département Informatique - CNRS URA 820,
46 rue Barrault, 75634 Paris Cedex 13, France.

Abstract. This paper introduces the current developments of the SPIF (Système de Prototypage à Implantation rapide et Faible coût) project. The goal of SPIF is to provide a low cost environment for quick prototyping of embedded distributed real-time applications. The hardware platform is built with reusable, standard off-the-shelf components. SPIF is the name of the testbed itself, a mobile autonomous robot controlled by an embedded real-time system, SPIF-OS. Ada95 is supported as an high level efficient tool to engineer real-time embedded software. Ada95 extends the original model by providing distribution capabilities.
Both hardware and software have been developed at the ENST Computer Science Department.

1 Introduction

1.1 Overview

Our concern is to address the problem of prototyping real-time embedded applications for computer science students as well as for engineers.

- In real-time applications the correctness of the results depends not only on the logical correctness of their computation but also on the time at which they are produced. In real-time embedded systems these timing constraints are set by the sensors and actuators which allow the application to communicate with the external world. If data inputs and outputs are not processed within the expected deadlines the applications will not be able to meet their objectives. It is worth stressing that embedded applications are not only software but comprehensive systems, tightly joining hardware and software. The hardware devices involved are of a great variety: miscellaneous sensors and actuators, engines, etc.
- The hardware board sets additional constraints: the available memory has generally a small size and there is no disk. The whole hardware must be compact, reliable and its power consumption must be low.
- The embedded software must guarantee that tasks activated by sensors or tasks triggering actuators will meet their timing requirements. In distributed embedded systems, the system must also address the problem of communicating with remote tasks while still offering timeliness guarantees.

- Embedded systems are developed in a specific way: the system and the high level applications are engineered on a host computer using a cross development suite and then downloaded to the target hardware platform. Simulation on the host computer checks the correctness of the overall design and the general behavior of the application. But the only way to prove the timeliness of external events handling and to assess the reliability of the system under unexpected situations is to download it on a hardware test platform.
- For embedded applications, prototyping is a mandatory stage after simulation because development and debugging are then handled under significant conditions: the system has to prove its correctness with regards to external stimuli, it does not get its input from simulated data. The developers can check and validate the behavior of both hardware and software under real-time critical situations.

1.2 Objectives

In fact, crafting an embedded system is a global approach wherein software and hardware are jointly designed under time, cost, physical performances and reliability constraints.

In many cases, embedded real-time applications are developed using low level languages and very difficult to maintain or to reuse on a different target. The aim of SPIF is to offer students and developers means to elaborate and test reusable hardware and software embedded components. The design of a hardware platform and its embedded software will be achieved by putting together basic hardware and software bricks. This allows a modular and scalable approach which fulfills the objectives of low cost and quick development.

To meet these objectives, we decided to use Ada95 as a development tool and to port an Ada95 run-time to the top of SPIF-OS.

Our prototyping architecture is layered as follows:

- the lower level: the hardware platform, a scalable mobile robot driven by a Motorola MC68302 processor,
- the low level software layer: the kernel, SPIF-OS, a real-time operating system,
- the "portability" layer: a C library and a POSIX [5] threads library. We chose the Florida State University one [4],
- the high level layer: an Ada95 run-time, the GNAT run-time.

This modular architecture makes it easy to change one of the layers: for instance we ported RTEMS [10] on top of the SPIF hardware.

The three upper layers make up the software platform. Figure number 1 shows the global architecture of SPIF.

1.3 Structure of the paper

Section 2 describes the first layer of the SPIF architecture: the hardware platform. This platform is a mobile robot. The modularity and scalability of the

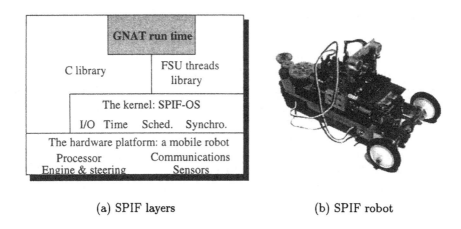

(a) SPIF layers   (b) SPIF robot

Fig. 1. The SPIF architecture

design gave the ability to build several versions of robots fitted with different sensors and actuators. In section 3 we present the second layer: the real-time kernel. The current one is SPIF-OS, developed at ENST. SPIF-OS implements real-time scheduling algorithms and synchronization policies in a simple and efficient way. The section 4 is a brief overview of the third layer which includes the POSIX thread library and the development tools: the GNU suite. In section 5 we explain why we chose to port a GNAT run-time library on top of the SPIF architecture. This section points up how Ada95 extended the original model, especially by providing distribution tools. Section 6 deals with the current teaching applications and works in progress: the use of GLADE and the porting of RTEMS on top of the SPIF hardware. Finally, section 7 concludes and presents the ongoing works.

2 The hardware platform

2.1 Design principles

The SPIF hardware platform is an autonomous mobile robot. All the components involved to build this robot fulfill the constraints of low cost, low consumption and are as close as possible to industry standards. The input/output devices are designed as hardware bricks plugged on the board giving the capability to easily reconfigure the hardware platform.

Indeed, our hardware offers a set of simple and cheap reliable sensors and actuators which can easily be combined to achieve skillful works.

2.2   Components

The current SPIF robot is driven by a Motorola MC68302 [6] processor equipped with 1M bytes of E-PROM and 1M bytes of RAM. At the moment, the following sensors are plugged on the board: an ultrasound device and a luminous sensor. One low consumption engine is in charge of the steering and another one powers the driving wheels. The power is supplied by an off-the-shelf battery.

Communications with remote real-time applications take place on a radio line. Two serial lines are used for tests and debugging.

Up to now, three different hardware boards have been built using the same processor and software platform, strengthening the expected scalability of the hardware components. We plan to design a new board equipped with a more powerful chip by the end of 1997.

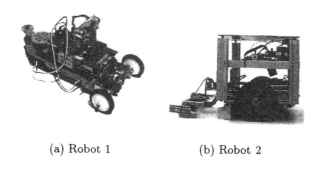

(a) Robot 1   (b) Robot 2

Fig. 2. SPIF different hardware platforms

More hardware information is available at : http://www.enst.fr/~spif.

3   The software platform

We briefly describe the low level software platform: SPIF-OS.

3.1   The kernel

Kernel design. SPIF-OS is a real-time kernel dedicated to embedded systems. We decided to keep it as simple as possible to reduce the overhead during basic kernel operations such as scheduling, synchronization and memory management. This kernel, the core of which is written in C, supports real-time scheduling (HPF, EDF) and synchronization policies (PCP) [2].

A special care has been given to input/output management: standard device drivers are provided (engine, steering, ultrasound, luminous sensor, serial line, radio line) or being developed (camera). A high level input/output library is built on top of these drivers.

Scheduling. Threads are managed at kernel level: the basic process of SPIF is very similar to a POSIX thread. The following scheduling algorithms have been implemented and tested: HPF (High Priority First), EDF(Earliest Deadline First). A sporadic server [1] has also been implemented and tested.

Synchronization. The semaphores can be given a priority in order to use the Priority Ceiling Protocol (PCP). This protocol has been implemented and tested with tasks scheduled by EDF.

Time management and alarms. To operate properly, many devices need to receive and send signals at a fairly high frequency. The ultrasound device, for instance, should be sampled at 100 microseconds (10 kHz). If the interrupt timer is set to this frequency, the system (running on MC68302) is overloaded with clock interrupts and is not fast enough to handle them. Time management is based on the joint handling of two counters: one dedicated to the regular clock and another one for the handling of fast events i.e events frequency of which is greater than the one of the regular timer. On the actual MC68302 platform, the main timer is set at 10 milliseconds, and the second one can be as accurate as 100 microseconds.

Input output. A real-time system can be regarded as a three stage machine: data acquisition from sensors, data processing and then data output to actuators. Indeed, input/output support must provide efficient, timely, fast and reliable operations. In real-time embedded architectures input/output management is the essential issue and must be carefully handled. SPIF offers high level sensors and actuators management routines written in Ada.

4 Libraries and development tools

At this level, the industry de facto standards have driven our choices.

The FSU POSIX threads library. For compliance with emerging standards, the FSU POSIX [4] threads library has been ported to the SPIF kernel.

Development tools. We are using the GNU development suite to build our system. We chose this suite for cost, efficiency and portability reasons. It's a fully integrated development environment and Ada95 is available in gcc. A loader has been developed to download the target code, and a shell make it possible to interact with the robot through a serial line during the tests.

C library. A C library is supplied with all the usual facilities.

5 Ada95 for SPIF

In order to give the developers (students or engineers) high level programming tools that provide well defined time, task and synchronization management, we decided to provide support for Ada95 on our embedded system.

5.1 Engineering embedded software

While engineering real-time software, developers have to tackle hard timing and synchronization problems [11]. They need to describe these constraints in a simple and precise way. If they are given a language like C, they will have to handle themselves the low level synchronization mechanisms by using system calls. They won't get any semantic checking to prevent them from usual mistakes. They will spend a lot of time to develop basic synchronization and time tools instead of focusing on their end application.

The real-time annex, the protected types, the selective accept and asynchronous transfer of control are powerful and simple tools that give developers the capability to express clearly the requirements of real-time tasks.

Indeed, Ada95 is a powerful tool for engineering embedded software:

- Ada's portability allows to test and develop the software modules that will run on the target in a self-hosted environment before testing them in the cross-compiled environment.
- Developing real-time applications in C language requires to use the threads library for synchronization, time management and events handling. With Ada95 this sensitive work can be carried out at language level, ensuring a greater consistency.
- Fault tolerance can be implemented through the Ada exception mechanism,
- Data concurrency can be handled by many facilities, including protected types.
- Very low level data structures as memory or registers location and their contents can be precisely defined, preventing any compiler side effect. Reading inputs from the actuators or sending outputs to the actuators is no more handling byte streams but processing data unit, size and dynamic of which are precisely defined and checked.

The Ada compiler we chose for SPIF is GNAT (The GNU Ada compiler) because it fully supports Ada95 and its real-time and distributed annexes and because it is integrated in the gcc suite which offers a free efficient cross development environment for most of market processors.

5.2 The port of a GNAT run-time

The GNAT (version 3.0.7) run-time library is roughly split in two parts : routines that interface with the underlying operating systems and the other ones (callable by the user or those for internal use only). Almost all the routines are written in Ada. The first part is the package System.OS_Interface. This package contains all the kernel dependent routines (time management, etc) and is different for each operating system. The key point is that there is a POSIX [3] version of System.OS_Interface. If the OS is POSIX compliant, the port of the GNAT run-time is quite straightforward.

We used the GNAT run-time library provided for Linux, which is POSIX compliant, and we successfully implemented it on top of the FSU SPIF POSIX threads library.

Our tests focused on the following services of the SPIF Ada run-time: exception handling, protected types, task management, basic memory management.

5.3 GNAT extends the original model

Ada95 extends the original SPIF model by adding new capabilities: semantic control, high level input/output and, as we detail in the next paragraph, distribution.

Distributing embedded real-time using GLADE. GLADE[1] is the implementation of the distributed annex, Annex E, for GNAT [12] [13] . In the SPIF architecture, the medium supporting the distribution is a bidirectional half-duplex radio-line.

The GLADE run-time is organized around protocols; a protocol is actually an object (in the object oriented sense) which exports a few primitive operations such as Connect or Send. A particular protocol object is in charge of communicating with the same protocol on another partition. It offers a reliable way to blindly transmit byte streams between partitions without operating on the content of the stream. A new protocol can be easily added by defining a new object and overriding the necessary primitive operations.

For the SPIF project, a new protocol called Serial has been designed and implemented. This protocol deals with non-reliable and possibly half-duplex serial lines (such as a wire or a radio) and is based on well-known token passing algorithms [7]. Once this protocol has been tested, we just had to add it into the GLADE run-time to be able to use the full power of the distributed systems annex without further coding.

The TriAda demonstration. During the last TriAda conference held in Philadelphia we set up a demonstration that showed the current state of our works. An outline of this demonstration is given in figure 3. An Ada application on the robot communicates with an Ada application on the workstation using a radio line. This bidirectional communication is achieved using either messages or RPC's. The main task of the robot is to avoid obstacles. It executes commands, sends its speed, direction and distance of the closest obstacle as detected by the ultrasound sensor. The size of the whole embedded software is about 250 Kbytes. The mobile autonomous robot used is the one displayed on figure 1(b).

---

[1] GLADE is maintained by ACT Europe (contact@act-europe.fr)

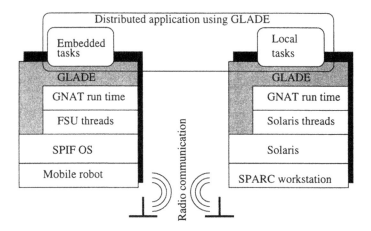

Fig. 3. Organization of the demonstration

6 Applications

6.1 Teaching

The GNAT run-time on top of the SPIF architecture is a convenient platform to acquire significant knowledge about crafting embedded real-time systems. The software is engineered under a methodic approach: the timing and synchronization constraints are consistently defined, the devices interfaces and the format of the data sent and received are precisely specified. The sensors and actuators behavior is non ambiguously described and this enables a positive feed-back from the software to the hardware design.

SPIF is one of the competitor of the yearly TV broadcast challenge where robots designed by high-school students friendly fight against each other. Before the porting of the GNAT run-time, all the embedded software controlling the robot was written in C, task and time management were handled at low level by calls to the thread library. Starting this year, critical parts of the fighting strategy will be programmed in Ada.

6.2 Research

GLADE. Addressing the problems of distributing real-time embedded software is a major improvement provided by the distributed annex. We demonstrated the capabilities of GLADE by building a distributed application involving tasks running on the ground station and the mobile robot which communicate by remote procedures calls.

RTEMS. We ported RTEMS [8] [10] [9] on the SPIF hardware platform and we are now testing a GLADE/GNAT/RTEMS toolset on one of our robots.

7 Conclusion

The joint usage of Ada95 and SPIF layers shows that it is possible to design scalable reusable components for both hardware and software on embedded systems. Students and researchers are given the opportunity to efficiently build complex systems using basic software and hardware bricks. The design and tests of a new embedded system are achieved by adding features in a modular and incremental way.

The integration of the GNAT run-time into our prototyping architecture not only improves the abilities of our toolbox for designing, prototyping and testing real-time embedded software, but also extends the original model. The Ada95 distributed annex provides great capabilities for straightforward implementations of distributed applications. Porting GNAT and GLADE to the SPIF platform using whether RTEMS or SPIF-OS allows to address the problem of distributing real-time applications.

8 Acknowledgements

The authors are very grateful to Patrick Busch and Gerard Mouret who are in charge of the whole hardware layer. They designed and realized the different versions of the mobile robot and their various peripherals keeping the whole board scalable and modular.

References

1. J. Lehoczky B. Sprunt, L. Sha. Aperiodic task scheduling for hard-real-time systems. *The Journal of Real-Time Systems*, 1989.
2. A. Burns and A. Wellings. *Real-time systems and their programming languages.* Addisson-Wesley Publishing, 1989.
3. T.P. Baker E.W. Giering, F. Mueller. Implementing Ada 9x features using POSIX threads: Design issues.
4. Florida State University Franck Mueller. Pthreads library interface, 1995.
5. IEEE. *P1003.1c POSIX Draft - Part1: System Application Program Interface*, 1994.
6. Motorola. *MC68302 Integrated Mutliprotocol Processor User's Manual*, 2nd edition, 1991.
7. S. J. Mullender. *Distributed Systems.* ACM Press, 1994.

8. Online Applications Research Corp. *RTEMS - C Applications Users' Guide*, January 1996.

9. Online Applications Research Corp. *RTEMS - Motorola MC68xxx C Applications Supplement*, January 1996.

10. M.Johannes P. Acuff, R. O'Guin and J. Sherril. *A Reusable Ada Real-Time Multiprocessing Executive for Military Systems*. Online Applications Research Corp., 1994.

11. J. Stankovic and K. Ramamritham. *Advances in Real-time Systems*. IEEE Computer Society Press, 1993.

12. L. Pautet Y. Kermarrec and E. Schonberg. Design document for the implementation of the distributed annex of Ada9x in GNAT. *Technical report, NYU*, 1995.

13. L. Pautet Y. Kermarrec and S. Tardieu. Garlic: generic Ada reusable library for interpartitions communication. *Proceedung of the TriAda conference, Anaheim*, 1995.

Developing Scripting Capabilities for an Ada-Based Simulator

Slobodan S. Jovanovic and Drasko M. Sotirovski

Hughes Aircraft of Canada, Ltd.
13951 Bridgeport Road,
Richmond, B.C. V6V 1J6,
Canada,
(ssjovanovic, dmsotirovski)@ccgate.hac.com

Pierre van Aswegen

MacDonald Dettwiler,
13800 Commerce Parkway,
Richmond, B.C. V6V 2J3,
Canada
pva@mda.ca

Abstract. The purpose of a system is, in a certain sense, contained in the interactions between the system and its environment. The role of a simulator is to provide an artificial but controllable environment usually for testing and training purposes. For that purpose, most testing and training simulators provide the user with a *scripting* mechanism, i.e. a means to compose the desired environment. Afterwards the simulator interprets the script, i.e. simulates the properties and behavior of a number of simulated entities that the desired environment is composed of. This paper describes a design which, instead of hard-coding script interpretation into the simulated entities, *derives* the scripting capabilities from the implementation of the simulated entities.

Keywords. Ada 95, Simulation, Scripting.

1 Introduction

A test or training simulator runs a test scenario or a simulation exercise. In both cases, the role of the simulator is to replace a variety of real-world entities and thus provide a realistic environment for testing or training. The simulated real-world entities are for training purposes often controlled by human operators, thus providing exquisite adaptability to unexpected turns that the exercise may take. The often large number of simulated entities, however, makes it virtually impossible to have humans control all of the simulated entities. If the simulator is used for testing purposes, human operators are usually avoided to increase predictability, repeatibility and reduce cost. One way or another, most of the entities that take part in a training or testing scenario as well as their planned actions and behaviour are defined by a script.

Scripting usually comprises a dedicated "scripting language" and a "compiler" which transforms the "scripted scenario" into some representation that the implemented simulator can understand (Figure 1). For that purpose, each simulated entity is traditionally provided with a hard-coded interpreter of the compiled scenario.

The focus of this paper is a design approach aimed at obtaining scripting support with minimal additional effort at the same time as when the basic capabilities of simulated entities are developed. It presents how scripting can be derived from the implemented capabilities of the simulated entities. Starting from a premise that the essence of a simulator is contained in the code which implements the simulated entities, it makes use of Ada's expressive power to capture the implemented simulation capabilities in a form suitable for scripting.

The fact that scripting is derived from the code has two important and advantageous consequences:

- The derived scripting is guaranteed to be consistent with the implemented simulation capabilities and, consequently, the energy that would be spent in maintaining compatibility between scripting and the implementation is freed for more productive purposes.
- Scripting is available as soon as the underlying simulation has been developed thus providing relatively primitive but gratifyingly early access to the simulation exercises.

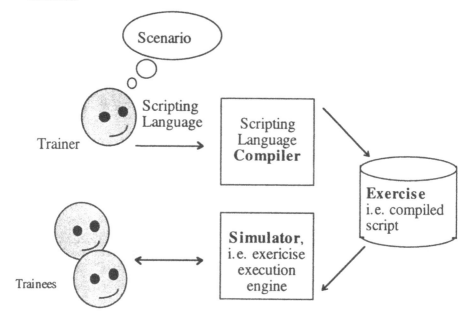

Fig. 1. Conceptual Model of a Testing or Training Simulator

2 Statement of the Problem

A real world entity exhibits self-motivated behaviour and also reacts to stimuli from other entities in accordance with its mission. In other words, the behaviour of an entity is defined by its mission, where a "mission" corresponds to an operational plan or procedure. For example, in an Air Traffic Control (ATC) environment an airline has a plan of all its flights and a computer telecommunication link to an area control centre. The real world airline's duty is, among others, to send the flight plans to the ATC service provider in a timely fashion for orderly proceed of the air traffic. Consequently, the simulated airline's mission is to send flight plans to the area control centre in due time. When simulating an entity, a mission can be regarded as a sequence of primitive operations. In the airline example, these primitive actions are "wait for the due time" and "send a message".

The design challenge is essentially contained in two very different facets (see Figure 2) that simulation exposes to the designer:

- Functional view. The essential capabilities of the simulator are built into the code implementing the simulated entities. Simulated real-world entities are represented as Ada types that captures the state of the entity and a number of procedures each simulating an atomic action that the real-world entity is capable of. Functional view focuses on execution which means that the real-world entities are given computationally efficient representation.

- Scripting view. Scripting requires that the very same functional capabilities of the very same simulated entities be expressed in a descriptive fashion. The state of the simulated real-world entities and the actions that these entities will conduct in the scope of a scenario have to be portrayed and stored for later execution. Scripting view focuses on achieving suitable expressive power.

```
-- The Airline package encapsulates the
-- basic functionality of a simulated
-- airline agency. An Airline agency can
-- be created and ordered to wait or to
-- send a message.

package Airline is

    type Object is private;

    procedure Create ...

    procedure Wait ...
    procedure Send ...

    ...

end Airline;
```

```
-- The essence of scripting lies in the
-- fact that an exercise can be defined and
-- saved so that later on it can be loaded
-- and executed.

package Script is

    ...

    type Exercise is ...

    ...

    procedure Save (This_Exercise: ...);
    procedure Load (This_Exercise: ...);

    procedure Execute;

end Script;
```

Fig. 2. Functional and Scripting View of a Simulator

This dualism raises a number of important questions. Is it possible to derive the scripting view out of the fundamental functional view of the Ada implementation? Isn't it that the Ada implementation of the simulated entities contains all the necessary information: the set of all entities and all the actions these entities can execute? Isn't it that the necessary information is there—alas—expressed in a functional instead of descriptive fashion?

3 Aggregating a Simulated Entity and the Script

First of all, the scripting view has to be aware of all the different entities contained in the Ada implementation of the simulator and of the mechanisms to be used to create such entities. In return, scripting will implement the notion of a mission and provide means for assigning missions to entities. This means that the "Airline" package and the "Script" package in our example have to be tied together in such a manner that the script can capture:

- all entities that participate in an exercise,
- the creation data for each of the entities,
- the creation "method" for each of the entities,
- the notion of a "mission" and
- a mechanism for assigning missions to entities.

```
-- The Airline package implements, among
-- other things, means for creating airline
-- agencies and captures the data to be
-- provided at creation.

package Airline is

    type Object is private;

    procedure Create
        (The_Object: in out Airline.Object;
         With_Name: in String);

    procedure Wait
        (The_Airline : in Airline.Object;
         The_Duration: in Duration);
    procedure Send
        (The_Airline : in Airline.Object;
         The_Message : in String);
    ...
private
    type Object ...
end Airline;
```

```
-- Each implemented entity will instantiate
-- into the scripting and thus provide the
-- scripting mechanism with a means to
-- create simulated entities and knowledge
-- of the data required at creation.

package Script is
    ...
    generic
        type Entity is private;
        type Creation_Data is private;
        with procedure Create
            (This : in out Entity;
             Using : in Creation_Data);
    package Simulated_Entity is
        type Object is ...;
        procedure Script_Creation
            (The_Entity : out Object;
             Using : in Creation_Data);

        type Mission is private;
        function Make_Mission
                    return Mission;
        procedure Assign
                    (This : in Mission;
                     To_Entity : in Object);
        ...
    end Simulated_Entity;
    ...
end Script;
```

Fig. 3. Simulated Entities and their Missions

The resulting design is presented in Figure 3 with the relevant information emphasized using italic print. The design asks for each simulated entity to be instantiated into the scripting mechanism. In the process, the information contained in the code of e.g. the "Airline" will be transformed from the functional view exposed through the "Airline" spec into descriptive view necessary for scripting.

An exercise is nothing but a set of simulated entities executing the missions they've been assigned. Irrespective of the actual front-end being used, exercise preparation is equivalent to executing the following Ada program:

```
package Airline_Entity is new Script.Simulated_Entity
                                (Entity => Airline.Object, ...);

procedure My_Exercise is
   ...
   Canadian_Airlines : Airline_Entity.Object;
   The_Mission : Airline_Entity.Mission := Airline_Entity.Make_Mission;
   ...
begin
   ...
   Airline_Entity.Script_Creation (Canadian_Airlines, "Canadian Airlines");
   Airline_Entity.Assign (The_Mission, Canadian_Airlines);
   ...
   Script.Save (This_Exercise => "Busy Day at JFK");
end My_Exercise;
```

4 Mission Commands

A simulated entity is capable of carrying out primitive actions — a fact that needs to be echoed in the scripting dimension and transformed into the 'substance' that missions are made of.

```
-- The Airline package implements the        -- Scripting provide a mechanism for each
-- atomic actions that an airline agency      -- atomic action to be transformed into a
-- can perform. The design challenge is to    -- mission command.
-- echo this information into the scripting
-- domain.                                     package Script is

package Airline is                               generic
                                                    ...
   type Object is private;                          type Commands is (<>);
                                                    ...
   procedure Create ...                          package Simulated_Entity is
                                                    ...
   type Commands is (Wait, Send, Etc);             generic
                                                       The_Command : in Commands;
   procedure Wait                                      type Parameters is private;
    (The_Airline : in Airline.Object;                  with procedure Action
     The_Duration: in Duration);                          (For_Entity : in Entity;
   procedure Send                                          Arguments : in Parameters);
    (The_Airline : in Airline.Object;             procedure Append_Command
     The_Message : in String);                       (To_Mission : in Mission;
    ...                                                With_Parameters : in Parameters);
end Airline;                                          ...
                                                 end Simulated_Entity;
                                                    ...
                                               end Script;
```

Fig. 4. Mission Commands

The resulting refinement of the Ada design (see Figure 4) is driven by the need to transform:

- the primitive actions that an entity can perform and
- the parameters each of the actions requires,

into commands that the missions can be composed of.

Using these refinements, exercise preparation enjoys the increased expressive powers needed to define the contents of the missions. An exercise preparation session now becomes equivalent to executing the following Ada program:

```
package Airline_Entity is new Script.Simulated_Entity
                                 (Entity => Airline.Object, ...);
procedure Append_Wait_Command is new Airline_Entity.Append_Command
                                 (The_Command => Airline.Wait, ...);
procedure Append_Send_Command is new Airline_Entity.Append_Command
                                 (The_Command => Airline.Send, ...);

procedure My_Exercise is
   ...
   Canadian_Airlines : Airline_Entity.Object;
   The_Mission : Airline_Entity.Mission := Airline_Entity.Make_Mission;
   ...
begin
   ...
   Append_Wait_Command (The_Mission, 30.0);
   Append_Send_Command (The_Mission, "(FLIGHT PLAN VANCOUVER-LONDON...)");
   ...
   Airline_Entity.Script_Creation (Canadian_Airlines, "Canadian Airlines");
   Airline_Entity.Assign (The_Mission, Canadian_Airlines);
   ...
   Script.Save (This_Exercise => "Busy Day at JFK");
end My_Exercise;
```

5 Exercise Execution

To complete the design, the execution of the following Ada code has to be considered:

```
   ...
   Script.Load (This_Exercise => "Busy Day at JFK");
   Script.Execute;
```

Assuming that the exercise "Busy day at JFK" was successfully prepared and stored, this code will:

- Use the creation data from the script and create each of the simulated entities defined in the exercise. (I.e. call Airline.Create with "Canadian Airlines" as creation data.)
- Assign each entity the mission(s) and, consequently, execute the first command of the mission. (I.e. call Airline.Wait with duration set to 30.0)
- As soon as one *command has been completed*, fetch the subsequent command and initiate its execution.

How will exercise execution know when to fetch the next mission command? The approach presented so far is suitable for actions which are executed instantly. For example, if the Send action only sends a message and doesn't wait for the response, the subsequent command can be fetched immediately. However, in order to meet specific requirements of asynchronous completion of many primitive actions without blocking the simulation exercise as a whole, the scripting support requires one last refinement (see Figure 5): a means for the simulated entity to signal when one atomic action has been completed. Please note that an entity may execute several missions concurrently and when a primitive action is completed only *the subject* mission goes ahead while all other missions remain blocked. (Concurrent mission execution is a topic in itself and further discussion is deemed outside the scope of this paper. More about concurrent missions and asynchronous mission commands can be found in [1,2].)

```
-- Not all actions are instantaneous. I.e.    -- Script execution implies launching the
-- some of them may take some time to         -- subsequent command as the preceding one
-- complete. Therefore, implementation of     -- has been completed. For that purpose, a
-- any such action requires a means to        -- mechanism for signalling completion is
-- signal completion so that the next         -- provided.
-- command in the mission can be initiated.
                                              package Script is
package body Airline is
                                                  ...
    ...
    procedure Wait
        (The_Airline : in Airline.Object;         type Command is private;
         The_Duration: in Duration) is
        ...                                        function Current_Command
    begin                                                        return Command;
        ...                                        procedure Signal_Completion
        -- For asynchronous commands,                          (This: in Command);
        -- remember the current command
        -- being executed                          procedure Execute;
        ... := Script.Current_Command;             ...
    end Wait;                                   end Script;
    ...
    -- At some later time, the command is
    -- completed and the scripting
    -- mechanism is told about it:
    Script.Signal_Completion (...);
    ...
end Airline;
```

Fig. 5. Asynchronous Command Completion

6 Conclusions

The presented design approach for scripting was successfully implemented in the Canadian Automated Air Traffic System (CAATS) where simulation is currently used for system integration and testing and is soon to be used to support user training. The simulated entities are implemented as a society of cooperating objects [3] that provide a realistic ATC environment for testing and training. The CAATS scripting mechanism is used to control a dozen or so simulated external systems and hundreds of simulated pilots flying the aircraft being controlled. To avoid manning all operator positions during testing and increase repeatability of the test exercises, scripting is also used to describe the desired behaviour of the operators.

Last but not least, developing support for script preparation (e.g. the script language, compiler or some sophisticated preparation tool) in parallel with the simulator introduces significant difficulties [4], since every change in the simulation execution data structure needs to be accompanied by a corresponding upgrade to the script preparation support (in particular when the simulator is developed in parallel with the system being developed). The implemented design approach to scripting relieved some of these difficulties through increased consistency and early access to scripted exercises. (Early on, before a sophisticated front-end for exercise preparation was available, CAATS scripts were built by simply writing Ada programs similar to the examples in previous sections. The imperfection of this scripting method was offset by its inherent consistency and immediate availability. After all, early access to scripting was gained at no additional cost since the user-friendly scripting tool that was eventually developed uses the same underlying mechanism.)

CAATS uses Ada 83 and the implementation of the scripting mechanism couldn't take advantage of Ada 95 access to subprograms. However, this design approach to scripting is not limited to Ada. The same design can be expressed in virtually any object oriented (OO) language with strong type checking. On the other side, the design assumes that the simulator is built using OO principles and heavily depends on well-defined, encapsulated simulated entities and their mutual interactions.

7 References

[1]   Nebojsa Vuksanovic, Marko Vuskovic and Vladimir Kukic. *APDL - A Formal Language for Cluster Behaviour Description*, Proc. of the 28th ISMM Applications of Microcomputers, February 5-7, Beverly Hills, 1986.

[2]   Vladimir Kukic and Nebojsa Vuksanovic. *APDL Interpreter*. Proc. of the 28th ISMM Applications of Microcomputers, February 5-7, Beverly Hills, 1986

[3]   Drasko M. Sotirovski, Slobodan S. Jovanovic and Philippe Kruchten. *Beyond Abstract Data Types: Giving Life to Objects*. In Marcel Toussaint, editor, Ada in Europe, First International Eurospace-Ada-Europe Symposium, Springer-Verlag, 1994.

[4]   Slobodan S. Jovanovic and Drasko M. Sotirovski. *Reuse Strategy for the Development of the Integration and Training Simulator for Large Systems*. In DASIA'96: Data Systems in Aerospace (organized by Eurospace), Conference Proceedings, pages 193—199, Rome, Italy, May 1996.

Systematic Unit-Testing of Ada Programs

Joachim Wegener, Ines Fey

Daimler-Benz AG
Research and Technology
Alt-Moabit 96 a
D-10559 Berlin
Germany

Tel.: +49 (0)30 39982-232/246
FAX: +49 (0)30 39982-107
{wegener, fey}@DBresearch-berlin.de

Abstract

The systematic test is an inevitable part of the verification and validation process for software. Overall support for all testing activities is currently not available in a single Ada testing tool. Hence, a combination of powerful testing tools is necessary to provide systematic and complete test process automation for the examination of Ada programs. The classification-tree editor CTE supports the systematic design of functional test cases. The strengths of AdaTEST are the comprehensive support for test execution and coverage analysis. The combination of both tools leads to systematic and well-documented test procedures. It has already been successfully applied to several real world examples including aerospace applications.

0. Introduction

In the aerospace and defence divisions of the Daimler-Benz Group, Ada is a widely used programming language. The systems developed with Ada are often safety-critical. Apart from a thorough way of proceeding during the development of the systems, the analytical quality assurance is of great importance for the avoidance of errors during the operation of the systems. The most important analytical method for the quality assurance of software-based systems is dynamic testing since it is the only method which allows a thorough examination of the actual run-time behaviour of such systems in their real application environment. Dynamic testing typically consumes 30 % - 50 % of the overall software development effort and budget.

Investigations of various software development projects in several divisions of the Daimler-Benz Group have shown that the costs for software testing mostly arise for unit testing, integration testing, and system testing. On average, about 35 % of the total testing expenses is spent on unit testing, 28 % on integration testing and approximately 27 % on system testing. The remaining 10 % is spent on specific tests like the examination of software-hardware interfaces.

A result of these statistics is that in practice up to 17 % of the overall development cost is allotted to unit testing. This significant quota of the entire development cost increases if integration testing is done bottom up and the integration is checked by testing higher level units. In this case the overall cost for unit and integration testing increases to an amount of 31 % of the entire development cost. This illustrates the importance of unit testing.

Significant savings can be achieved, and the product quality can be improved by tools which systematize and automate the unit testing process. Therefore, many computer-aided software testing tools exist for the testing of Ada programs. Most of these provide specialist support for distinct test activities such as test execution, monitoring, and test evaluation. Overall support for all testing activities is not currently available in a single tool. Moreover, none of the tools offers methodological support for the functional test case determination. Hence, a combination of powerful testing tools is necessary to provide systematic and complete test process automation from test case design to test evaluation.

In the first chapter this paper gives an introduction to the test activities necessary for the systematic test. Furthermore, the classification-tree method and the classification-tree editor CTE which support the systematic test case determination for the functional test are explained. In the next chapter a survey of the existing tools for unit testing of Ada programs is given. It is shown what test activities are automated by the respective tools. For an integration with the CTE, AdaTEST from IPL was chosen since it produces particularly good results in the fields of test execution and monitoring. The integration of both tools is described in chapter 3. The following chapter presents the first practical experiences with this tool combination. The paper closes with a short summary of the most important results and an outlook on future work.

1. Systematic Testing and the Classification-Tree Editor CTE

The systematic test is an inevitable part of the verification and validation process for software. Testing is aimed at finding errors in the test object and giving confidence in its correct behaviour by executing the test object with selected input values. The overall testing process can be structured into the following central test activities: test case design, test data selection, expected values prediction, test case execution, monitoring, and test evaluation. In addition, accompanying activities like test organization and test documentation are of importance. This structure facilitates a systematic procedure and the definition of intermittent results [Wegener and Pitschinetz, 1995].

During test case design the input situations to be tested are defined. A test case abstracts from a concrete test datum and defines it, only in so far as it is required for the intended test. In the course of test data selection concrete input values which meet the test case conditions are chosen. Determining the anticipated results for every selected test datum constitutes expected values prediction. The test object is run with the test data and thus the actual output values are produced. The test results are then determined by comparing expected values and actual values. Additionally, monitoring can be used to obtain information about the behaviour of the test object during test execution. A common method is to instrument the program code according to a white-box test criterion.

The most important prerequisite for a thorough software test is the design of relevant test cases since they determine the kind and scope and hence the quality of the test. A test case defines a certain input situation to be tested. It comprises a set of input data from the test object's input domain. Each element of the set should, for example, lead to the execution of the same program functionality, the same program branch, or the same program state, depending on the test criteria applied. Functional testing is of particular importance since it is the only method which allows to examine appropriately whether or not all specified requirements have been implemented in the test object. The classification-tree editor CTE supports the systematic design of functional test cases. It is based on the classification-tree method.

1.1 Classification-Tree Method

The classification-tree method [Grochtmann and Grimm, 1993] is a special approach to (black-box) partition testing partly using and improving ideas from the category-partition method defined by Ostrand and Balcer [1988]. By means of the classification-tree method, the input domain of a test object is regarded under various aspects assessed as relevant for the test. For each aspect, disjoint and complete classifications are formed. Classes resulting from these classifications may be further classified – even recursively. The stepwise partition of the input domain by means of classifications is represented graphically in the form of a tree. Subsequently, test cases are formed by combining classes of different classifications. This is done by using the tree as the head of a combination table in which the test cases are marked. A major advantage of the classification-tree method is that it turns functional test case design into a process comprising several structured and systematized steps – making it easy to handle, to understand, and also to document.

The use of the classification-tree method will be explained by testing a sample Ada function: *is_line_covered_by_rectangle*. The function checks whether or not a line is covered by a given rectangle with its sides parallel to the axes of the coordinate system. Input parameters of the test object are two records. The first one of type *line_data* describes the line by the positions of its two end points, the second one of type *rectangle_data* describes the rectangle using the position of its upper left corner, its width and its height. If the line is covered by the rectangle, the test object should return *True*, otherwise *False*. Figure 1 illustrates the task of the test object by means of an arbitrary rectangle and several sample lines. The figure also defines regions to describe the possible positions of the line end points with respect to the rectangle.

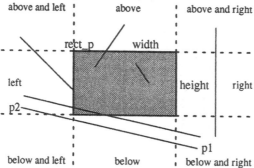

Figure 1: Rectangle with sample

The possible inputs are various lines and rectangles. Appropriate test aspects in this particular case are the positions of the line end points *p1* and *p2* with respect to the rectangle as well as the properties of the line like its course, orientation and gradient. Furthermore, the input domain of the test object is distinguished according to the existence and degree of coverage (Figure 2).

The classification based on the aspect *degree of coverage*, for instance, leads to a partition of the input domain into three classes: *complete coverage* (both line end points are covered by the rectangle), *one end point covered* (only one line end point is covered by the rectangle, the other one is located outside the rectangle), and *no end point covered* (both line end points are not covered, but some points in the middle of the line are covered). The classifications based on the positions of the line end points produce each a partition into two classes: *line end point located outside the rectangle* and *line end point located inside the rectangle*. Figure 2 shows a refinement for the case that p2 lies outside the rectangle. This case is further distinguished according to the position of the respective line end point with respect to the rectangle and according to the distance of p2 from the rectangle. The *properties of the line* are also specified in a refinement. According to the *course of the line* it is, first of all, distinguished between *horizontal*, *vertical*, and *slanting* lines. Horizontal and vertical lines are further subdivided according to their orientation, horizontal lines, for example, into lines running *from left to right* or *from right to left*. For slanting lines the *gradient of the line* is also taken into account. The various classifications and classes are noted as classification tree.

Afterwards, the test cases are defined by combining classes of different classifications in the combination table. Each row in the table represents a test case. For *is_line_covered_by_rectangle* 49 test cases were determined. The second test case, for example, defines a test with the special case that the line end point p1 is the only point of the line which is covered by the given rectangle. P1 is located on the left side of the rectangle. P2 is located far away from the rectangle. Its position is left from and above the rectangle. A corresponding sample line is shown in Figure 1.

A comprehensive description of the classification-tree method and related works was given by Grochtmann and Grimm [1993].

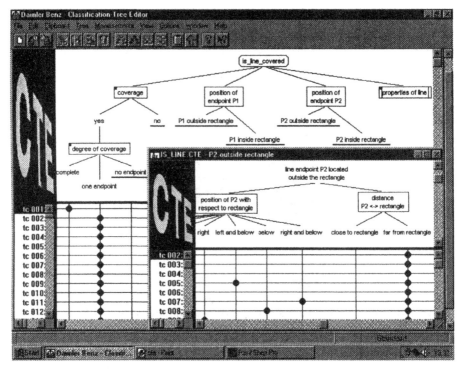

Figure 2: Test Case Design for *is_line_covered_by_rectangle* using the CTE

1.2 Classification-Tree Editor CTE

The classification-tree editor CTE (Figure 2) is based on the classification-tree method and supports systematic test case determination for functional testing. The two main phases of the classification-tree method – design of a classification tree and definition of test cases in the combination table – are both supported by the tool. For each phase a suitable working area is provided. To give the user optimal support, editing is done in a syntax directed and object based way. Several functions are performed automatically. These include drawing of connections between tree elements, updating the combination table after changes in the tree, and checking the syntactical consistency of table entries. The CTE also offers features which allow large-scale classification trees to be structured in order to support the test case design for large testing problems efficiently.

As test documentation plays an important role in systematic testing, the CTE offers suitable support for this activity. For example, the test case design can be documented easily by printing out the trees and tables. Furthermore, the tool can automatically generate text versions of the test cases, based on the test case definition in the combination table. For example, the text version of test case 2 of the example is shown as:

```
- coverage: yes
    - degree of coverage: one endpoint
- position of endpoint P1: line endpoint P1 located inside the rectangle
    - position of P1 in the rectangle: on one side (no corners)
        - which side: left
- position of endpoint P2: line endpoint P2 located outside the rectangle
    - position of P2 with respect to rectangle: left and above
    - distance P2 <-> rectangle: far from rectangle
- Course of line: slanting
    - direction of line: bottom right -> top left
    - gradient of line: medium.
```

On the one hand these text versions serve as documentation, on the other hand they provide a basis for the subsequent activities of software testing like the generation of concrete test data. As the CTE only supports test case determination, additional tools are required for an efficient test process which automates most of the test activities.

2. Survey of Existing Ada Testing Tools

Many different Ada testing tools are available for the examination of Ada programs (cf. [Graham et al., 1995]). This chapter summarizes the results of a detailed study of existing Ada testing tools regarding their support for the various test activities. Commercially available tools as well as non-commercial tools were included in the study in order to cover a broad spectrum of different approaches to the test. The following tools were examined on the basis of literature, vendor information, evaluation licences and demo-versions: AdaCAST (Vector Engineering), AdaTEST (Information Processing Ltd), DARTT (Daimler-Benz Aerospace AG), DEVISOR (Dassault Electronique), LDRA Testbed (Liverpool Data Research Associates Ltd), LOGISCOPE (Verilog), STW Coverage (Software Research), TAOS (University of California), TBGEN and TCMON (Testwell Oy), as well as UATL (ITT Avionics).

2.1 AdaCAST

AdaCAST [Vector Engineering, 1995] can be used for unit tests as well as for integration tests. AdaCAST integrates four components: the Test Environment Constructor, the Test Case Editor, the Test Execution Manager, and the Test Report Generator. With the help of the Test Environment Constructor the environment for the test is defined. It is determined, for example, which Ada library will be used and what the name of the test object will be. When all relevant information is available, the Environment Constructor automatically parses the unit under test, generates test driver and stubs, and compiles a complete Ada test harness. The Test Case Editor serves for giving test data. The test cases consist of data values for each formal parameter for each subprogram within the unit under test, and any dependent units that were stubbed by the Environment Constructor. With the Execution Manager the test is carried out, using any previously created test case. The Report Generator is used to construct text file reports which summarize the results of a specific test case. The main emphasis of AdaCAST is on the execution and documentation of function oriented tests. The instrumentation of the program code and a monitoring of the test coverage are not supported. A possibility of monitoring the test is to execute the test cases under control of the Compilation System Debugger. Moreover, it is not possible to specify the expected behaviour. Consequently, the test evaluation is not supported by the comparison of expected and actual values either. There is, however, the possibility of an automatic test evaluation for regression tests. Positive about this test system is that all its functions are provided via a graphical user interface.

This information was compiled on the basis of the demo-version 1.4 of AdaCAST. Test organization, stub as well as test driver generation could not be evaluated with this version.

2.2 AdaTEST

AdaTEST [IPL, 1995] is a product which has been developed to assist primarily with the unit and integration testing stages of an Ada software project. It comprises facilities in three main areas, namely the production of test drivers and stubs, test coverage analysis and also static analysis. Consequently, the main emphasis of AdaTEST is on the activities test execution, test evaluation, monitoring, and test documentation. AdaTEST offers a script-driven approach to encourage repeatability, containing automated checks on data object values and exception behaviour. Scripts can be created in two different ways. The first one requires the tester to write his scripts as an Ada main procedure, calling the unit under test directly and using the AdaTEST Harness directives accessed via the normal Ada package mechanisms. The second approach involves the generation of the Ada main test procedure from test case data supplied by the user in the form of a Test Case Definition (TCD) file. AdaTEST scripts can be run in any validated Ada environment which confers the portability characteristic.

AdaTEST supports about ten different forms of coverage, including code and data coverage types like statement coverage, branch coverage, and condition coverage. The software under test is instrumented automatically and test results are generated. There is a graphical option for the display of coverage against code.

2.3 DARTT

DARTT ([Gerlich and Fercher, 1993], [Gerlich, 1995]) is a tool for statistical testing. It is used primarily for the execution of stress tests for units. The test data are generated automatically for this according to the value domains of the input parameters. The test execution is also automated. As a basis for the manual test evaluation, DARTT provides an analysis of the outputs generated by the test object. In the course of this, discontinuities occurring in the output behaviour of the test object are detected and documented.

Using DARTT has its limitations. All definitions are supported except discriminant and variant records. For type "address" currently the address value "0000:0000" is returned and neither random nor incremental initialisation is done. Due to these restrictions and the general weaknesses of random testing the tool is not meant to be an alternative to other test systems but shall rather be used additionally.

2.4 DEVISOR

DEVISOR [Dassault Electronique, 1994] is a product which links functions for the debugging and the software test. The test support concentrates on test execution and test evaluation. An interpreter as well as a compiler for the DEVISOR specific test language are the most important parts. The test execution is based on a test script which can either be interpreted directly or compiled to an executable program. DEVISOR offers the possibility of drawing up the script manually but also makes it possible to generate the script automatically by using the DEVISOR-A extension. A symbol data basis generated automatically on the basis of the test object makes the access to the test object variables easier and supports test execution and test evaluation. With DEVISOR only those programs can be tested which are complete and in an executable form. DEVISOR does not offer a suitable possibility of documenting the test results.

The common criteria for structural testing as, for example, branch testing are offered optionally with the extension DEVISOR-B. Additional functions for the testing of real-time applications are provided by DEVISOR-C. The details on DEVISOR result from an evaluation of its basic version 9.0.0 and also from information provided by Dassault Electronique.

2.5 LDRA Testbed

LDRA Testbed [LDRA, 1993] is orientated towards structural testing and static analysis. The most important coverage measurements like statement coverage, branch coverage, and condition coverage are considered. Apart from the achievements in the field of monitoring, the main emphasis is on test evaluation and test documentation. The extensive functions for summarizing the generated results in a textual and graphical form need to be stressed here. LDRA Testbed provides all functionalities via a graphical user interface.

The basic version of LDRA Testbed restricts the possibilities of its use considerably because only one source file can be handled at a time. This does not apply when using the additional component TBset. The achievements of TBset are not contained in the graphical user interface. A more extensive test automation is offered by another component called TBrun which makes an automatic generation of the test program possible.

As a basis of this assessment, the test system LDRA Testbed, version 4.9, was evaluated including the extension TBset.

2.6 LOGISCOPE

LOGISCOPE [Verilog, 1993] combines support in the fields of static analysis and structure oriented tests. It is designed for the use subsequent to functional testing. The test functionality therefore concentrates on monitoring and test documentation. LOGISCOPE can be used at the level of the unit test as well as the integration test. As an aid for the integration test, LOGISCOPE offers a function-call graph which makes the selection of test objects easier and also shows clearly the progress of the test.

As criteria for white-box testing, statement coverage, branch coverage, and also condition coverage are available. In order to support the attainment of a complete test coverage, LOGISCOPE generates a list of program conditions for branches that have not been executed during the test so far. This list can be consulted for deriving test data which cause the execution of certain parts of the program that have not been reached before. LOGISCOPE provides a modern graphical user interface. It was evaluated in version 2.0.

2.7 STW Coverage

STW Coverage is a test coverage analysis tool from the Software Test Works (STW) tool suite which provides support for structure oriented tests. STW Coverage can be used for unit and integration tests. The functionality offered lies mainly in the fields of monitoring and test documentation. Apart from branch coverage and path coverage, the coverage of function calls is offered as a test criterion for the integration test. For documenting the coverage results, STW Coverage generates an overall view in tabular form. Additionally, the executed parts of the program can be visualized in call graphs and control-flow graphs. STW Coverage can be used via a graphical user interface but also through extensions of compiler and linker commands.

2.8 TAOS

The test system TAOS [Richardson, 1994] combines statistical tests with structural tests. Program dependencies concerning the control flow as well as the data flow of the test object are in the centre of the test with TAOS. These are first of all analysed and shall then be covered as completely as possible in the course of the test. Therefore, the functionality of TAOS supports test data generation, test evaluation on the basis of test oracles, and test documentation. The user interface of TAOS consists of several graphical editors.

The test data are either determined manually, for example on the basis of the program structure, or generated automatically by means of a test data generator. Statistical tests with simultaneous coverage analysis can therefore be carried out in addition to regular structure tests. The evaluation takes place by comparing the actual values with the values given by the test oracle. TAOS contains a set of test oracles which can be adapted to the respective tests. The test results are documented in different reports. All resulting data are stored in a repository.

2.9 TBGEN and TCMON

TBGEN and TCMON [Testwell Oy, 1996] are two separate tools which in this combination support function and structure oriented tests. Their achievements include test execution, test evaluation, monitoring, and test documentation.

The main emphasis of TBGEN is on functional testing for the unit and integration test. TBGEN consists basically of a Testbed Generator which automates the generation of a test environment. In this environment a number of TBGEN specific test instructions are provided. These instructions can be dealt with separately or can be summarized in a test script. For documenting the test results a clear report can be generated according to the needs of the user.

With TCMON structural tests such as statement coverage and condition coverage are supported. An overall view of the test coverage achieved is part of the documentation.

The given details are based on an evaluation of the demo-versions of TBGEN 5.0 and TCMON 2.3. The Testbed Generator and the report generator were not part of the demos.

2.10 UATL

The UATL (Universal Ada Test Language) is a test language developed especially for the integration test of Ada programs [Ziegeler et al., 1989]. It is orientated primarily towards the automation of function oriented, real-time closed-loop tests. With the functionality of the UATL, tests in the host environment as well as on the target system are supported. The main emphasis is on test execution, monitoring, test evaluation, and test documentation.

The UATL consists of a set of Ada packages that provide the user with a complement of reusable test functions. It also includes an interactive test manager and interactive program generation tools which simplify the test program development process. Further components are a tool for the instrumentation of the source code according to white-box test criteria, a tool for real-time data recording, and a component for data reduction analysis. A graphical presentation of the test results in different kinds of charts is also supported.

2.11 Comparison of the Testing Tools

The study shows that a lot of tools are available for the automation of test execution and monitoring. More powerful tools also offer support for test evaluation and test documentation. A systematical test case design in particular is not supported by any of the tools evaluated. None of the tools supports expected values prediction extensively. Only one tool has a component for test data selection but several tools offer functionalities for the automatic generation of random test data. Several testing tools add static analysis features. It becomes clear that the tools, as a rule, are specialized in separate areas. Table 1 summarizes the individual functionalities of the different test systems and shows for the separate tools the scope of support for every test activity.

One of the most powerful commercial tools is AdaTEST from IPL. AdaTEST's strengths are the comprehensive support for test driver generation, the high degree of automation for test execution, and the large number of different coverage criteria provided by the monitoring component. Furthermore, AdaTEST offers an interface for the integration with other tools like the CTE, the TCD file. On the basis of an existing TCD file and the source code of the unit under test, most test activities can be performed automatically.

3. Integration of CTE and AdaTEST

The aim of integrating the classification-tree editor CTE with AdaTEST is to achieve systematic and comprehensive support for the functional test of Ada units with a high degree of automation. To integrate the classification-tree editor CTE with AdaTEST, extensions to the CTE were implemented. An export interface was added to the classification-tree editor which is based on a template file containing global as well as test case specific statements. The export interface facilitates the automatic generation of TCD files corresponding to the test cases specified graphically with the classification-tree method. For each test case the specific commands from the template file are duplicated. Along with the test case numbers, the textual representations for the test cases are generated and saved into the TCD file. Names and comments for test cases which the tester entered in the CTE can be exported to the TCD file optionally.

	AdaCAST	AdaTEST	DARTT	DEVISOR	LDRA Testbed	LOGISCOPE	STW Coverage	TAOS	TBGEN, TCMON	UATL
Test Organization	++	−	+	−	+	++	+	+	−	++
Test Case Determination	−	−	−	−	−	−	−	−	−	−
Test Data Selection	+	−	++	−	−	−	−	++	−	+
Expected Values Prediction	+	+	−	+	−	−	−	−	+	+
Test Execution	++	++	++	+	+	−	−	−	+	++
Monitoring	−	++	−	+	++	++	++	++	++	+
Test Evaluation	+	++	−	++	+	−	−	++	++	+
Test Documentation	++	++	++	−	++	+	++	++	++	++

++ activity extensively supported   + activity partly supported   − activity not supported

Table 1: Functionalities of the different test systems

The generated TCD file can further be used by AdaTEST directly for the generation of the test driver. In most cases, however, the user must add test data and expected values for the individual test cases to the TCD file. This is necessary because the test cases generated with the CTE usually represent an abstract description of the input situations to be tested and do not yet contain any concrete test data or expected values. In addition to the generation of the test driver, AdaTEST also executes automatically the instrumentation of the test object. The instrumented test object and the test driver are then compiled and linked together to an executable test program which automates test execution, test evaluation, and monitoring. As a result the test documentation containing the test results is generated. In the following the use of both tools is illustrated using the example *is_line_covered_by_rectangle*.

3.1 Example

In the course of the test of the sample function *is_line_covered_by_rectangle* the systematic test case design carried out by means of the CTE is the first step. The determination of the test cases for *is_line_covered_by_rectangle* has already been described in chapter 1. First of all, a classification tree covering the test relevant aspects is developed. Afterwards the test cases are determined by combining classes of different classifications in the combination table. 49 test cases were defined for the test of the sample function. Figure 2 shows a part of this classification tree and the combination table belonging to it.

For the next step a TCD file is generated by the CTE. For doing so the user enters the name of the TCD template to be used for AdaTEST into a dialogue box of the CTE. He then selects the *Export* operation of the CTE's file menu. The TCD file produced contains instructions in the AdaTEST specific Test Case Definition Language as specified in the corresponding template file. For each test case the TCD file contains the specification and a framework for calling the test object and giving the test data and the expected values. The order of the test cases is analogous to that in the CTE. The following paragraph shows a part of the generated TCD file along with the instructions generated automatically for the first test case.

```
%%TEST_CASE 1;

-- Test Case description
  %%PURPOSE "- coverage: yes";
  %%PURPOSE "  - degree of coverage: complete";
  %%PURPOSE "- position of endpoint P1: line endpoint P1 located inside the rectangle";
  %%PURPOSE "  - position of P1 in the rectangle: inside the rectangle";
  %%PURPOSE "- position of endpoint P2: line endpoint P2 located inside the rectangle";
  %%PURPOSE "  - position of P2 in the rectangle: inside the rectangle";
  %%PURPOSE "- Course of line: slanting";
  %%PURPOSE "  - direction of line: bottom left -> top right";
  %%PURPOSE "  - gradient of line: medium";

  %%CALL   graphics.is_line_covered_by_rectangle, " ";

  %%INPUTS
     rectangle :=  ;
     line :=  ;
  %%OUTPUTS
     ATS_RETURN :=  ;
```

As a next step the test data and the expected values for each test case are added by editing the TCD file. In case the test data and the expected values have been entered completely, the test driver can be generated automatically from the TCD file by means of the Ada-TEST script generator. Test execution, coverage analysis, test evaluation and documentation will then take place automatically in the framework of the AdaTEST functionality.

By executing the 49 test cases no error was detected in *is_line_covered_by_rectangle*. 100 % branch coverage as well as 100 % operand coverage were achieved with this test which hints at the good quality of the functional test. A part of the documentation generated with AdaTEST is shown in Figure 3. Figure 3 also shows parts of the three main files which were constructed or generated automatically combining CTE and AdaTEST. The interrelation between the specified test cases, the test run, and the test results is documented for the first test case.

4. Practical Experience

The classification-tree editor CTE has been used successfully in various projects for the systematic test case design for more than four years now (cf. [Grochtmann and Wegener, 1995]). In comparison with previous tests, perceptible savings could be achieved: the number of test cases could be reduced and their quality has been improved considerably. Thus the cost for the entire tests has been diminished substantially. Because of the positive user acceptance, a product version of the CTE has been developed and can be obtained from ATS (Automated Testing Solutions) since 1995.

The CTE-AdaTEST integration has already been successfully applied to several real world examples including aerospace applications and internal software products of Daimler-Benz Research. An application in the field of aviation was a rate limiter. For this example 28 test cases were determined systematically with the CTE. In the course of the test carried out on the basis of these test cases, 100 % coverage was measured for all structural test criteria supported by AdaTEST. In a further aerospace example a function of the complex COLUMBUS SW Development Environment (SDE) was examined. 16 test cases were determined. The execution of these test cases led to 97 % statement coverage. At the same time it was discovered that the exception coverage amounted to only 33 %. Those parts of the program that had not been reached could, however, be easily identified with the help of the clear presentation of the coverage analysis results in the test documentation. On the basis of the program information additional test cases could be determined which then led to 100 % exception coverage. One part of the functionality of this test object is the processing and the comparison of dates. In the course of the test it turned out that the unit under test did not recognize that some dates like April 31 were false.

The combined use of CTE and AdaTEST proved to be very helpful in the sample applications mentioned above. The quality of the tests and the number of test cases are influenced

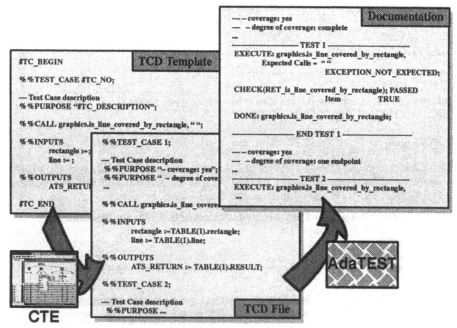

Figure 3: Interface between CTE and AdaTEST

considerably by the systematic test case determination. Moreover, the functionalities of AdaTEST offer an appropriate environment for an efficient test execution. The coverage analysis provided by AdaTEST offers a further evaluation criterion for the test. The systematically generated test cases, the test results, and the results of the coverage analysis summarized in the test documentation give a suitable overall view of the test which also allows to detect errors quickly. Furthermore, confidence in the function of the test object is established provided that no errors were found.

5. Conclusion

A number of professional tools exists for the unit testing of Ada programs. None of these tools, however, offers overall support for all test activities. Moreover, the tools evaluated lack methodological support for the important activity of functional test case design. Most of the tools concentrate on structure oriented test case determination on the basis of the results obtained from coverage analysis. In order to fill this gap the classification-tree editor CTE can be combined with existing tools.

The CTE is a graphical editor for the functional test case determination and supports the application of the classification-tree method. It has already proved very worthwhile in many different areas of application in the industrial practice and also has a flexible interface which facilitates the combination with other tools. An integration of the CTE with AdaTEST has been presented in this paper. An integration of the CTE with the test system TESSY for the testing of C programs is described in [Wegener and Pitschinetz, 1995].

The combination of the CTE with IPL's AdaTEST covers most of the activities which are essential to the unit testing and integration testing of Ada programs. Due to the methodological basis and the high degree of automation, the combination of both tools leads to systematic, well-documented, and efficient test procedures. Future work will focus on extensions for test data selection and expected values prediction as well as the automatic generation of test cases and test data. Furthermore, an integration of the CTE with the Test

Manager from SQA is in preparation to support systematic test case design also for the examination of applications with graphical user interfaces.

Acknowledgements

We are grateful to the following persons for their assistance with the different Ada test systems: Dr. Vieser and Mr. Hennell (LDRA Testbed), Mr. Gerlich (DARTT), Mrs. Buisson and Mr. Lernoud (DEVISOR), Mr. McCaffrey (AdaCAST), and finally Mr. Poutanen (TBGEN and TCMON).

References

Dassault Electronique (1994). DEVISOR System Tutorial and User Manual, DEVISOR System Test Language Reference Manual Version 9.4, DEVISOR Software debug and test system, 1994, Dassault Electronique, Saint-Cloud, France.

Gerlich, R. (1995). DARTT User's Manual Version 2.0, 1995, Dornier GmbH, Friedrichshafen, Germany.

Gerlich, R., and Fercher, G. (1993). A Random Testing Environment for Ada Programs. *Contribution to Forth EUROSPACE symposium on "Ada in Aerospace"*, 8 - 11 November 1993, Brussels, Belgium.

Graham, D., Herzlich, P., and Morelli, C. (1995). CAST Report – Computer Aided Software Testing. 1995, Cambridge Market Intelligence, London, UK.

Grochtmann, M., and Grimm, K. (1993). Classification Trees for Partition Testing. *Software Testing, Verification and Reliability*, Vol. 3, No. 2, pp. 63 - 82.

Grochtmann, M., and Wegener, J. (1995). Test Case Design Using Classification Trees and the Classification-Tree Editor CTE. *Proceedings of Quality Week '95*, 30 May - 2 June 1995, San Francisco, USA.

IPL (1995). AdaTEST Harness Version 3.0 User Guide & Reference Manual, AdaTEST Analysis Version 3.0 User Guide & Reference Manual, 1995, Information Processing Ltd., Bath, UK.

LDRA (1993). LDRA Testbed Technical Description, 1993, Liverpool Data Research Associates Ltd., Liverpool, UK.

Ostrand, T., and Balcer, M. (1988). The Category-Partition Method for Specifying and Generating Functional Tests. *Communications of the ACM*, 31 (6), 1988, pp. 676 - 686.

Richardson, D.J. (1994). TAOS: Testing with Analysis and Oracle Support. *ACM SIG-SOFT Software Engineering Notes: Proceedings of the 1994 International Symposium on Software Testing and Analysis*. 1994, Seattle, Washington, USA.

Testwell Oy (1996). What's new in TBGEN 5.0 ?, 1996, Testwell Oy, Tampere, Finland.

Vector Engineering (1995). AdaCAST Product Overview, 1995, Vector Engineering, North Kingstown, USA.

Verilog (1993). LOGISCOPE Ada Analyzer 2.0 Reference Manual, 1993, Verilog SA, Toulouse, France.

Wegener, J., and Pitschinetz, R. (1995). TESSY – An Overall Unit Testing Tool. *Proceedings of Quality Week '95*, 30 May - 2 June 1995, San Francisco, USA.

Ziegler, J., Grasso, J.M., and Burgermeister, L. (1989). An Ada Based Real-Time Closed–Loop Integration and Regression Test Tool. 1989, ITT Avionics, Washington, USA.

Ada 95 as a Base to Architect Systems in O4S™ (Objects For Systems)

Ingmar Ögren, Romet AB
Fridhem 2, S-76040 Väddö, Sweden
phone: +46 176 54580, fax: +46 176 54441,
e-mail: iog@romet.se, URL: www.romet.se

Work presented here has been sponsored by the Swedish Defence Material Administration and the Swedish National Board for Industrial and Technical Development. The text is also part of the O4S™ development handbook, part 3.

1 Abstract

Traditional "architecture" for buildings is studied to find what "architecture" should mean for complex information systems with a high software content. Different architectural qualities are presented and referenced to Ada 95-based work.

The system development O4S™ (Objects For Systems) is presented as a method that handles not only the information aspect of software and/or software, but complete systems including missions and operator's roles. In connection to O4S™, the Ada 95-inspired design language Odel is presented as a means to describe structure and behaviour of complex systems.

The concept of "architectural base" is introduced as a necessary base to architect and describe systems. It is shown how the architectural base for systems work can be connected to software standards:

- Ada 95 to provide semantics, syntax and formal base.
- MIL-STD-498 (Software development and documentation) to govern structure and documentation for systems work..

An applicatory example is given to show how the "architectural base" can be used to architect and describe complex systems on different levels.

Conclusion and message of this paper is: Ada 95 and MIL-STD-498 can be used, not only for software development, but also to create an architectural base for systems work concerning information systems work in general. This work can be extended to create a formal base for the information aspects of total systems.

2 Introduction

Engineering of complex systems means that you must create an architecture, composed from components of categories operator, software and hardware that co-operate to complete missions. The architecture must be described in a way that is readily understood by end users, system engineers and component implementors, such as software engineers.

The O4S™ systems engineering method uses the Odel (Object Design Language) that is defined in reference to Ada 95 (formalised English). This creates a way to architect and document complex systems.

3 What is Architecture?

When you study various papers on software and systems architecture, it is easy to get the impression that "systems architecture" can be anything. To get some idea what "architecture" should mean it can be a good idea to return to traditional architecture.

In architecture textbooks you will find some information about traditional architecture that is relevant also for software and information systems architecture (IT architecture):

Architecture encompasses all kinds of human building (thus including software and systems in general).

Architecting an information system should thus include not only software, but also humans and hardware when these take part in the information processing and/or are important for understanding the information in the software.

Architecture combines functionality with aesthetics

An architected system with its software must not only meet its functional requirements, but should also include an element of aesthetics. Aesthetics will concern both the user's impressions of the system and the system structure, as experienced by the analyst, designer and supporter.

An architectural implementation concerns components, design method and tradition.

The architecture should give a clear coupling between a completed product and its components. Architectural implementations can be grouped depending on design method and tradition. One such group, for information systems can be based on the combination of object-oriented methods and Ada.

Architectural work is basically a description of a product that is to be built. You can use models to clarify the description.

You can describe information systems with e g graphs, pseudo code, etc. Models can be software prototypes.

Architecture contains the three aspects design, function and form.
- The development process includes the design aspect.
- Requirements handling and verification of information systems represent the functional aspect.
- The form for information systems can vary. One possibility is to use a standardised form based on Ada 95 and MIL-STD-498.

4 What is Architecture good for?

4.1 Human needs

Architecture concentrates on human needs. For traditional architecture this means mainly dimensions like ceiling height, step heights, etc. that are adjusted to suit the average human.

Sometime you will find architectures seemingly adjusted for giants like in the government buildings in Washington DC or the imperial palace in Vienna, Austria. These exceptions, however, are motivated by the human need to express the gigantic power of the politicians in office.

The human need for a systems architecture is basically to support understanding. [3, 6 the "hrair" factor]. The "hrair limit" tells us that the limit to the number of entities a human can process at one time is roughly seven. To be able to develop and understand, we will thus need abstractions. An architectural base will then be helpful to create these abstractions.

4.2 Comfort

A good architecture contributes to comfort for its builders and users.

Comfort in a systems architecture means:

- system builders feel comfortable with their ability to express and understand the designs and system models
- system users feel comfortable with their user's interfaces and with their understanding of system functionality.

In the Ada community, comfort means that you work with the familiar programming concepts, not only in implementation, but also in analysis and design.

4.3 Economy

A good architecture is economical. In traditional architectures this can mean that you base an architecture on locally available materials and skills.

For systems architectures in the Ada community, locally available material is Ada components and legacy systems while an important local skill is to understand Ada's semantics and syntax.

4.4 Usefulness

A good architecture is useful, meaning that it fulfils its requirements.

For an information systems architecture this means both that it must fulfil its requirements and that it must be possible to show that it fulfils its requirements.

For a good systems architectural base, we require that it makes it possible to describe a system exactly and unambiguously. This can be achieved with an architectural base, derived from Ada 95.

4.5 Impression

A good architecture shall give the right impression. For example a shopping centre should look inviting and bank should look secure.

For information system architectures this means that the user shall get an understandable and correct impression of the information handled, for example through intuitive icons. This is *extremely important* as the user will have difficulties to trust a system, that does not give him a correct and readily understandable impression of the information available.

A systems architecture, based on a the programming language Ada 95 can give the impression: "this is code and thus only understandable for software experts". To give a correct expression, we need intuitive graphs to complement the textual form to describe systems. These graphs must be formally coupled to the Ada syntax. Examples of useful graphical syntax are given below.

4.6 Requirements Meeting Implementation

A traditional architecture is an interpretation of the proprietor's requirements. It also sets the requirements for and guides the construction work.

The same concerns any information system architecture that must interpret a set of requirements (written or not) and distribute and derive requirements on implementation modules.

The software standards Ada 95 and MIL-STD-498 contain modularisation concepts that can be used for requirements distribution (CSCI, SU, Package).

4.7 Multi-level Understanding

Traditional architecture concerns several levels like area, building, interior, etc. The levels connect to each other.

The same goes for information systems architectures that should be applicable on several levels with connections between the levels.

Ada 95, mainly the "with" construct that couples packages on different semantic levels to each other, is useful to structure systems on multiple levels.

4.8 Organisation of Building Blocks

A rational architecture makes maximal use of existing building blocks and sometimes contains definitions of new building blocks for reuse.

The same goes for information systems architectures where the building blocks can be for example Ada packages or COTS (Commercial Off The Shelf) modules.

Standards are helpful to get an understandable and accepted organisation of IT-architectures. Applicable standards are Ada 95 and MIL-STD-498. These standards will provide forms for building blocks:

- Subprogram and Package from Ada 95
- CSCI (Computer Software Configuration Item) and SU (Software Unit) from MIL-STD-498.

4.9 Similarity and Difference

As shown above it is easy to find a set of similarities between traditional architecture and Information System architecture (IT-architecture). These similarities basically depend on the common need to fulfil human needs.

The main difference is that traditional architecture concerns physical layout, structure and functionality while IT architecture concerns logical layout, structure and behaviour.

5 O4S™ and Odel to Architect Complex Systems

O4S™ (Objects For Systems) is an object-oriented system development method. The figure shows how the method views systems engineering as centred around the user's engagement. Some of the main characteristics of O4S™ are: System concept, iteration, recurrence and user's engagement. This means:

- System concept in O4S™ means that you work, not only with software, but with systems constituted from Operators, Software and Hardware, co-operating to complete Missions. These are all modelled as objects in a system hierarchy.

- Iteration means that the method presupposes that the developer and the user learn during development. O4S™ is thus structured in activities, not in phases. You are allowed, recommended and supported to redo activities for an object, while the object evolves from draft to delivery version.
- Recurrence means that you apply the same activities to all objects in a system structure, from system level to component level.
- User's engagement means that users are allowed and expected to take part in system development. Also that the O4S™ notations are easily understandable.

To architect a system in O4S™, you use the language Odel (Object design language). Odel is a language, inspired from Ada 95 with a graphical and a textual form:

- The total architectural structure of a system is shown with three graphs
- The structure for a single object with an offered interface as a set of actions and required interface as a set of required support object interfaces is shown with object graphs and as Ada-inspired pseudo code
- The behaviour for an object is shown per action as Ada-inspired pseudo code.

"Ada-inspired" in Odel means that the semantics and syntax of Ada 95 are followed as far as possible in order to make the Odel language easily readable by anyone who is literate in Ada. It also means that some simplifications, as compared to Ada 95, have been introduced to hide programming details and to make the language readable for end users, who are not literate in Ada. They normally experience Odel as "formalised English".

This means that the Odel description gives the programmer a framework for his work with interfaces and requirements on software behaviour. Still, it leaves the programmer freedom to solve the programming problems, that may not be very well understood by a system designer.

6 The O4S™ Architectural base

6.1 The Object

The object, or rather the object type, should naturally be a central concept in an object-oriented architectural base. The object type concept gives a form that is useful on any level from complete system to a low level system component.

Note that an object type here represents a collection of related actions and data, as compared to the more limited "object" concept in Ada 95 [ref. 1], that is limited to data objects (ADTs). The "object type" described here maps most closely to Ada's "package" concept.

Each object type defined can be implemented in one or more instances (like an Ada package type).

The entity-relationship graph below shows the object type with related concepts:

The relations in the figure are:

Object can support object
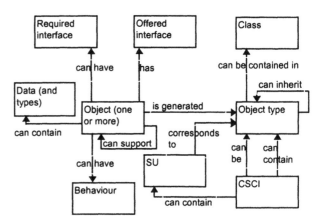
When the actions in object use actions in another object, the second object is a "support object".

Object has offered interface

An object's offered interface contains the actions that the object offers to the "outside world".

In Ada 95 this corresponds to the package specification, that defines the actions a package offers "to system".

Object can have required interface

When an object is supported by other objects, this means that the actions, contained in the current object, invokes actions in the support objects. The sum of the actions used in the support objects is the required interface of the current object.

In Ada 95 this corresponds to a package's "with list", combined with the actions used to support the current package.

Note that offered and required interfaces allow parameter passing "both ways".

Object can contain data (and types)

To architect an IT-system, you must know what information it shall handle. You define this as types and data, contained in objects.

In Ada 95, this corresponds to type and data declarations.

Object can have behaviour

An object that contains actions, also has a behaviour, that is determined from its actions and from data contained in the object.

In Ada 95, this corresponds to package bodies where behaviour is defined as a reaction to input data and current state of the package's actions.

Object is generated from object type
When you define an architecture, you define objects as object types, from which object instances are created.

In Ada 95, this corresponds to generation of package instances from a package type.

Object type can be contained in class
Like in Ada 95 [1], a set of object types, derived from each other trough inheritance, can be contained in a class.

Note that this differs from many object-oriented notations that use "class" for "object type".

Object type can inherit object type
An object type can inherit another object with addition and/or redefinition of actions, contained in the object type.

SU corresponds to object type
In MIL-STD-498 [7], SU means "Software Unit".
Here, the meaning of SU is widened to "System Unit". The SU can then be used, not only for software, but also for hardware and operator system parts.

CSCI can be object type
CSCI, according to MIL-STD-498 [ref. 7], means "Computer Software Configuration Item". Here, the meaning of CSCI is widened to "Complete System Configuration Item". The CSCI can then contain, not only for software, but also hardware and operator system parts.

CSCI can contain object type
From an architectural point of view, a CSCI is a useful concept for grouping a number of object types together. You can do this grouping for structural reasons, but also for organisational reasons.

CSCI can contain SU
As the CSCI is a wider concept, as compared to the SU, a CSCI will normally contain a number of SUs.

6.2 Compositive Arrangement of Objects with "Contained/Attached"

In O4S™ (Ada 95), you can describe any system structure as a structure of objects (packages) supporting each other. Some of the objects are CI-objects (CI = Configuration Item), while others are ordinary objects. The CI concept is then mainly used to structure systems and to organise work. An object can be supported by other objects within (contained) or outside (attached) the CI that contains the current object.

Each object has an offered interface and can have a required interface:

- The offered interface is constituted from the actions, offered by the object to its environment

- The "required interface" is the parts of the offered interfaces in the support objects that are used to complete the behaviour of the current object.

This is shown graphically in a syntax based on Booch 83 [3]:

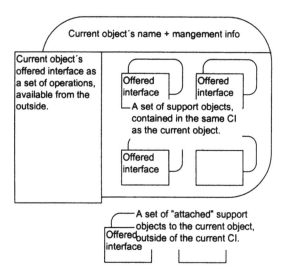

6.3 Inheritance with the Class Concept

You can derive an object type from another object type through inheritance. Inheritance then means the derived object contains the actions of the original object type, possibly with changed functionality. The derived object can further contain new actions.

As an example is shown the system "Carrier company" where we consider the class "carrier_vehicle", that contains two object types: boat and truck.

Both objects are of category "hardware objects" In PDL language Odel this is expressed:

```
object Carrier_boat is
-- inherits (Boat:Vehicle)
```

Note that the textual and graphical notations for inheritance in Odel are informal. The reason for this is that Odel is intended for architecting systems, while inheritance details are best expressed in the programming language(s) used.

6.4 Dynamic Binding

Dynamic binding is a result of the fact that an action can be redefined when inherited. The action with same name can then be invoked in different object types, with different implementation of the action.

An object graph for the object Carrier_company, containing the objects Carrier_boat and Carrier_truck will then look like this:

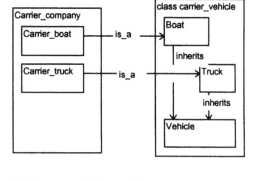

Note that the boat and the truck offer the same actions, although they are obviously implemented with different behaviour, depending on vehicle type. The concept of dynamic binding will thus help to architect systems where similar actions are carried out by objects with different behaviour.

6.5 Handling Different views from an Architectural Viewpoint

Need for different views
A traditional architecture is described from different views like e g plans, projections, component lists, models, etc. The same goes for an IT architecture. Some of the different views needed are presented in reference [5]. Below, some of the possible views are presented, with a discussion of how their respective needs can be satisfied with the "architectural base".

Logical view
The logical view concerns structure and behaviour. This is covered by object types (System Units) combined with behaviour per object type, expressed in Odel, alternatively in state charts or some other presentation form.

Static view
The object type structure has two levels: CSCI level and SU level where Odel's object type concept is used on both levels. These two levels can be used to give a static view of any system.

Scenario view
For description of scenarios or "use cases" [ref. 4], the Odel concept of object type is used again, as "mission objects". Inclusion of scenarios as "missions" formally in the object structure gives three important advantages as compared to working with a separate "use case" or "scenario" structure:

- the same syntax is used for scenarios as for any other object
- missions can be included and integrated in a systems architecture on several levels
- operator roles can be included in the system description.

Dynamic view
The dynamic view of a system has several aspects like:

- dynamic behaviour per object type
- dynamic creation/deletion of object instances as a result of events and internal object states
- fulfilment of non-functional requirements concerning capacity, load, etc.

Behaviour and creation/deletion of object instances are handled through Odel behavioural descriptions per object type. Non-functional requirements are handled as any other requirement through requirements definition per object type. Dynamic object behaviour can further be visualised through simulation.

Physical view

Traditionally you handle hardware and software differently. From an IT-architectural point of view this is not necessary as you can handle the hardware as object types with logical structure, behaviour, etc.

It is thus possible to include hardware elements as any other element (object type) in an IT-architecture. This however does not concern "real physical" qualities like for example weight, size, etc.

7 Use of the Architectural base to Describe Different kinds of Objects

Above are shown principles to use the standards Ada 95 and MIL-STD-498, to create an architectural base. This architectural base can be applied in systems work on different levels as shown below. Systems work then includes definition of structure and behaviour from an information management viewpoint of object categories:

- mission, to define objectives and scenarios on different levels
- operator, to define operator's roles
- software, to describe software as a basis for implementation
- hardware, limited to the information handling aspects of hardware, but including information handling capacity.

Architecting systems is difficult. The difficulties have been experienced very clearly in software work. The difficulties have further led to development of syntax and semantics for handling of software, like in Ada 95 and MIL-STD-498.

This work, that has been done primarily to handle the software problems, can be applied to complete IT systems. This is done simply through extension of the object type concept to include, not only software objects, but also:

- Mission objects to describe missions (scenarios)
- Hardware objects to describe hardware objects, using or used by other parts of an IT system
- Operator objects to describe operator's roles included in IT-systems as a logical part.

8 Multi-level Application of the Architectural base

8.1 Detail Level

On the detail level, the object type is the system component. To meet the basic requirements for understandability and reusability, the size of each object type description is limited. This limitation is expressed as two limit recommendations in O4S™ [ref. 9 + 10]:

- limit the number of support objects for any object to less than ten [ref. "hrair limit" in 3]
- limit the behaviour complexity per object type through limitation of its PDL description to about two pages.

On the detail level, the architectural base thus gives a mechanism to describe system components with their content and connection.

The principle to connect supporting objects also makes it possible to describe a system of any size as a single object.

8.2 Domain Level

A domain is an area that represents a usage area. In such a usage area, several applications are possible. In a domain, system elements for the usage area concerned are gathered.

You can use the architectural base in two ways in domain work:

- to describe system elements included in the domain
- to structure and describe the total content of the domain.

8.3 Application Level

On the application level, you can use the architectural base to structure and describe any application system. You use the architectural description:

- to document and understand the system
- to evaluate a system solution
- as a base for implementation of the system
- as a guide and "road map" during development and support of the system.

An often heard objection is that real systems are not strictly hierarchical, but that the system structure is "more complicated".

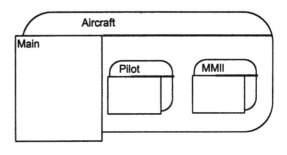

This objection is based on the misunderstanding that the object type structure with offered and required interfaces leads to a "strict hierarchy". As an example consider the interaction between a pilot and his MMI when a main warning is flashed. This situation can be seen from the pilot and from the panel:

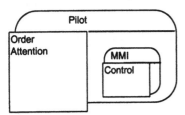
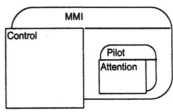

The structure can also viewed as a tree graph. It shows how "Pilot" and "MMI" are active in parallel and depend on each other.

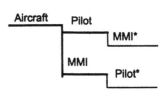

9 Experiences

O4S™ has been used to architect various military projects. Experiences are:

- Building the architectural structure early in a project helps to reveal problems.
- The object structure makes it simple to distribute requirements as fulfilment requirements per object. This makes it simple to specify tests.
- The principle with offered and required interfaces per object, makes it possible to apply traditional methods for analysis of fault tolerance like FTA and FMEA.
- The architectural description with interfaces and behaviour, described per object, gives a good level of formality. It is quite useful as a basis for software engineering and programming in Ada 95 or other languages.
- Simple software tools like the GNAT and MS Word can be used to support systems enginering.

10 Conclusions

The basic conclusion is that the difficulties to structure and develop software now has led to development of software-oriented standards to such an extent that you can apply these standards not only to software, but also to describe complex system architectures. This makes it possible to architect and document complex systems, where operators co-operate with software and hardware to complete missions, in a uniform way, based on Ada 95 and MIL-STD-498.

The Ada 95-based system description syntax gives a good level of formality as it is possible to analyse with conventional software tools. Still, the descriptions are readable for end users, system engineers and implementors (software and hardware).

The principle with offered and required interfaces per object makes it possible to apply traditional FTA and FMEA for fault tolerance analysis of critical systems.

11 References

[1] Ada 95, Reference manual

[2] Ada 95 Rationale

[3] Grady Booch: Software Engineering with Ada, Benjamin Cummings 1983

[4] I Jacobson: Object-Oriented Software Engineering - A Use Case Driven Approach, Addison-Wesley 1992

[5] P. B Kruchten and C. J. Thompson: An Object-Oriented, Distributed Architecture for Large Scale Ada Systems, TRI-Ada 1994

[6] G. A. Miller: The Magical Number Seven, Plus or Minus Two, Psychological Review, Vol. 63, No 2, March 1956

[7] MIL-STD-498, 5 December 1994.

I Ogren: O4S™ development handbook (available through URL www.romet.se):
[8] part 1   Overview and introduction
[9] part 2   Activities in the development process
[10] part 3 Fundamental concepts
[11] part 4 Compliance with standards

[12] Proceedings IEEE 1994 Tutorial and Workshop on Systems Engineering of Computer-Based Systems

Including Non-functional Issues in Anna/Ada Programs for Automatic Implementation Selection

Xavier Franch

Universitat Politècnica de Catalunya
Department Llenguatges i Sistemes Informàtics
Pau Gargallo 5. E-08028 Barcelona (Catalonia, Spain)
e-mail: franch@lsi.upc.es

Abstract. We present an enrichment of the Anna specification language for Ada aimed at dealing not only with functional specification of packages but also with non-functional information about them. By non-functional information we mean information about efficiency, reliability and, in general, any software attribute measuring somehow the quality of software (perhaps in a subjective manner). We divide this information into three kinds: definition of non-functional properties, statement of non-functional behaviour and statement of non-functional requirements; like Anna annotations, all of this information appears in Ada packages and package bodies and their syntax is close to Ada constructs. Non-functional information may be considered not only as valuable comments, but also as an input for an algorithm capable of selecting the "best" package body for every package definition in a program, the "best" meaning the one that fits the set of non-functional requirements of the package in the program.

1 Introduction

Component programming [Jaz95, Sit+94] is a useful and widely employed way of building complex software systems by means of combining, reusing and producing software components. What a component does is stated by its functional properties. Different implementations must satisfy them, but they will differ in some non-functional aspects, such as execution time or reliability.

Among other possibilities, we are interested in software components as an encapsulation of *abstract data types* (*ADT*) [Gut75], described by algebraic specifications and implemented using an imperative or object-oriented programming language. To be more precise, we view software components consisting of: a) the *definition* of an ADT stating both functional and non-functional characteristics, and b) one or more *implementations*, each one including a description of its non-functional behaviour.

In this paper, we propose component programming with ADTs using:

- Ada [Ada83] as the programming language. Then, definitions of ADTs are encapsulated in packages while implementations appear inside package bodies[1].

- The Anna specification language [LH85, Luc90] for stating functional properties of ADTs.

- Some new constructs [Fra96, FB96, FB97] for dealing with non-functionality.

We consider three kinds of non-functional information:

- *Non-functional property* (short, *NF-property*): any attribute of software which serves as a means to describe it and possibly to evaluate it; for instance, time efficiency of a procedure or portability of a package body.

- *Non-functional behaviour* of a component implementation (short, *NF-behaviour*): any assignment to the NF-properties which have been declared of interest for the implemented software component.

- *Non-functional requirement* imposed on a software component (short, *NF-requirement*): any constraint referring to a subset of the NF-properties which have been declared of interest for the software component.

In order to make our approach more attractive, we integrate these last new constructs into the Anna notation, providing then an integrated framework where functional and non-functional aspects of software are uniformly considered, as we think they always should be.

The rest of the paper is structured as follows. We review in section 2 the main features of the Anna specification language. Sections 3, 4 and 5 introduce non-functional properties, behaviour and requirements, respectively. Section 6 shows how our packages are managed to produce different files distinguishing the non-functional part from the functional one. Section 7 gives an outline of the automatic selection algorithm. Finally, section 8 provides the conclusions.

2 The Anna Specification Language

The Anna specification language (ANNotated Ada) [LH85, Luc90] is a language extension of Ada that includes features supporting functional specification such that:

Anna program = Ada program + formal comments

Formal comments are just comments from the Ada point of view, and so Anna programs are acceptable by Ada compilers with no changes at all. However, these comments obey some syntactic rules and they have a semantic meaning. There are two types of formal comments:

---

[1] Hereafter, we use the words "definition" and "package" interchangeably, and the same with "implementation" and "package body".

- Virtual Ada text. Definition of virtual concepts by means of usual Ada subprogram constructs. These virtual concepts are used in annotations (see below) to state functional specifications, and their definition can be either by a (virtual) Ada body or by means of annotations; in the first case, they are executable as usual Ada subprograms. Syntactically, lines in virtual Ada text begin with '--:'.

- Annotations. Statement of functional specifications, possibly involving virtual concepts introduced with virtual Ada text. There are many kinds of annotations, identified by means of key words. We remark:

  - Object annotations. They constrain the value of one or more program variables.

  - Subtype annotations. They support the formulation of representation invariants [Hoa72] of types.

  - Statement annotations. To formulate arbitrary assertions in the middle of Ada code.

  - Subprogram annotations. A kind of pre post specification of functions and procedures that may include constraints on their formal parameters, function results, etc.

  - Axiomatic annotations. Classical algebraic specification of ADTs by means of conditional equations.

  Syntactically, lines in annotations begin with '--|'.

A package representing mappings (mathematical functions) is shown in fig. 1; we will suppose in the rest of the paper that we have operations to create the mapping, to add a pair <key, information>, to remove a pair given its key, to obtain the information associated to a key and also to get the list of defined keys; to simplify some details that are not relevant to our work, we suppose that both keys and information are integer numbers. We present a private type representation by means of a bounded array with a cursor to the first free position; pairs are stored in order of arrival. So, addition of new pairs must take care of lack of space; for this reason, we introduce two virtual Ada functions, one to compute the number of pairs already in the array and the other to find out if a key is already defined. As part of the type representation, we provide a representation invariant which states the valid values of the cursor (this could be made with Ada code) and also that keys do not appear more than once in the data structure (this part could not be written with Ada code); the last fact uses two quantifiers provided by Anna. Note that, as stated in [Hoa72], some relationships implicitly hold as pre and post conditions of ADT operations, coming from the invariant.

As a convention, we use lowercase identifiers (except for initials) for virtual Ada text, annotations and also non-functional information. For the sake of brevity, we do not include the package body, which could provide code for the virtual Ada subprograms in order to obtain executable annotations (in this case, the code is easy to write and not too inefficient, which could be a problem when executing annotations).

```
package MAPPING_ADT is
   use LIST_OF_INTEGER;  -- for the GET_ALL_KEYS operation
   type MAPPING is private;
   --: function NbKeys (M: MAPPING) return NATURAL;
   --: function DefinedKey (M: MAPPING; K: INTEGER) return BOOLEAN;
   ...
      procedure ADD_PAIR (M: in out MAPPING; K, V: in INTEGER);
   --|    where in not DefinedKey(M, K) => (NbKeys(M) <= MAX_KEYS),
   --|        out DefinedKey(M, K);
   ...
   private
     type MAPPING is
        record A: array (1..MAX_KEYS) of record k, v: INTEGER end;
             FREE: INTEGER;
        end record;
   --| where M: MAPPING =>
   --|    (M.FREE > 0) and (M.FREE <= MAX_KEYS + 1) and
   --|    for all K: INTEGER =>
   --|        (1 <= K < M.FREE =>
   --|              not exist R: INTEGER =>
   --|                  (R <> K) and (M.A[R].k = M.A[K].k))
end MAPPING_ADT;
```

Fig. 1. An Anna specification for mappings

From this description, we may conclude that Anna is a powerful and easy-to-use notation for stating functional specifications of ADTs implemented with Ada. However, it does not provide any mean to deal with non-functional aspects of packages, such as efficiency or reliability. So, in the rest of the paper we enrich Anna with some new constructs to obtain what we think it is a complete specification language, by putting functional and non-functional specifications together.

3 Declaration of Non-Functional Properties

NF-properties attached to software components may be of many different kinds: 1) *boolean*, to represent software attributes which simply hold or fail (ex.: full portability of an implementation); 2) *integer*, to introduce software attributes that can be measured (ex.: reliability of an implementation); 3) *by enumeration*, to represent software attributes which can be classified into some categories (ex.: type of user interface); 4) *string*, to associate arbitrary identifiers as value of NF-properties; 5) *asymptotic*, to establish the execution time and space of types and operations.

Asymptotic NF-properties need not to be explicitly declared; their existence is inferred from the definition: there is an NF-property for every type measuring the space of its representation, and there are two NF-properties for every public procedure, one for its execution time and the other for its auxiliary space. In the ADT framework, we measure efficiency with the *big-Oh asymptotic notation* [Knu76, Bra85], defined as:

$$O(f) = \{g: \mathcal{N}^+ \to \mathcal{N}^+ \: / \: \exists c_0 \in \mathcal{N}^+, \: \exists n_0 \in \mathcal{N}^+: \forall n \geq n_0: g(n) \leq c_0 f(n)\}^2$$

($\mathcal{N}^+$ stands for non-zero natural numbers.) Values of this kind of NF-properties are given in terms of some *measurement units*, which represent problem domain sizes and which must also appear in definitions.

A set of possible NF-properties for the *MAPPING_ADT* package is shown in fig. 2. Their names, together with the comments we include, are self-explanatory enough. Some of the numerical and by enumeration properties declare the valid values they can take. In the case of *reliability*, there is an implicit ordering (writing ordering) which allows later to write expressions as "reliability >= medium". We introduce a measurement units for the keys[3]. Note that we declare the properties as virtual Ada text, as is usually done when working with Anna.

```
package MAPPING_ADT is
    ... declaration of interface with Anna annotations
    --: properties
    --:     boolean error_recovery, fully_portable;
    --:     string supplier;  -- "own" stands for software produced in the company
    --:     integer reusability_degree [0..5];
    --:     integer month [1..12], year;   -- date of delivery of the component
    --:     enumeration reliability = (none, low, medium, high);
    --: measurement units nb_keys;
end MAPPING_ADT;
```

Fig. 2. Declaration of NF-properties for mappings

In order to allow programmers to define their own catalogue of NF-properties, it is possible to introduce them in separate packages which do not contain real Ada code; these packages may be used inside any other one. Although we are not going to show this in the paper, it is possible to form hierarchies with these packages. For instance, we can reformulate the *MAPPING_ADT* package as in fig. 3.

---

[2] We may extend this definition for the case of having more than one parameter to measure efficiency.

[3] This measurement unit does not have the same meaning as the *NbKeys* virtual function of fig. 1: the first one concerns asymptotic sizes, while the second one counts the actual number of keys.

```
package CREATION_ISSUES is
  --: properties
  --:     integer month [1..12], year;   -- date of delivery of the component
  --:     string supplier;  -- "own" stands for software produced in the company
end CREATION_ISSUES;

package MAPPING_ADT is
  ... declaration of interface with Anna annotations
  --: properties
  --:     use CREATION_ISSUES;
  --:     boolean error_recovery, fully_portable;
  --:     integer reusability_degree [0..5];
  --:     enumeration reliability = (none, low, medium, high);
  --: measurement units nb_keys;
end MAPPING_ADT;
```

Fig. 3. An equivalent declaration of NF-properties for mappings

4 Statement of Non-Functional Behaviour

Each package body implementing an ADT should state its NF-behaviour with respect to the NF-properties declared in the definition package, including efficiency ones. For instance, the behaviour of the implementation for *MAPPING_ADT* using the representation shown in fig. 1 may look as in fig. 4. Note that non-asymptotic NF-properties and also the asymptotic space of the type representation are listed altogether, while efficiency of operations is stated in the operations themselves. See the use of arithmetic operators to state efficiency, which are interpreted in the big-Oh notation [Bra85]; the equality $time(x) = E$ means $time(x) \in O(E)$ (the same for *space*).

```
package body MAPPING_ADT is
  --| behaviour
  --|     error_recovery; fully_portable; reusability_degree = 4; reliability = high;
  --|     month = 8; year = 1996; supplier = "own";
  --|     space(mapping) = nb_keys;
  ...
  procedure GET_ALL_KEYS ...
  --| time(GET_ALL_KEYS) = pow(nb_keys, 2); space(GET_ALL_KEYS) = 1;
  ...
end MAPPING_ADT;
```

Fig. 4. Non-functional behaviour of an implementation for mappings

5 Statement of Non-Functional Requirements

NF-requirements state constraints imposed on implementations of software components. Syntactically, they are Ada boolean expressions enriched with some *ad hoc* constructs for non-functionality (see examples below). They may appear both in packages and package bodies.

NF-requirements in packages state the conditions that every implementation of the component must fulfil in order to be useful in the system. Put it in other words, they form the non-functional part of the specification of the component. Below, we enrich the *MAPPING_ADT* package with some relationships between NF-properties: execution time of individual operations must not exceed linear cost, while the time of obtaining the list of all the keys is (asymptotically) bounded by the square of the number of keys; also, some constraints about the value of *reliability* are stated. Note that all of these relations are up to the specifier, although sometimes there are relationships which are inherent to the ADT.

```
package MAPPING_ADT is
   ...
   --: properties
   --:    use CREATION_ISSUES;
   --:    ...the same as before
   --: relations
   --|    time(ADD_PAIR, REMOVE_PAIR, LOOK_UP) <= nb_keys;
   --|    time(GET_ALL_KEYS) = pow(nb_keys, 2);
                 -- "pow" means power; here, symbol "<=" stands for set inclusion
   --|    not error_recovery => (reliability <= medium);
   --|    (not fully_portable and supplier <> "own") => reliability = none;
end MAPPING_ADT;
```

Fig. 5. Non-functional specification for mappings

NF-requirements appearing in a package body V state the conditions that the implementations of all the software components used by V must fulfil in order to be useful in V. Their purpose is to represent the environment into which implementations are to be introduced. They should be complete enough to select a single package body (i.e., a single implementation) for each imported software component. In the general case, V will include a list of NF-requirements over every imported component[4]; the importance of NF-requirements in the list corresponds to their order of appearance.

---

[4] This corresponds with the usual case of having requirements with different degrees of importance.

For instance, an NF-requirement imposed on lists in the package body for *MAPPING_ADT* could be: first, list implementation must be as reliable as possible; next, the cost of the operations to build a list (*EMPTY* and *PUT*) must be constant (i.e., O(1)); last, list traversal should be as fast as possible. To state this requirement, we can use a few predefined operators, such as *max* and *min*, which have an intuitive meaning.

```
package body MAPPING_ADT is
  use LIST;
  --| behaviour   ...the same as before
  --| requirements on LIST_OF_INTEGER:
  --|     max(reliability);
  --|     time(EMPTY, PUT) = 1;
  --|     min(time(TRAVERSAL));
  ... package body using Ada and Anna features
end MAPPING_ADT;
```

Fig. 6. Non-functional requirements on lists inside *MAPPING_ADT*

6 Package Organisation and Processing

Packages and package bodies are analysed in a pre-process step and they generate two different files:

- An Anna/Ada package, where every appearance of non-functional information has become just a comment. This file can be then processed by a standard Anna toolset.

- A file containing non-functional information in an abstract-syntax tree form. These kinds of files are the ones managed by the selection algorithm presented in the next section.

Some words should be said about the existence of multiple implementations for software components. In standard Anna/Ada programs, it is not possible to have more than one package body for the same package, which contradicts our definition of software component. To solve this problem, we allow more than one pair package - package body to exist for a given ADT. Every pair shares the same identifier in the package (although the name of the files will differ), but they have different identifiers for the package bodies (*MAPPING_BY_LISTS*, *ORDERED_MAPPING*, etc.). To make explicit that a package body is an implementation of a package, we add a new key word, "implements", to appear in the header after the identifier, as in:

package body MAPPING_BY_LISTS implements MAPPING_ADT is...

So, our tool is able to keep track of the package bodies corresponding to a given ADT, which is necessary to select the best implementation for an ADT in a program in an automatic manner. When generating Anna/Ada packages, headers and identifiers are manipulated to follow Ada conventions.

7 Automatic Selection Algorithm

We have built an algorithm to select implementations of ADTs in a program. If all packages have their non-functional information completely defined, the algorithm may proceed starting from the package body that contains the main procedure down to the hierarchy of packages that form the whole program.

Every time a package body M is reached, it is necessary to select which implementations to attach to the packages that M uses: for every package D used in M, the algorithm proceeds by computing the list of NF-requirements for D appearing inside M. NF-requirements in the list are applied in order of appearance until one of the following conditions holds:

1) a single implementation is selected;

2) applying the next NF-requirement would yield an empty set of implementations;

3) all the NF-requirements have been applied. In the last two cases, more than one implementation may satisfy a given list, with the result that requirements may have to be reviewed.

The result defines the set of valid implementations for D; if there is more than one, NF-requirements for D appearing in other packages will choose one of them. The implementation finally selected may also use other packages, which are processed in the same way; so, selection of an implementation becomes selection of a tree of implementations.

The algorithm may fail for any of the following reasons (apart from purely lexical, syntactical or type errors in the source code):

• NF-behaviour has been left incomplete (or even does not exist) in some packages.

• An NF-requirement imposed on a package is not satisfied by any of its implementations[5]. The programmer must decide whether this NF-requirement can be relaxed somehow; otherwise, a new implementation satisfying it must be built.

---

[5] We consider that a list of NF-requirements is violated if the first NF-requirement in the list is not satisfied by any implementation.

- There is not a single implementation satisfying all the NF-requirements imposed on its definition [Fra94]. The programmer must decide how NF-requirements can be relaxed somehow to obtain an implementation valid in all its contexts of use. Also, the algorithm may be tuned to examine only the first NF-requirement in the lists of NF-requirements, which may enlarge the set of implementations locally satisfying the requirements.

It is worth mentioning that the algorithm may select multiple implementations of the same ADT in different places of the program. This coexistence is allowed, provided that there is no interaction between objects of the same type but different implementations. To make possible this scenario, different copies of the same definition package must be done, with different names to avoid clashes.

8 Conclusions

A language for adding non-functional information of software components into Anna/Ada programs has been presented. Non-functional information is expressed in a consistent way with respect to Anna/Ada programs and complements the functional specification part, which is well covered by Anna. The kind of non-functional information provided is complete enough to support automatic selection of the best implementations of components in every context where they appear.

We think that our work offers two main contributions:

- We provide a complete, easy-to-use (at least, for Ada programmers) and formally defined notation [Fra96] to state non-functional issues of software systems. This notation improves software understandability, reusability and maintenance, since more information appears in the software itself. In spite of many claims to this effect [Sha84, Win90, MCN92, Jaz95], we do not know of any approach providing a programming language with the same features as ours. There are many non-formalised or partial proposals [Mat84, LG86, Win89, CGN94, Sit94, SY94] the results of which are subsumed in our work. Also, [CZ90] present a very interesting framework, close to our selection algorithm but restricted to non-functional properties taking numerical values; they do not integrate their approach into any programming language.

- The best implementations for software components can be automatically selected. The existence of such an algorithm supports software development and also software maintenance [FB97], because non-functional modifications in the environment of the system or in the components themselves (i.e., as implementations become more carefully tested or their efficiency is improved) require no more than re-running the algorithm to update the software. A few proposals have been made in this direction [Sc+86, Kan86], but they are bound to languages with major restrictions (a few implementations for a few types).

Currently, an initial prototype of the selection algorithm exists. This algorithm, in fact, may be applied to any Ada-like programming language, provided that we change the Lex and Yacc files that generate the abstract-syntax tree internal representation from non-functional information.

There is a lot of future work to be done. First, we would like to adapt our approach to Ada95, to support inheritance. Also, we would like to allow interaction between objects of the same type but different implementations. Finally, the constructs concerning non-functionality may be enriched in many ways: by defining derived NF-properties, by building predefined catalogues of NF-properties, etc.

References

[Ada83]   U.S. Departament of Defense. *Reference Manual for the Ada Programming Language*. American National Standards Institute/MIL-STD-1815A-1983, 1983.

[Bra85]   G. Brassard. "Crusade for a Better Notation". SIGACT News, 16(4), 1985.

[CGN94]   D. Cohen, N. Goldman, K. Narayanaswamy. "Adding Performance Information to ADT Interfaces". In *Procs. of Interface Definition Languages Workshop*, SIGPLAN Notices 29(8), 1994.

[CZ90]   S. Cárdenas, M.V. Zelkowitz. "Evaluation Criteria for Functional Specifications". In *Proceedings of 12th ICSE*, Nice (France), 1990.

[FB96]   X. Franch, X. Burgués. "Supporting Incremental Component Programming with Functional and Non-Functional Information". In *Proceedings of XVI Computer Science Chilean Conference (SCCC)*, Valdivia (Chile), 1996.

[FB97]   X. Franch, P. Botella. "Supporting Software Maintenance with Non-Functional Information". In *Proceedings of 1st Euromicro Conference on Software Maintencance and Reengineering*, Berlin (Germany), 1997.

[Fra94]   X. Franch. "Combining Different Implementations of Types in a Program". In *Proceedings Joint of Modular Languages Conference*, Ulm (Germany), 1994.

[Fra96]   X. Franch. "Automatic Implementation Selection for Software Components using a Multiparadigm Language to state Non-Functional Issues". Ph.D. Thesis, Universitat Politècnica de Catalunya (Catalonia, Spain), 1996.

[Gut75]   J.V. Guttag. *The Specification and Application to Programming of Abstract Data Types*. Ph.D. Thesis, University of Toronto, 1975.

[Hoa72]   C.A.R. Hoare. "Proof of Correctness of Data Representations". In *Programming Methodology*, Springer-Verlag, 1972.

[Jaz95]   M. Jazayeri. "Component Programming - a Fresh Look at Software Components". In *Proceedings of 5th ESEC*, Barcelona (Catalonia, Spain), 1995.

[LH85]   D.C. Luckham, F.W. von Henke. "An Overview of Anna, a Specification Language for Ada". Software IEEE, March 1985.

[Luc90]   D.C. Luckham. *Programming with Specifications: an Introduction to ANNA, a Language for Specifying Ada Programs*. Texts and Monographs in Computer Science, Springer-Verlag.

[Kan86]   E. Kant. "On the Efficient Synthesis of Efficient Programs". In *Readings in Artificial Intelligence and Software Engineering*, Morgan Kaufmann, 1986.

[Knu76]   D.E. Knuth. "Big Omicron and Big Omega and Big Theta". SIGACT News, 8(2), 1976.

[LG86]   B. Liskov, J. Guttag. *Abstraction and Specification in Program Development*. The MIT Press, 1986.

[Mat84]   Y. Matsumoto. "Some Experiences in Promoting Reusable Software". IEEE Transactions on Software Engineering, 10(5), 1984.

[MCN92]   J. Mylopoulos, L. Chung, B.A. Nixon. "Representing and Using Nonfunctional Requirements: A Process-Oriented Approach". IEEE Transactions on Software Engineering, 18(6), 1992.

[Sc+86]   J. Schwartz et al. *Programming with Sets: Introduction to SETL*. Springer-Verlag, 1986.

[Sha84]   M. Shaw. "Abstraction Techniques in Modern Programming Languages". IEEE Software, 1(10), 1984.

[Sit94]   M. Sitaraman. "On Tight Performance Specification of Object-Oriented Components". In *Proceedings 3rd International Conference on Software Reuse*, IEEE Computer Society Press, 1994.

[Sit+94]   M. Sitaraman (coordinator). "Special Feature: Component-Based Software Using RESOLVE". ACM Software Engineering Notes, 19(4), Oct. 1994.

[SY94]   P.C-Y. Sheu, S. Yoo. "A Knowledge-Based Program Transformation System". In *Proceedings 6th CAiSE*, Utrecht (The Netherlands), LNCS 811, 1994.

[Win89]   J.M. Wing. "Specifying Avalon Objects in Larch". In *Proceedings of TAPSOFT'89, Vol. 2*, Barcelona (Catalonia, Spain), LNCS 352, 1989.

[Win90]   J.M. Wing. "A Specifier's Introduction to Formal Methods". IEEE Computer 23(9), 1990.

Semantics-Based Support Tools for High Integrity Ada Software

W L Yeung

Lingnan College
Hong Kong
Email: wlyeung@ln.edu.hk

Abstract. This paper introduces a rigorous approach to developing high integrity software with Ada and the Jackson System Development (JSD) method. The approach involves the use of a specification language, called FJSD, in expressing JSD designs. FJSD is introduced and illustrated with a simple example in this paper. A semantic analysis tool and an Ada code generator have been developed based on the denotational semantics of FJSD. The semantic analysis tool translates an FJSD specification into the formalism of Communicating Sequential Processes (CSP) for formal reasoning and the Ada code generator produces Ada code from an FJSD specification. The strength of the approach lies in the rigour of FJSD and its semantic definition which have allowed the highly systematic development of the support tools.

1 Introduction

There has been much interest in the use of formal methods in software development in recent years, particularly in applications that require a high-level of safety, reliability, and integrity. Indeed, the UK MoD Standard 00-55 [1] stipulates how safety critical software procured by the MoD should be developed and it places great emphasis on the use of formal development methods, rather than the conventional testing approach.

Ada is a general-purpose programming language originally developed for military and other types of embedded systems which are very often safety critical and require high integrity software. A software development process that incorporates formal methods in the specification and design stages together with rigorous transformation of designs into Ada programs seems most desirable. However, the wholesale adoption of the "specify-and-verify" approach with formal methods is still subject to many practical constraints. On the other hand, there exist some well-tried structured methods, such as Yourdon SA/RT [2], HOOD [3], and JSD [4, 5], together with their associated commercial off-the-shelf (COTS) tools. It would seem natural for a software development process to incorporate both structured and formal methods in a complementary and integrated way, together with appropriate support tools.

The integration of structured and formal methods has taken many forms:

1. Structured and formal methods are applied in different stages or aspects of the development process [6].

2. Formal specifications are embedded into structured specifications to the lower-level designs more rigor [7].
3. Formal methods are visualized to give a structured "flavor" [8].
4. Structured specifications are formalized to allow formal verification [9].

The support tools discussed in this paper address the last form of method integration above. We shall look at a tool which generates Ada code from a given design expressed in a structured notation. The structured notation has a formal semantics which allows every design expressed in that structured notation to be translated into a formal notation for formal verification and analysis purposes. The translation process is automated by another support tool. Hence, using the pair of support tools just mentioned, a developer can use the structured method to formulate a design according a pre-existing specification, verify and analyze the design formally by first translating it into the formal notation, and then generates Ada code from the design for the implementation.

The particular structured and formal methods discussed in this paper are the Jackson System Development (JSD) method and Communicating Sequential Processes (CSP) [10], respectively. However, the approach to method integration and tool support demonstrated in this paper should also be applicable to other structured and formal methods.

The next section considers briefly the formal semantics of FJSD, a textual version of the JSD notation. Sections 3 and 4 illustrate the use of FJSD in specifying JSD designs. Section 5 considers the design of a semantic analysis tool for FJSD and section 6 describes the design and testing of the Ada code generator. Section 7 discusses some experience on the development of both support tools. Section 8 gives a conclusion of the paper.

2   Formal semantics for JSD

FJSD, which stands for Formalised JSD, is a language developed for specifying process networks (see Section 3) and their transformations (see Section 4) in JSD. It has a denotational-semantic definition [11] which serves as a basis for building the support tools discussed in this paper. A denotational-semantic definition consists of three parts, namely, abstract syntax, semantic domains, and semantic functions. The abstract syntax of a language describes the "phrase structures" of the language without concern of parsing. A phrase in the language is identified as an element of a particular syntactic domain. For example, an (entire) FJSD specification is identified as an element S of the syntactic domain System.

An FJSD specification begins with a name I $\in$ Identifier and can be regarded as a combination of three parts as stated by the BNF rule for System

$$S ::= I = D : X : T$$

where D $\in$ SystemSpecificationDiagram, X $\in$ Transformation, and T $\in$ StructureText. These three parts correspond to the process network, transformations, and definition of individual processes, respectively. Given the abstract syntax of FJSD, its semantics is defined by a set of semantic functions that map each syntactic domain into an appropriate semantic domain construction. For each syntactic domain, there is one semantic function which is defined by a functionality and a set of equations, one per option in the corresponding BNF rule. The functionality of a semantic function indicates the semantic domain into which elements of the syntactic domain are mapped. For example, the functionality of semantic function S

$$S : \text{System} \rightarrow CSPdefns$$

tells us that the syntactic domain **System** is mapped to the semantic domain $CSPdefns$ (CSP definitions). On the other hand, the equations of a semantic function define the semantics of the syntactic domain in terms of the semantics of the constituent syntactic domain(s). This is the reason why the style of such a semantic definition is known as "denotational". For instance, the semantics of **System** is defined in terms of the semantics of its three constituents, D, X and T which are in turn defined by the semantics functions $\mathcal{D}$, $\mathcal{X}$, and $\mathcal{T}$, respectively, as follows

$$S[\![I = D : X : T]\!] = \text{let } (e_1, p) = \mathcal{D}[\![D]\!] \text{ in}$$
$$\text{let } (e_2, d) = \mathcal{X}[\![X]\!] e_1 \text{ in}$$
$$\langle ([\![I]\!], p) \parallel par^*(fst^*(d)) \rangle \frown d \frown \mathcal{T}[\![T]\!] e_2$$

3 Specification

JSD consists of three phases, namely, modelling, specification, and implmentation. The modelling phase deals with the entity-life modelling [12] of relevant real-world objects and results in a set of "model" processes which communicate their corresponding real-world objects. In the specification phase, "function" processes are created and connected to the model processes in order to provide the system's functions. The resulting specification becomes a network of communicating processes interconnected by two kinds of connection. A datastream connection is a one-way communication channel with (potentially) unbounded buffering between two processes. The operations for sending and receiving messages through a datastream are **write** and **read**, respectively. In a state-vector connection, one process inspects (reads) the value of the state-vector of another process by issuing a **getsv** operation. The state-vector of a process consists of all local variables declared in the process and the so-called text-pointer, which is logically equivalent to the program counter.

Figure 1 shows a simple system taken from [5]. In a process network, a rectangle represents a process or a process type (see below) whereas a directed line with a circle represents a datastream connection. The behaviour of the individual processes in Figure 1 is specified informally as follows:

- The input datastream A contains integer records in ascending order without duplicate.
- P writes alternate records of A to B and C, writing the first record to B.

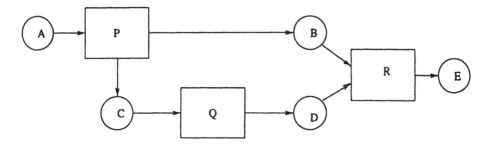

Fig. 1. A simple process network

- Q copies the records of C to D, adding 8 to each integer.
- R merges the records of B and D, eliminating duplicates, to give the output datastream E of records in ascending order.

Figure 2 shows the FJSD specification of the above system. In the specification, line 1 gives a name of the overal system. Lines 2-7 correspond to the process network in Figure 1. Line 2 defines the process types of the system, whereas lines 3-7 define the data stream connections (A, B, C, D, and E). Lines 8-11 specify some transformations to the process network (to be discussed in Section 4). The remaining lines contain the behavioral specification of processes P, Q, and R. Note that there are three basic constructs for specifying the behaviour of processes in JSD, namely, sequence (seq ... end), selection (sel ... alt ... end), and iteration (itr while ... end).

4 Transformations

Given a process network, JSD provides a number of transformation techniques by which a sub-network of processes can be implemented on a single sequential processor without any support for concurrency. This reduces the amount of concurrency in the implementation and could help reduce the amount of computing resources required and overheads associated with concurrency. In extreme cases, the entire process network can be transformed into a single processor implementation.

Transformations applied to a sub-network are expressed in FJSD in the form:

{I: V: U: G}

where I denotes the name of a scheduler process, V denotes inversion, U denotes scheduling transformations, and G denotes transformations for guarding concurrent access to state-vectors.

For example, the process network in Figure 1 can be transformed into a single processor implementation as shown in Figure 3. First, P and Q are transformed into coroutines with respect to datastream C by inversion. Then, a scheduler process, SCHEDULER, is provided to schedule all the processes. The interaction between SCHEDULER and all the processes are summarised as follows:

```
EX1 =                               R seq
[P], [Q], [R] :                       R-IREAD seq
(A) -> [P],                             iread B into x;
[P] -> (B) -> [R],                      read D into y;
[P] -> (C) -> [Q],                    end
[Q] -> (D) -> [R],                    R-BODY itr (true)
[R] -> (E) :                            R-MERGE sel (x>y)
{ SCHEDULER :                             R-D seq
 C :                                        write y to E;
 / P : A /, / R : B, D / :                  read D into y;
}:                                        end
P seq                                   R-MERGE alt (x<y)
  P-IREAD seq                             R-B seq
    iread A into x;                         write x to E;
  end                                       read B into x;
  P-BODY itr (true)                       end
    P-SPLIT seq                         otherwise
      write x to C;                       R-BOTH seq
      read A into x;                        write x to E;
    end                                     read B into x;
  end                                       read D into y;
end                                       end
Q seq                                   end
  Q-IREAD seq                         end
    iread C into x;                 end
  end
  Q-BODY itr (true)
    Q-ADD seq
      write (x+8) to D;
      read C into x;
    end
  end
end
```

... continue here with next column

Fig. 2. FJSD specification for a simple system

- SCHEDULER is given control initially.
- SCHEDULER transfers control to either P or R, depending on the status
  of the datastreams A, B and D. (Datastreams B and D are implemented as
  FIFO buffers).
- P, as it runs, relinquishes control to SCHEDULER before every read opera-
  tion on datastream A.
- R, as it runs, relinquishes control to SCHEDULER before every read oper-
  ation on datastream B and D.
- P and Q interact as coroutines with respect to datastream C.

The transformations shown in Figure 3 can be specified in FJSD as shown

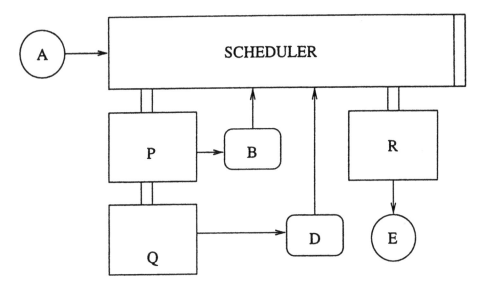

Fig. 3. An implementation with a single processor

in Figure 2 (lines 8-11), repeated as follows:

{SCHEDULER: C: /P: A/, /R: B, D/: }

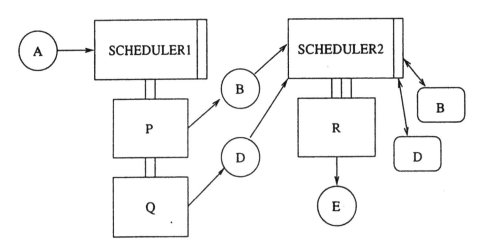

Fig. 4. An implementation with two Ada tasks

Figure 4 shows a different implementation of the same system involving two Ada tasks. P and Q are transformed into coroutines running as a single task and R now runs as a separate task under the scheduling of SCHEDULER2. Since

```
((("EX1" nil)
  ((("P" nil) "||" (("Q" nil) "||" ("R" nil)))
   "||" (("SCHEDULER" nil) "||" (("B" nil) "||" ("D" nil)))))
 (("SCHEDULER" nil)
  (((SKIP) ";" (SKIP)) ";"
```

... lines omitted ...

Fig. 5. Sample output of the semantic analysis tool

communications between Ada tasks are unbuffered (synchronised), SCHED-ULER2 also manages the buffering of the inter-task datastreams B and D. The necessary transformations for this implementation can be specified in FJSD as:

{SCHEDULER1: C: /P: A/: }, {SCHEDULER2: : /R: ?B, ?D/: }

Note that datastreams B and D are marked as inter-task connections by the "?" symbol.

5   A Semantic Analysis Tool

A semantic analysis tool has been developed in parallel with the FJSD language in order to provide a convenient way to translate the language into the formalism of Communicating Sequential Processes and also to test and exercise the denotational-semantic definition of FJSD. It was designed in such a way that it would be:

- easy to implement, and
- easy to modify as the semantic definition changes.

The tool has been developed in the UNIX environment and its design was inspired by Wand's Semantic Prototyping System [13]. It includes:

- a bottom-up parser generated by *yacc* [14],
- a translator written in Franz LISP [15], and
- the Franz LISP applicative order lambda expression evaluator.

The translator is essentially an implementation of the semantic functions for FJSD. It inputs the syntactic structure of a FJSD specification and outputs the result of applying the semantic functions to the input. Figure 5 shows the first few lines of the output of the tool given the FJSD specification in Figure 2 as input. The output represents the CSP definitions in Figure 6. Note that such a list of CSP definitions can be executed symbolically, given a suitable implementation of CSP such as [16, 17, 18].

$$EX1 \cong P \parallel Q \parallel R \parallel SCHEDULER \parallel B \parallel D$$
$$SCHEDULER \cong Skip;\ Skip;\ \dots$$

Fig. 6. CSP definitions for the simple system

6   An Ada Code Generator

The Ada code generator accepts FJSD specifications written in the same concrete syntax recognised by the semantic analysis tool discussed in Section 5. Given an FJSD specification as input, it produces executable Ada code in a single-pass of the input. The UNIX utilities *yacc* and *lex* were used to generate code for the parsing functions; the code generation functions were written in C and embedded in the *yacc* specification. The design of the code generation algorithm is based on the denotational-semantic definition of FJSD and it realises the mapping of FJSD into Ada. The mapping of FJSD into Ada is described in detail in [11]; it follows the structure of the denotational-semantic definition: each semantic function corresponds to a code generation function written in C.

6.1   Testing

The testing of the Ada code generator made use of the elevator control system first discussed in [5] and subsequently in [12, 19]. The testing involved writing FJSD specifications for three different implementations of the elevator control system which would control a single perpetually travelling elevator serving six floors. These FJSD specifications were supplied to the code generator to produce Ada code. The physical elevator system was actually simulated in software and the simulation was animated in real-time on the terminal screen. Figure 7 shows how the animation screen looks like. The simulated elevator (animated by a rectangle moving up and down the screen) and floor buttons (each animated by a "0" or "1" depending on its state) could be activated through the terminal keyboard. Both the simulation and animation were implemented as packages which could be conveniently interfaced with the different implementations of the elevator control system.

A few observations were made during the testing:

1. The animation of the elevator system exhibited the expected behaviour using the generated Ada code.
2. The testing suggested a model for the proper use of Ada tasking facilities for JSD. The current form of mapping of concurrent processes into tasks is actually the most satisfactory form amongst the few alternatives which have been experimented with the case studies. The rejected forms tended to suffer from poor system response.

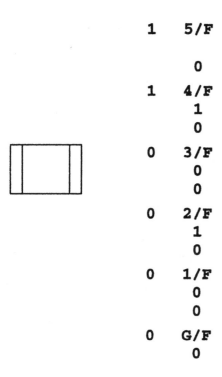

1   5/F

0

1   4/F
1
0

0   3/F
0
0

0   2/F
1
0

0   1/F
0
0

0   G/F
0

Fig. 7. Animation of the elevator system

3. Evidence for the Ada code generator being a useful tool is provided by the ease of specifying different transformation schemes in FJSD specifications and the well structuring of the generated Ada code which requires a minimal amount of additional code. In fact, apart from the top-level procedure, the only additional code required for the generated code is the addition of renames clauses for local variables in blocks or procedures that implement coroutines. Supplementary code for constants, data types, etc. is supplied in separately compiled packages which can be reused for different implementations of the same system.

7 Discussion

The semantic analysis tool has been used to experiment with various versions of the denotational-semantic definition of FJSD. The experiments involved writing FJSD specifications for the case studies given in [5] and producing their denotations using the tool. The strategy of these experiments was to exercise all the features of FJSD so as to reveal any errors in the denotational-semantic definition. Many errors were revealed by carefully reading the output of the tool and they were were often non-trivial and typically included inconsistencies between different parts of the definition and unhandled cases. Apart from errors, the experiments also helped reveal limitations, redundancies, and complexities, which were all very important for the evaluation and subsequent refinement of each version of the denotational-semantic definition. There have been four major versions of the definition and its size has diminished through the versions. That has been the result of removing many undesirable redundancies and complexities, as well as improving the semantic domains.

In devising the mapping of FJSD into Ada for the code generator, the primary objective was to produce a correct implementation of the denotational-semantic definition of FJSD. Under this condition, however, there was still considerable scope for choosing between different mapping schemes and the following sub-objectives were aimed at:

- The mapping should allow an efficient, preferably one-pass, code generation algorithm.
- Although additional code, mainly for data typing and state-vector definition, would be necessarily supplied in conjunction with a FJSD specification, the generated Ada code should be as compilable as possible.
- The generated Ada code should be structured in a way that additional code could be conveniently supplied, preferably as separate compilation units.
- The generated Ada code should follow good programming practice and should be as readable as possible.

Although it is difficult, if not impossible, to evaluate how well these sometimes conflicting sub-objectives have been achieved, it is felt that the effort spent in pursuing these sub-objectives has been fruitful. On the other hand, the mapping and hence the code generator is biased towards real-time embedded applications. As a result, it actually fails to address the need of batch-processing application for which JSD is also suitable. Other mapping schemes have been proposed [20, 21] but they lack any formal basis.

The design of the code generation algorithm has actually influenced the mapping in many respects. These influences often stemmed from the desire to produce a one-pass code generator and this could not have been achieved without Ada's separate compilation facility which allows task and procedure bodies to be generated simultaneously in different files and to be compiled separately. Although no attempt has been made to formally verify the correctness of the code generator algorithm with respect to the denotational-semantic definition, the style of the denotational-semantic definition which combines abstraction, formality, and modularity, does provide very strong support toward producing a correct code generator. For the interest of the reader, Table 1 shows the approximate sizes of the denotational-semantic definition and the code generator.

The PRESTIGE Workbench [22] is a CASE tool for JSD that also generate Ada code from JSD specifications. It differs from the Ada code generator discussed in this paper in the following significant ways:

1. PRESTIGE does not has any formal basis whereas the Ada code generator discussed in this paper is based on the denotational semantics of FJSD.
2. PRESTIGE supports transformations with so-called implementation hierarchies (IHs). An IH is applied to a process network as a whole whereas the use

Denotational definition		Code generator	
Section	Lines	Section	Lines
		main	20
abstract syntax	45	*yacc* and *lex* spec	377
semantic domains	42	symbol table and aux.	669
semantic functions	426	code generation	1800
Total	513	Total	3550

Table 1. Size of semantic definition and code generator

of FJSD in specifying transformations on the level of sub-networks provide greater control over the behaviour of an implementation.

3. PRESTIGE uses a graphical notation for JSD specifications whereas FJSD is a textual notation.
4. PRESTIGE comes with a graphical user interface for its operation whereas the Ada code generator has a very simple command line interface.

While the Ada code generator discussed in this paper is arguably more rigourous (1) and flexible (2), further work should be directed towards improving its usability in the respects of (3) and (4).

8 Conclusion

This paper has introduced the specification language FJSD for specifying transformations in JSD and has discussed the development of two support tools based on the denotational semantics of FJSD. The semantic analysis tool has been used to help develop the FJSD language and can be used as a tool for translating FJSD specifications into CSP for formal reasoning. The Ada code generator offers automated support for implementation by generating executable code directly from FJSD specifications. Together, they provide a rigorous approach to supporting the implementation phase of JSD. The strength of this approach lies in the rigour of FJSD and the use of denotational semantics as a basis for the systematic development of the support tools.

References

1. Ministry of Defence. The Procurement of Safety Critical Software in Defence Equipment. INTERIM Defence Standard 00-55, April 1991.
2. Edward Yourdon. *Structured Systems Analysis*. Prentice Hall, 1990.
3. HOOD Technical Group. *HOOD Reference Manual*. Prentice Hall and Masson, 1999.
4. J.R. Cameron. An Overview of JSD. *IEEE Trans. Software Eng.*, SE-12(2), 1986.
5. M.A. Jackson. *System Development*. Prentice Hall, 1983.
6. J. A. McDermid et al. Tool Support for High Integrity Ada Software. In *1st International Eurospace - Ada-Europe Symposium*, September 1994.

7. A. Alapide et al. Applying Teamwork/Ada and RAISE for Developing an Air Traffic Control Application. In *2nd International Eurospace - Ada-Europe Symposium*, October 1995.

8. J. Dick and J. Loubersac. Integrating Structured and Formal Methods: A Visual Approach to VDM. In *3rd European Software Engineering Conference*, October 1991.

9. W.L. Yeung et al. Theoretical Basis for Jackson System Development. *Information and Software Technology Journal*, 34(8), August 1992.

10. C.A.R. Hoare. *Communicating Sequential Processes*. Prentice Hall, 1985.

11. W.L. Yeung. *System Development with Communication Sequential Processes: Formalisation and Related Studies*. PhD thesis, Staffordshire University, Stafford, England, October 1991.

12. B. Sandon. An Entity-Life Modeling Approach to the Design of Concurrent Software. *Communications of ACM*, 32:330–343, 1989.

13. M. Wand. A Semantic Prototyping System. In *SIGPLAN '84 Symp. on Compiler Construction*, pages 213–221, 1984.

14. S.C. Johnson. Yacc: Yet Another Compiler-Compiler. CSTR 32, Bell Laboratories, Murray Hill, NJ, 1975.

15. J.K. Foderara, K.L. Skowler, and K Layer. *The Franz LISP Manual*. University of California, Berkeley, CA, 1983.

16. C.J. Fidge. A LISP Implementation of the Model for Communicating Sequential Processes. *Software Practice and Experience*, 18(10):823–943, 1988.

17. M.E.C. Hull. Implementations of the CSP Notation for Concurrent Systems. *Computer Journal*, 29(6), 1986.

18. K.L. Wrench. CSP-i: An implementation of Communicating Sequential Processes. *Software Practice and Experience*, 18(6):545–560, 1988.

19. W.L. Yeung and G. Topping. Implementing jsd designs in ada - a tutorial. *ACM SIGSOFT Software Eng. Notes*, 13(3):25–32, July 1990.

20. J.R. Cameron. Mapping JSD network specifications into Ada. *Ada User*, 8(Supp):S91–S99, 1987.

21. J.R. Lawton and N. France. The Transformation of JSD Specification into Ada. *Ada User*, 9(1):29–39, 1988.

22. B. Ratcliff and M. Boyle. The PRESTIGE workbench: CASE support for the implementation phase of JSD. *Software Engineering Journal*, 1993.

An Alternative Toolset for Analysis of Ada Programs

Alex E. Bell

Hughes Aircraft of Canada, Systems Division
13951 Bridgeport Rd.
Richmond, BC V6V 1J6 Canada
email: aebell@ccgate.hac.com
phone +1 604 231 3091
fax: +1 604 278 5625

Abstract. There are a number of tools available on the market today that provide a means of documenting or enforcing the design and coding policies of Ada programs. Alternatively, there are *few* tools that provide insight into how such policies impact the low-level details of program execution, particularly with respect to performance. It is the objective of this paper to present the elements of an alternative toolset that provide the software engineers developing the Canadian Automated Air Traffic System (CAATS) program at HCSD with precisely this insight.

It will be suggested that tools of the nature created on the CAATS program should be provided, or at least supported, by the Ada vendor community so that all software development organizations can realize their benefits. Vendor support would relieve customers from the burden of maintaining tools that are based on proprietary, and often dynamic implementations.

1 Introduction

In the absence of adequate vendor support, a toolset has evolved which provides the software engineers of the CAATS program with assistance in performing CPU and memory utilization analysis of Ada programs. Additionally, there are components in the toolset that provide extended debug capabilities used to support unit and integration test activities.

The elements of the toolset fall into either of two categories: the *static* set or the *dynamic* set. The elements that belong to the static category analyze the executable image itself, defying the traditional perception of static analysis being performed on Ada source code. The dynamic analysis components of the toolset capture runtime data that is subsequently analyzed off-line. Each of these tools is described in this paper and fragments representative of their output are provided as well.

Many of the metrics reported by the CAATS toolset are in terms of a *subsystem*, a unit of the CAATS Static Architecture (also known as an element of the Development View in the *4+1 View Model of Architecture* [1]). A subsystem is a container which groups together closely related Ada units that support a complete abstraction. It usually consists of several thousand lines of source code and is supported by 3-4 developers.

2 Static Analysis of Ada Programs

As previously stated, the static analysis of an Ada program involves the use of tools that examine the executable image itself. There is a great deal that can be learned about a program without having to execute even a single one of its instructions.

- **Frame Size Analyzer**

The Frame Size Analyzer reports the *static* stack frame requirements of each subprogram in an executable. Of particular interest are those subprograms that demand unusually large stack frames. Of course, allocation of a large stack frame is not necessarily bad in itself, but there are often performance implications associated with subprograms having excessive stack frame size requirements. It is emphasized that the Frame Size Analyzer currently focuses on stack frame demands that are statically known at compilation time as opposed to those demanded dynamically at runtime. Future extension of this tool to support analysis of dynamic stack frame demands will proceed based on results of feasibility analysis.

It was based on output of the Frame Size Analyzer that the CAATS program recognized problems with its policies relating to self-initializing Ada types as well as compiler deficiencies that considerably aggravated these problems. Also, a number of dubious data structures were discovered, as well as several flagrant coding errors that may not otherwise have been discovered for some time. Finally, a number of frequently invoked functions copying large and complex data structures into the caller's stack frame were identified and are candidates for re-implementation using access types.

A fragment produced by the Frame Size Analyzer follows. The format of the report from which this fragment was extracted specified that frame size demands for each subprogram should be grouped by subsystem and listed from most demanding to least demanding.

•
•

```
Now Processing Subsystem => FLGT
 The Frame Size => 23168  The Subprogram => auth_progress.update_position'n(3)
 The Frame Size => 23040  The Subprogram => auth_progress.update_position'n(1)
 The Frame Size => 12608  The Subprogram => auth_clearance.flight_plan_changed.execute
 The Frame Size => 8256 The Subprogram =>  auth_system_parameter.vsp_collection.update
```
•
•

A demanded frame size of 23,168 bytes, such as one shown above, is of suspicious magnitude by CAATS standards and is motivation for visually inspecting the associated Ada unit. The following fragment is an excerpt from the declarative region of the unit in question:

```
The_Profile : Common_Profile.Object := Common_Profile.Nil_Object;
The_Post_Processing_Data : Post_Processing_Data := Nil_Post_Processing_Data;
```

Upon inspection of the associated assembly, it was discovered that the declarations above accounted for 5,950 bytes of the 23,168 demanded. Further analysis of the assembly revealed that these declarations were doing much more than causing frame allocation, they were consuming over 30,000 CPU cycles in support of initialization, only to be overwritten in their entirety soon after.

Variable initialization, whether implicit or explicit, is extremely common across the CAATS implementation and a potential cause of performance problems if ignored. Instead of yielding to the philosophy of removing initialization altogether, which would likely create a different class of problem, a smarter initialization strategy continues to evolve. Private types, such as Common_Profile.Object above, do not necessarily need to self-initialize each and every one of its nested components individually. Instead, only a single field is necessary to represent initialization state, *initialized*, which is set to false upon object declaration. Subsequent client requests for services validate an object's initialization state before proceeding. Requesting services upon an uninitialized object are grounds for initiating error processing.

In some cases, such as in declarations of large arrays that are only partially returned as function arguments, no initialization at all is required. The implementation controls the extent of the array that is to be returned and guarantees to its client that it is filled with semantically correct data. The CAATS program continues evolving guidelines on the initialization of variables as new patterns are recognized.

- **Subprogram Size Analyzer**

The Subprogram Size Analyzer outputs information that specifies the instruction segment memory requirements associated with each subprogram in an executable image. Due to the implementation of the CAATS' compiler, however, there is only limited information that can be reported detailing a unit's data size requirements. In the interest of minimizing the time spent on linking, copying, debugging, and elaborating excessively large executables, the CAATS program uses Subprogram Size Analyzer output to manage the size of its executable images.

It was based on the output of the Subprogram Size Analyzer that the CAATS program recognized the implications of limited compiler support for shared generic bodies. The output also identified data structures that should have been relegated to heap residence, as opposed to occupying static memory and contributing directly to the size of the executable.

Finally, the output of this tool was used to recognize and correct some undesirable packaging dependencies that contributed to unnecessarily large executable sizes. The importance of Subprogam Size Analyzer output to identify sub-optimal packaging is heightened by the fact that the CAATS' linker does not support dead code elimination.

There are a number of report options made available by the Subprogram Size Analyzer. The report option from which the fragment below was extracted specified that subprograms be listed from largest to smallest, partitioned by subsystem.

•
•

Now Processing Subsystem => FLGT
The Subprogram Size =>4288 The Subprogram => flgt_clearance_notices.add_category_set
The Subprogram Size =>3896 The Subprogram => flgt_filter.filter."not"'n(1).non_trivial_not
The Subprogram Size =>3736 The Subprogram => flgt_flight_diob.communication.read
The Subprogram Size =>1840 The Subprogram => flgt_flight_plan.create_filed_flight_plan

•
•

Processed 8636 Subprogram(s) Which Consumed 4,300,800 Bytes in Subsystem => FLGT

•
•

The Aggregate Size of All 52754 Subprograms Processed => 28,468,260 Bytes

As previously noted, use of the Subprogram Size Analyzer has been instrumental in reducing the size of the CAATS executable images. At one time, the executable image responsible for supporting the air traffic controller user interface functionality ballooned to over 90 megabytes! As the result of studying Subprogram Size Analyzer reports, the size is down to 70 megabytes and still shrinking.

The most important observation derived from the reports involved the side effects of combining CAATS' heavy generic usage with a compiler having limited support for shared generic bodies. For example, analysis of the CAATS Simulation process showed that a particular generic package supporting linked list services was instantiated over 200 times. Because each instantiation cost approximately 30 kilobytes, it was recognized that over 6 megabytes of the 60 megabytes associated with the Simulation executable were attributable to unnecessary replication of the generic package body! The same code replication phenomenon, but to a lesser degree, was recognized for several other popular generic services used in the CAATS implementation as well.

Because the compiler implementation would not be extended to support shared generic body semantics and due to uncertainty of whether or not CAATS could endure the lower performance associated with a shared generic body implementation anyway, the resolution to the problem was to achieve a shared implementation *manually*. The means by which this shared implementation was realized involved creating a very thin generic wrapper on top of underlying *type independent*, common services. Specifically, the thin wrappers interchange the typed parameters into the general parameters accepted by the underlying type independent services. Usage of this strategy reduced the CAATS executable sizes by over 15% with further savings expected as more units are *degenerified*.

The output of the Subprogram Size Analyzer also contributed to the reduction of CAATS executables simply by enumerating the subprograms contained within a subsystem. Because of heavy generic usage on CAATS and the fact that developers were not always aware of the additional baggage absorbed when instantiating a particular generic unit, clear enumeration of all subprograms resident in a subsystem resulted in heightened awareness of actual subsystem content. As a direct side effect, the developers campaigned for more focused and streamlined generics to reduce the size of their subsystems.

3   The Dynamic Analysis

The tools that support analyzing the dynamic aspect of an Ada program rely on data captured at runtime that is subsequently analyzed off-line.

• Leak Detection

The CAATS memory leak detection capabilities identify the units responsible for this unwelcome phenomenon. For grievous leaks causing storage error in minutes, to slow leaks that eventually incapacitate a system like an unforgiving cancer, the *Leakmeister* identifies the call sequences with the most memory allocated, as well as the call sequences with the greatest number of *outstanding* heap transactions. It is with this information that memory management anomalies, traditionally extremely difficult to isolate, become painlessly apparent.

In addition to serving as a tool during the integration and acceptance testing phases, the Leakmeister provides memory management analysis support during the unit test phase as well. The testing of all units that embody polylithic data structures can be executed under the auspices of the Leakmeister to report if any outstanding memory allocations exist at the conclusion of a test and provide the client *signatures* responsible for the allocations.

A typical output fragment produced by the Leakmeister follows below. An important term to understand for interpreting the report is a *client signature*. A client signature is the sequence of all callers leading up to a memory allocation or deallocation. In the example below, the 7 element signature had 2 outstanding memory allocations associated with it that totaled 524 bytes upon test completion. It must be emphasized that the Leakmeister can only report the signatures responsible for the memory allocations contained within a particular data acquisition. It is a developer responsibility to determine if and where previously allocated memory should be deallocated.

•
•
Number of Allocated Entries with the Following Client Callframe Signature => 2

The Client Signature is:
    1 => 000BC1638 tesu_unwind_stack.get_call_tree + 000000020
    2 => 000BC85EC tesu_heap_transaction_history.report_allocation + 00000007C
    3 => 000D33618 allocate_cell + 0000002B0
    4 => 000D3334C allocate_fixed_cell + 000000024
    5 => 000176E80 baty_byte_stream_allocation.new_byte_array + 000000408
    6 => 00017B220 baty_byte_stream_support.assign_contents + 0000000A0
    7 => 000216724 syse_work_order.put + 0000002FC
•
•
The Number of Bytes Allocated to This Client Signature => 524
•
•

If one of the more verbose presentation options had been chosen to generate the report from which the element above was extracted, the size and time associated with *each* heap transaction would be indicated. Additional report options allow the user to specify the order in which outstanding memory allocations should be presented, specifically, by the client signature with most bytes or most transactions associated with it.

The implementation of the Leakmeister depends on the ability to hook into the system heap manager for access to the details of each transaction. Specifically, access to details such as number of words requested, number of words allocated, allocation address, and deallocation address are required to support the currently available reports. In addition to the details directly related to the heap transaction itself, the client signature must also be extracted by unwinding the callframe. It is the combination of client signature and transaction parameters that are output to a file for subsequent off-line analysis.

It is unfortunate that the creation of an important tool such as the Leakmeister was only possible because the CAATS runtime vendor happened to provide access to the heap manager. Had this not been the case, as likely true for many other runtimes, alternative means by which to isolate heap usage anomalies would have been very limited for the CAATS program. Less importantly, but still worth noting, vendor provision of a stack frame unwinder, as opposed to having had to write one, would have reduced development time of the Leakmeister and would eliminate the potential for future maintenance efforts.

- **Heap Usage Profiler**

The unit by which CAATS currently measures its heap activity is based on the *subsystem*. The Heap Usage Profiler provides insight into which subsystems are the most active with respect to heap transactions. Future extensions of the Heap Usage Profiler will show heap transaction activity on a more granular level, presenting the most active client signatures. An example output fragment of the Heap Usage Profiler follows:

●
●

```
Summary for Subsystem => FLGT
  Heap Allocation Involvement  => 13495 Allocations
  Byte Allocation Involvement  => 1995201 Bytes
  Largest Allocation Involvement => 213012 Bytes
  Allocation Involvement Percentage => 66.98267732169
  Byte Usage Involvement Percentage => 63.37701618667

Summary for Subsystem => GEOM
  Heap Allocation Involvement => 13147 Allocations
  Byte Allocation Involvement => 1206934 Bytes
  Largest Allocation Involvement => 268 Bytes
  Allocation Involvement Percentage => 65.25537300839
  Byte Usage Involvement Percentage => 38.33792968941
```
●
●
```
***** Subsystem Heap Allocation Transaction Summary *****

The Number of Allocations => 20147
The Number of Bytes Allocated => 3148146
The Sample Collection Duration => 29.338127000 Seconds
The Allocation Frequency => 686.7173217977 Allocations per Second
```

A brief interpretation of the information above shows that the FLGT and GEOM subsystems were involved in 13,495 and 13,147 allocations, respectively, of the 20,147 occurring in this example. FLGT's 13,147 heap allocations represent *participation* in ~65% of the total while GEOM's involvement in 13,147 allocations represents a percentage of ~38%. Because many subsystems can be involved in a single heap transaction, the concept of *participation* is used to refer to a single subsystem's involvement in a particular transaction. Of the 3,148,146 bytes allocated during this test, FLGT's involvement in the allocation of 1,995,201 bytes represents ~63% while GEOM's byte usage involvement represents ~38% of the total.

The output of the Heap Usage Profiler unexpectedly identified the low level provider of CAATS geometrical services, the GEOM subsystem, as a leading heap memory user in terms of transaction frequency. As a result, the GEOM implementation's usage of dynamic memory is under scrutiny and is likely to migrate to a strategy, for example, where static arrays replace short-lived linked lists.

An alternative report option of the Heap Usage Profiler presents a lower level summary of heap allocations and deallocations occurring during a data acquisition interval. Specifically, the report presents information providing insight into the relative frequencies associated with each transaction size:

Outputting Summary of Allocations...
    The Transaction Size => 8 The Number of Transactions => 2191
    The Transaction Size => 9 The Number of Transactions => 13211
    The Transaction Size => 24 The Number of Transactions => 5168
                •
    The Transaction Size => 268 The Number of Transactions => 6118

Outputting Summary of Deallocations...
    The Transaction Size => 8 The Number of Transactions => 1560
    The Transaction Size => 9 The Number of Transactions => 3504
    The Transaction Size => 24 The Number of Transactions => 1393
                •
    The Transaction Size => 268 The Number of Transactions => 1516

Outputting Summary of Outstanding Allocations...
    The Transaction Size => 8 The Number of Transactions => 631
    The Transaction Size => 9 The Number of Transactions => 9707
                •
    The Transaction Size => 268 The Number of Transactions => 4602

Total Allocations in Bytes => 4,001,451
Total Deallocations in Bytes => 899,698
Total Allocation Transactions => 60,218
Total Deallocation Transactions => 16,064
Number of Active Allocations => 44,154
Number of Currently Allocated Bytes => 3,101,753

The CAATS program has taken advantage of this information to identify the pool sizes necessary for optimal performance of its own memory manager.

- **Heap Transaction Registrar**

The Heap Transaction Registrar is used to support analysis into the causes of heap corruption. The means by which the Heap Transaction Registrar supports this analysis is by providing all client signatures previously having custody of a specified heap memory address. The most frequent cause of heap corruption occurs when an application makes a *copy* of an access variable, deallocates the original, and subsequently writes to the *copy*, most often annihilating the context of the current owner. The historical information associated with a particular memory address often eases the pain associated with solving heap corruption problems by significantly reducing the set of units under investigation.

The Heap Transaction Registrar can also be used as a debug tool to show the *footprints* taken by a program during execution. Because heap transactions are captured at runtime, the corresponding symbolic callstack and timestamp are available for each transaction and can be extracted off-line to provide an alternate means of chronicling program execution.

- **Footprints**

In addition to the *incidental* footprints that occur as the result of heap transactions, application code can be instrumented to *explicitly* create footprints which provide complete call frame details at the point of service invocation. An off-line footprint post-processor is available that translates the hex callstack into fully qualified symbolic references. Footprints are most frequently used as temporary debug instrumentation in code that is difficult, impractical, or inconvenient to monitor within the context of a debugger.

The advantage of using *footprints* over traditional insertion of a *put_line* is evident when investigating an anomaly in a low level service that can be invoked by many clients. Instead of having to instrument all client software that invokes the lower level service to find out which one is the caller at time of failure, a single, strategically inserted footprint will provide the otherwise elusive client signature.

The following fragment represents typical usage of footprint services. The circumstances under which it was produced involved pursuit of an anomalous condition not repeatable in the debugger. It was through instrumenting the software under suspicion at strategic points that the necessary footprints were produced to identify the precise sequence of events leading up to a failure.

TESU FOOTPRINTS REQUESTED : Trace Zooming Deactivation

Time of Event: 1997-01-17-15:20:07.282_362 UTC

```
The Callstack:
  1 => 00306EC64 => usit_situation_display.when_zooming_deactivated + 0000001D4
  2 => 00303DEC4 => usit_situation_display.deactivate_zooming_thread + 00000010C
  3 => 0006170E8 => syse_pivot.thread_action_subprogram.invoke + 000000038
  4 => 002D704C0 => ucon_pick_resolver.response.dispatch + 0000003B8
  5 => 000617688 => syse_pivot.response_subprogram.invoke + 000000038
  6 => 000623000 => syse_pivot.spin + 000000570
  7 => 00062B58C => inco_pivot_scheduler.perform_periodic_processing + 000000034
```

- **Storage Demand Monitor**

Although this tool has not yet been created, its intention is to provide the user with information reflecting a program's demand for heap and stack memory. It is critical to understand if the heap and stack sizes allocated for programs and tasks, respectively, are tuned to comfortably absorb demand spikes. The output of this tool will likely be periodic in nature and provide the maximum and minimum extremes of heap and stack usage for the program.

- **Exception Interceptor**

The Exception Interceptor is a component of the CAATS toolset that significantly reduces the number of program failures going unsolved due to lack of sufficient supporting data. Based on optional resource data that identifies the action to be taken upon specified exceptions, the Exception Interceptor either reports the complete callstack and register context at the time of exception, forces a core dump, or silently ignores its occurrence. To facilitate the interpretation of callstack outputs, the Exception Post Processor tool has been written to translate addresses into fully qualified subprogram references.

An important characteristic of the Exception Interceptor is that it is layered on top of application code, providing its user with selective non-interference of underlying exception handlers. Because the Exception Interceptor is called back by the runtime *before* application level exception handlers take control, it can disposition an exception as parameterized, optionally allowing resumption of processing or immediately dumping core.

The Exception Interceptor was implemented to overcome a perceived deficiency of the CAATS runtime as provided by the vendor. This tool could not exist if a similar deficiency existed with respect to the availability of runtime services that supported application callbacks in the event of exception. The Exception Interceptor is not only dependent upon the runtime for exception callback services, but also for access to the context required to unwind the callframe that was active at the time of exception.

An example output fragment of a post-processed Exception Interceptor report for a constraint_error follows below. The associated fields are relatively self-explanatory with further clarification only required to explain that not all registers are available upon application callback and that the trace reads from deepest to shallowest frame.

```
EXCEPTION INTERCEPTED
Time of Event: 1997-01-10-19:50:33.799_636 UTC
Exception Name: constraint_error
The Location: 00077B120 => geom_vector."*"'n(1) + 000000048
The Registers:
  r0  =>                r1  =>                r2 => 00077EA7B   r3  => 041D20BE8
  r4  => 044386C70      r5  => 041D20828      r6 => 000000001   r7  => 041D1ED04
                             •
                             •
  r24 =>                r25 =>                r26 =>            r27 =>
  r28 => 0403E3BC0      r29 =>                r30 => 041D20CE8  r31 =>

The Callstack:
  1 =>  001EC1428  => uflt_event.report.image_of + 000000080
  2 =>  00306EC64  => usit_situation_display.when_zooming_deactivated + 0000001D4
  3 =>  00303DEC4  => usit_situation_display.deactivate_zooming_thread. + 00000010C
  4 =>  0006170E8  => syse_pivot.thread_action_subprogram.invoke + 000000038
  5 =>  002D704C0  => ucon_pick_resolver.response.dispatch + 0000003B8
                             •
                             •
```

The report above was generated based on the default parameterized exception action specifying that normal processing should be resumed following report to standard output.

A debugger, of course, is invaluable for providing similar stack trace services in the event of failure, but it is most frequently the case that no debugger is attached to a process when it fails. The natural course of events, in this case, is to reload and attach a debugger, and hope that the problem re-occurs. It is often the case, however, that the anomaly is not reproducible because the exact sequence of events causing it is unknown, leaving a defect in the system that will choose the worst possible time to recur in the future.

Courtesy of the Exception Interceptor, CAATS developers have much more than the string *constraint_error* available to them in the system log to support failure investigation. Failures that once would have gone unsolved due to insufficient supporting data are now rare.

- **Gprof Hierarchical Translator**

The CAATS program has made extensive use of the gprof tool to support execution profiling of some performance sensitive components, specifically, geometrical intersections of trajectories and volumes. A typical fragment of gprof output showing callgraph parents and callgraph children follows:

```
                                •
                                •
             0.00      0.00    300/300      geom_2d_polyarc.intersections_of'n(1) [17]
[502]  0.0   0.00      0.00    300          geom_2d_directed_arc.angle_at_the_arc_plane
             0.00      0.00    300/13772    geom_2d_directed_arc.angle_of [139]
             0.00      0.00    900/125884   geom_2d_coordinate.unit_vector_of'n(1) [11]
--------------------------------------------------------------------------
             0.00      0.00    15/853       geom_ 2d_polyarc.common_paths [564]
             0.00      0.00    838/853      geom_ 2d_polyarc.append'n(3) [84]
[503]  0.0   0.00      0.00    853          geom_ 2d_polyarc.polyarc_paths.lists_containing
             0.00      0.00    853/3268     geom_ 2d_polyarc.polyarc_paths.user_of [435]
                                •
                                •
```

The output above reports the activity associated with the functions tagged as nodes [502] and [503]. Taking node [503] as an example, the data shows that node [564] invoked node [503] 15 of the total 853 times it was invoked. The remaining 838 of 853 invocations are attributed to node [84]. Nodes [564] and [84] are referred to as the *call graph parents* of node [503]. Similarly, node [503] has one *call graph child*, node [435], which *it* invokes 853 times out of the total 3,268 times node [435] is invoked. Because sufficient *time* was not spent executing the code associated with these nodes and their children, there is no timing data available and is displayed as zeroes (please see gprof *man* page for further details on these fields).

While the format of the data above is useful for certain types of analysis, it is difficult to derive the big picture when there are hundreds of such related node summaries. The Gprof Hierarchical Translator was written to transform the node oriented, standard gprof output, into a hierarchical format, one that is much easier to visualize as a whole. The hierarchical fragment associated with the node [503] example above has been extracted from the complete report and is provided below. The applicable nodes have been emphasized to show how they fit into a hierarchical format.

Frame Level	Self Time	Child Time	Call Counts	Subprogram
				•
				•
11	0.02	0.14	798/855	**geom_internal_2d_polyarc.append'n(3) [84]**
12	0.04	0.00	8541/235814	geom_2d_polyarc.polyarc_paths.view_of [24]
12	0.00	0.02	6865/232186	geom_2d_polyarc.polyarc_paths.next [26]
13	0.73	0.00	217693/281862	geom_2d_polyarc.polyarc_paths.assign [25]
14	0.01	0.00	9816/125884	geom_2d_coord.unit_vector_of [111]
12	0.00	0.00	7703/234161	geom _2d_polyarc.polyarc_paths.is_at_end [132]
12	0.00	0.00	855/15749	geom _2d_polyarc.polyarc_paths.initialize [169]
12	0.00	0.00	838/2720	geom_ 2d_polyarc.polyarc_paths.tail [453]
13	0.01	0.00	2720/281862	geom _2d_polyarc.polyarc_paths.assign [25]
12	**0.00**	**0.00**	**838/853**	**geom _2d_polyarc.polyarc_paths.lists_containing [503]**
13	**0.00**	**0.00**	**853/3268**	**geom _2d_polyarc.polyarc_paths.user_of [435]**
12	0.00	0.00	7703/499961	geom_2d_directed_arc.length_of'n(2) [92]
12	0.00	0.00	838/41653	geom _2d_directed_arc.end_of'n(2) [162]
				•
				•

In addition to providing a hierarchical view of execution, the Gprof Hierarchical Translator also provides the stack frame level associated with each invocation. This information can be used to identify candidates for manual in-lining for cases the compiler does not do so automatically. The *Self Time*, *Child Time*, and *Call Counts* fields are unmodified from the standard gprof output and, as previously stated, defined in the gprof *man* page.

4   Conclusion

It is difficult to quantify the amount of time that will have been saved by the existence of this toolset upon CAATS delivery, but there is no question that it will be significant. How many other organizations using Ada to develop their products have duplicated the CAATS' efforts in developing their own toolsets to realize the same benefits? How many organizations know nothing of the existence of such tools and are not developing software as efficiently as they could be?

If vendors do not assume responsibility for providing tools such as those described above, at least the building blocks must be provided so that their customers can build such tools themselves. For example, the means by which to receive a callback with sufficient supporting context upon exception must be available to support extended error analysis. Also, the means by which to hook into heap management services must be provided to access the transaction details necessary to support dynamic memory usage analysis tools. The vendor community needs to be supportive of the evolving and creative means by which their customers are trying to meet their schedules while at the same time trying to provide a quality product.

If Ada is to continue to be considered a good language upon which to base large scale software development, vendors need to take responsibility for proprietary dependencies and provide or support tools that address the issues discussed in this paper. The argument proclaiming Ada as the language of choice for large scale software development efforts is further reinforced with the provision and support of such tools as standard components of the development environment.

5   References

[1]   Philippe Kruchten, "The 4+1 View Model of Architecture." *IEEE Software*, v 12, no 6, pages 42-50 November 1995.

Implementing Application-Level
Sporadic Server Schedulers in Ada 95

By: M. González Harbour, J.J. Gutiérrez García, and J.C. Palencia Gutiérrez

Departamento de Electrónica y Computadores
Universidad de Cantabria
39005 - Santander
SPAIN
email: {mgh, gutierjj, palencij}@ctr.unican.es
phone: +34 42 201483 - fax: +34 42 201402

Abstract[1]. The sporadic server is a scheduling algorithm which is designed to schedule aperiodic activities in hard real-time systems, and which can also be used to schedule periodic activities in distributed hard real-time systems. In distributed systems the total schedulability can be increased substantially, up to 50% more schedulable utilization, by eliminating with the sporadic server the delay effects caused by jitter. Most of the real-time schedulers included in commercial operating systems or Ada run-time systems do not provide a scheduler-level implementation of the sporadic server algorithm, and thus an application-level implementation must be used. In this paper we present several implementations of this scheduling algorithm that can be accomplished using the features defined in the Ada 95 language. The different implementations are designed using extensible data types, to take advantage of the inheritance and polymorphism features of the language.

Keywords: Scheduling, Real-Time, Sporadic Server, Ada 95, Jitter

1 Introduction

Most of the hard real-time scheduling theory relies on analysis methods for periodic tasks. When aperiodic activities are executed in the system it is necessary to provide some way to bound the effects of these activities on other lower priority tasks that have hard real-time requirements, so that the results of the schedulability analysis remain valid. Also of importance is to limit the delay effects caused by jitter, which are frequently found to diminish the schedulability in distributed systems. In these systems many of the tasks are activated upon the finalization of a previous activity, which may have a great degree of timing variability. Therefore, although the tasks and messages remain basically periodic, they are activated at irregular instants; this causes a delay effect on lower priority tasks, which can severely damage the schedulability of the system, reducing the schedulable utilization in many cases even by a factor of 50% [2].

The sporadic server scheduling policy was designed to schedule the execution of aperiodic activities in hard real-time systems in the context of fixed-priority scheduling. It

---

1. This work has been funded in part by the *Comisión Interministerial de Ciencia y Tecnología* of the Spanish Government under grant number TAP94-996

is a bandwidth-preserving algorithm that can provide relatively fast responses to external events. The effects of processing aperiodic activities using a sporadic server can be no worse than the effects of an equivalent periodic task. Thanks to this property, the sporadic server can be used to schedule periodic activities in distributed systems, because it eliminates the delay effects caused by jitter on lower priority tasks. This allows us to achieve much higher utilization levels than if jitter is not properly scheduled.

The sporadic server scheduling policy as originally defined by Sprunt *et al.* [7] should be implemented in the task scheduler, because it is necessary to measure the CPU-time consumed by the different tasks. However, since most real-time operating systems or Ada run-time systems do not provide this scheduling policy, it is possible with some restrictions to implement it at the application level [1][4]. Other scheduling algorithms that have been proposed for scheduling aperiodic activities in real-time systems, and which provide better performance than the sporadic server [5] cannot be easily implemented at the application level with small overhead, and that is the reason why we have chosen the sporadic server.

In this paper we present several application-level implementations of the sporadic server scheduling algorithm, which represent different compromises between performance and complexity. These implementations take advantage of the new features defined in the Ada 95 language, such as protected objects, to accomplish a much more efficient data synchronization, and object-oriented programming primitives, which enable an easy design of the different implementation variations, and allow the user to write the application code in an implementation-independent way. In distributed systems, in addition to the task sporadic server schedulers it is necessary to use the sporadic server algorithm to schedule the messages in the communications network, if we wish to eliminate the effects of jitter. The implementation of the communications sporadic servers and their description can be found in [3].

The paper is organized as follows. In Section 2 we give a brief overview of the sporadic server scheduling algorithm, and we describe the different operations that will be used by the application code. In Section 3 we discuss the basic aspects of three sporadic server implementations, without taking into account the mechanism used for replenishing the consumed execution time; these implementations correspond to the different kinds of event-receive operations that may be available for a particular application. Section 4 discusses the implementations of the replenishment policies, which are a fundamental part of the sporadic server schedulers; we will see that the different implementations correspond to different levels of service and overhead. Section 5 presents the results obtained with these implementations, including their timing performance. Finally, Section 6 gives our conclusions.

2 The Sporadic Server Scheduling Algorithm

The sporadic server is an algorithm defined for scheduling aperiodic activities in hard realtime systems. This algorithm reserves a certain amount of execution time (the *exe-*

cution capacity) for processing aperiodic events at any given priority level. The algorithm also limits the preemption effects on lower priority tasks, thus allowing us to predict their worst-case response times, even in the presence of aperiodic events with unbounded arrival rates (i.e. with a potentially large number of requests in a short time interval). Fig. 1 shows a comparison of the timing behavior of a high priority task scheduled with different methods. As it can be seen, if the events are scheduled directly at a high priority (Fig. 1-a) the response times are short, but excessive preemption may occur for lower priority tasks when a burst of aperiodic events arrives. If the periodic polling method is used, i.e. a task is used to periodically poll for the event arrivals, (Fig. 1-b), the amount of preemption per polling period is bounded even in the presence of a burst of aperiodic events, but the response times get worse. With the sporadic server scheduler (Fig. 1-c) the average response times are better, and the amount of preemption on lower priority tasks is also bounded because when several aperiodic events arrive very closely, their execution is spaced apart (by an amount called the *replenishment period*) to give lower priority tasks the opportunity to execute.

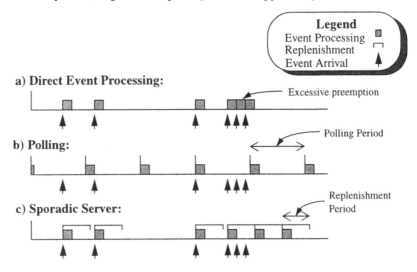

Fig. 1. Timing behavior of several aperiodic schedulers

The sporadic server algorithm has the two basic attributes that were mentioned above: the *execution capacity* and the *replenishment period*. The execution capacity is the amount of execution time that is reserved for processing the application task that is being scheduled, at the desired priority level. When an aperiodic (or periodic) event arrives, it activates the execution of this application task, and the arrival time of the event is recorded for future reference. As the task is processed, the execution time spent is subtracted from the capacity, until it gets exhausted. At this point, execution of the aperiodic task is suspended. Each portion of execution capacity that was consumed is replenished, i.e., added back to the available capacity, at a later time. This time is equal to the instant when the portion of consumed capacity became active (usually the arrival time of the triggering event), plus a fixed time called the replenishment period.

In some implementations, the application task that has no available execution capacity can continue executing at a background priority level, below the priority of any other task with hard real-time requirements. In other implementations, the task with exhausted capacity is simply suspended until a replenishment operation increases its execution capacity.

An interesting property of the sporadic server is that its effects on the schedulability of lower priority tasks cannot be worse than the effects of an equivalent periodic task with a period equal to the replenishment period and an execution time equal to the initial execution capacity. Suppose a periodic task that suffers from deferred activation (jitter). If this task is scheduled using a sporadic server with a replenishment period equal to the task's period and an initial capacity equal to the task's worst-case execution time, then its effects on lower priority tasks cannot be worse than that of the equivalent periodic task, with no jitter. The worst-case completion time of the task itself is equal to the worst possible deferral in the activation, plus the worst-case completion time of the equivalent periodic task, which is easily obtained from the usual RMA schedulability analysis [4].

When the sporadic server is implemented at the application level, it is not possible to keep track of the consumed execution time, and thus a worst-case assumption must be made that the consumed execution time is equal to the worst-case execution time for each event. This pessimistic assumption is necessary to guarantee the results of the worst-case real-time analysis.

From the implementation point of view, the sporadic server scheduler is an object that defines several operations which must be invoked by the application tasks wishing to execute under its control. The object has three public attributes (the *Initial_Capacity*, the *Replenishment_Period*, and the *Worst_Case_Execution_Time*); the latter one is necessary for the application-level implementations because if the available execution capacity is less than the worst-case execution time, then the task is not allowed to execute at its normal priority level. The operations defined for the sporadic server object are:

- *Initialize*: Sets the initial values of the attributes and initializes the replenishment manager.

- *Prepare_To_Wait*: Performs the operations that are necessary before the task suspends itself to wait for the arrival of the triggering event.

- *Prepare_To_Execute*: Performs the operations that are required after the event has arrived, and before it is processed.

- *Schedule_Next*: Performs the scheduling operations that are required before the task is ready to wait for the next event.

The pseudocode of an application task that runs under the application-level sporadic server is shown in Table 1. The sporadic server scheduler is designed as an abstract class of objects with the four operations described above, and all the different imple-

Table 1. Application task using a sporadic server

```
task body Application_Task is

   SS : Sporadic_Server.Scheduler;
begin
   Initialize(SS);
   loop
      Prepare_To_Wait(SS);
      Wait_For_Event;
      Prepare_To_Execute(SS);
      Do_Task's_Work;
      Schedule_Next(SS);
   end loop;
end Application_Task
```

mentations are derived from it. In the following sections we will describe these implementations.

3 The Sporadic Server Implementations

Depending on the operations that are available to wait for the event that triggers the application task, we may have three basic implementations of the sporadic server:

- *Simple*: If the triggering event is timestamped with its arrival time, then the calculation of the activation time of the task is straightforward: it is the maximum of the event's timestamp and the last time at which the task had no execution capacity available. This gives way to the simplest of the sporadic server implementations, which we call *Simple*. In order to use the timestamp of the event, the pseudocode of the main loop of the application task must be like the one show in Table 2. The actions performed by the different sporadic server operations are shown in Table 3. The *S* parameter in these operations is the scheduler.

Table 2. Application task with timestamped events

```
loop
   Prepare_To_Wait(SS);
   Wait_For_Event (Timestamp);
   Prepare_To_Execute(SS,Timestamp);
   Do_Task's_Work;
   Schedule_Next(SS);
end loop;
```

- *High_Priority*: If a timestamp associated with the triggering event is not available, the activation time of the task can be recorded after the event has arrived, by reading the clock. However, the task may get preempted between the arrival of the

130

Table 3. Operations in the *Simple* implementation

```
Prepare_To_Wait (S) is null;

Prepare_To_Execute
      (S,Timestamp) is
begin
   S.Activation_Time:=
      Max(Timestamp,
         S.Next_Start);
end;
```

```
Schedule_Next (S) is
begin
   S.Next_Start:=
      S.Activation_Time+
      S.Replenishment_Period;
   delay until Next_Start;
end;
```

event and the recording, and thus the activation time recorded would be later than it should, causing the sporadic server to schedule the next event too late. This problem can be partially solved by recording the activation time at an increased priority level. In the *High_Priority* implementation, the operation *Prepare_To_Wait* increases the priority of the task to the highest priority, and *Prepare_To_Execute* decreases it to its normal level after recording the activation time of the task. In addition, since the task may get preempted before it raises its priority, thus causing a wrong recording of the activation time of events that may have arrived during the delay statement in the *Schedule_Next* operation, this delay statement is moved to the *Prepare_To_Execute* operation (this is possible because the requirement for this statement is that it occurs before the event is processed). Table 4 describes the operations for this implementation. In this implementation, the application task has the same pseudocode that was shown in Table 1.

Table 4. Operations in the *High_Priority* implementation

```
Prepare_To_Wait (S) is
begin
   S.Current:=Get_Priority;
   Set_Priority(Highest);
end;

Schedule_Next (S) is
begin
   S.Next_Start:=
      S.Activation_Time+
      S.Replenishment_Period;
end;
```

```
Prepare_To_Execute (S) is
   Timestamp:=Clock;
begin
   Set_Priority (S.Current);
   delay until S.Next_Start
   S.Activation_Time:=
      Max(Timestamp,
         S.Next_Start);
end;
```

With the *High_Priority* approach, the difference between the actual arrival time of the event and the recorded activation time is minimised. The creation in this approach of a segment of high priority code introduces an extra delay on the other tasks, but it is small and bounded, basically equal to the time it takes to handle the event, record the time, and decrease the priority. Although the activation time is recorded at a high priority level immediately after the event has arrived, there is a small difference between the arrival and the recorded activation time, caused by the overhead of waiting and recording the time. This implies that the next event may be scheduled slightly late, unless the replenishment period is reduced to take into account the overhead effect.

- *High_Priority_Polled*: One solution that can be used to solve the suboptimality of the *High_Priority* implementation when the events cannot be timestamped is applicable if the events can be polled to determine whether they have arrived or not. In this case, the sporadic server requires a new operation, *Execute_Without_Waiting*, which is invoked if the event had already arrived when the task polled for its arrival. This operation calculates the activation time of the event as the activation time of the previous event plus the replenishment period. For this implementation, the pseudocode of the main loop in the application task must be like the one shown in Table 5.

Table 5. Application task with polled events

```
loop
    Poll_For_Event_Arrival
    if available then
       Execute_Without_Waiting;
    else
       Prepare_To_Wait(SS);
       Wait_For_Event;
       Prepare_To_Execute(SS);
    end if;
    Do_Task's_Work;
    Schedule_Next(SS);
end loop;
```

The operations in this implementation are similar to the ones for the *High_Priority* implementation, except that the delay statement used to enforce the replenishment period is moved back to the *Schedule_Next* operation. The reason is to invoke the *Poll* operation as late as possible, to increase the probability of it finding that the event had already arrived. Table 6 shows the implementation of the operations for this case.

In addition to the three different kinds of implementations, the policy used to replenish the consumed execution capacity may have different degrees of complexity and level of service. Four kinds of replenishment policies have been defined, which are discussed in the next subsection. The combinations of the three basic implementations and the four replenishment policies give way to 12 different implementations of the sporadic server. Fig. 2 shows the diagram of the different classes with their attributes and operations, according to Rumbaugh's OMT notation [6]. Since Ada 95 does not support multiple inheritance directly, each sporadic server object has an access attribute to point to the desired replenishment manager, if one is needed. A mixin inheritance approach could have been used here by defining each of the replenishment

Table 6. Operations in the *High_Priority_Polled* implementation

```
Prepare_To_Wait (S) is null;


Schedule_Next (S) is
begin
    S.Next_Start:=
        S.Activation_Time+
        S.Replenishment_Period;
    delay until S.Next_Start
    S.Current:=Get_Priority;
    Set_Priority(Highest);
end;
```

```
Execute_Without_Waiting(S) is
begin
    S.Activation_Time:=
        S.Next_Start;
    Set_Priority (S.Current);
end;

Prepare_To_Execute (S) is
    Timestamp:=Clock;
begin
    S.Activation_Time:=
        Max(Timestamp,
        S.Next_Start);
    Set_Priority (S.Current);
end;
```

managers as a generic package that extended a sporadic server scheduler with the appropriate replenishment manager. This approach would allow us to avoid repeating the code of many of the operations, but would prevent us from using inheritance or polymorphism for the replenishment managers, since they would no longer be tagged objects. This is why we did not use the mixin approach.

4 The Replenishment Policies

We have defined four replenishment policies for our sporadic server implementations. The simplest one is the *Single* policy in which the initial capacity of the sporadic server equals the worst-case execution time of the event. In this case the replenishment policy is extremely simple, because the capacity is consumed completely when the event is processed, and it is replenished completely one replenishment period after the event arrival. This policy is used by the implementations called *Simple_1*, *High_Priority_1*, and *High_Priority_Polled_1* (see Fig. 2), and corresponds to the sporadic server operations shown in Table 3, Table 4, and Table 6.

The other three replenishment policies correspond to the case in which the initial capacity allows *Multiple* event executions before it becomes exhausted. We have defined these three policies as three different replenishment management objects derived from the same class, each with three operations (see Fig. 2): *Initialize*, *Schedule_Replenishment*, and *Request_Execution*. The three different replenishment managers are:

- *Non_Queued*: This manager does not keep track of the activation times of the different portions of consumed execution time. Instead, when there is not enough execution capacity to service one event, the *Request_Execution* operation suspends the application task until one replenishment period after the activation time of the last processed event and, after the suspension, it fully replenishes the

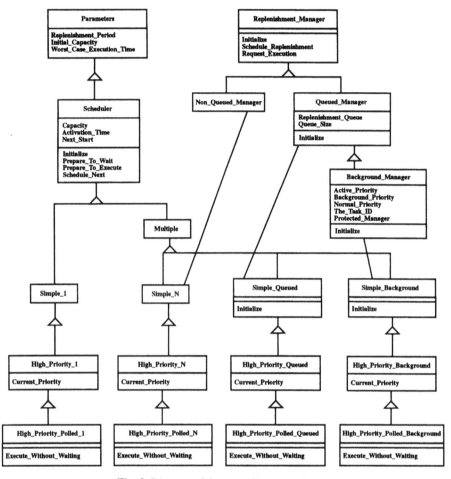

Fig. 2. Diagram of the sporadic server classes

execution capacity. *Schedule_Replenishment* just subtracts the consumed execution time from the available capacity.

- *Queued*: In this manager there is a queue of replenishment operations. Each time an event is processed, *Schedule_Replenishment* subtracts the consumed execution time from the available capacity, and inserts a replenishment operation in the queue, scheduling it to occur one replenishment period after the activation time of the event. The *Request_Execution* operation processes the pending replenishments and, if there is not enough capacity available, suspends the application task until the time when a replenishment operation would cause the available capacity to become sufficient to process the next event. A replenishment operation is processed by dequeuing it, and adding back the consumed capacity to the available capacity. The replenishment queue is organized as a priority queue in which the priority is the time at which the replenishment is due.

- *Background*: This is an extension of the queued manager, in which we allow the application task to execute at a background priority level when its execution capacity is exhausted. A special task (the *Rooster*) takes care of awaking (i.e., raising the priority of) the application tasks when a replenishment operation that increases the available capacity is due. Communication between the application tasks and the *Rooster* is done through a protected object called the *Wakeup_Manager*, to minimize the number of context switches, and thus the overhead. In addition, each sporadic server scheduler has its own protected object, called the *Protected_Manager*, to manage accesses to both the replenishment queue and the sporadic server parameters. Fig. 3 shows the basic architecture for this implementation.

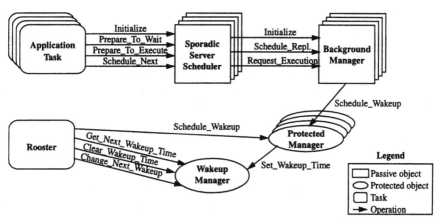

Fig. 3. Basic architecture of the implementations using the *Background* manager

The sporadic server operations need to be changed with respect to the operations described for the *Single* replenishment policy in the following way: the *Schedule_Next* operation invokes the *Schedule_Replenishment* operation instead of calculating the *Next_Start*; and the delay statement is replaced by a call to the *Request_Execution* operation.

5 Performance of the Different Implementations

When evaluating the performance of the different sporadic server implementations, it is necessary to take into account the different requirements that the application tasks may have. For example, we may have aperiodic sporadic tasks that have a guaranteed minimum interarrival time between events. In this case the task may have hard deadlines imposed, and the way to guarantee that they are met is to create a sporadic server that is capable of processing all the events arriving at the system, even at their highest possible rate. The sporadic server is created with a capacity of one event, and a replenishment period equal to the minimum interarrival time. The replenishment policy may in this case be the simplest one (the *Single* policy) because only one event per replenishment period may be processed. We must choose the *Simple_1* sporadic server implementation, if the events are timestamped, or the *High_Priority_Polled_1* implementation, if we can poll to check whether the event has arrived or not. If none of these are available, we can chose the *High_Priority_1* implementation, in which case we must reduce the replenishment period by an amount equal to the worst-case delay between the arrival of the event and the recording of its arrival time. This delay can be calculated using RMA [4]. Of course, the reduction of the replenishment period has a small negative impact on the schedulability of lower priority tasks.

In the case of periodic tasks with jitter we also require that the sporadic server be capable of processing one event per period, because otherwise the events would accumulate at the sporadic server scheduler and would have increasingly high response times. In this case, the requirements and solutions are the same as for the sporadic tasks with hard deadlines, which we have mentioned above.

For those periodic or aperiodic tasks with soft real-time requirements, we can use a sporadic server to enhance the average-case response times, while keeping the effects on lower priority tasks bounded. In this case we will probably want a server capable of processing several events per replenishment period, and thus a *Multiple* replenishment manager must be chosen. If the system has a low utilization level and there is enough slack time between the response times and the deadlines for hard deadline tasks, we may want to include the background manager, which can make use of idle CPU cycles at the cost of a higher overhead. If the deadlines are tight or the system already has a very high utilization level, the queued manager is probably the best choice. The sporadic server implementation (*Simple*, *High_Priority* or *High_Priority_Polled*) is chosen according to the event-receive operations that are available in the system.

Table 7 shows the overheads associated with each of the operations. The execution times are in μs, and the platform used to measure them was GNAT 3.05 under Linux 1.2.13 on a 486 CPU at 100 MHz. These numbers can help in selecting the implementation that is more appropriate for a particular application. A more complete description of all these performance metrics, including all the data that is required to apply the RMA techniques [4][8] that determine if the timing requirements will be met, is available from the following site, together with the implementation code: *ftp://ftp.unican.es/pub/misc/mgh/*

6 Conclusion

The sporadic server scheduling algorithm is very well suited for processing aperiodic events with a relatively short response time while the deadlines of all lower priority activities can be guaranteed to be met. The sporadic server can also eliminate the effects of jitter in periodic tasks. This is specially important in distributed systems, where the jitter effect may reduce the schedulability of the system by more than half. Although the sporadic server is intended to be implemented at the task scheduler level, very few commercial systems offer this scheduling policy. To solve this problem, in this paper we present different strategies that may be used to implement the sporadic server algorithm at the application level.

Table 7. Performance metrics of the sporadic server operations (µs)

Implementation	Prepare _To_ Wait	Prepare _To_ Execute	Schedule _Next	Execute_ Without_ Waiting
Simple_1	10	51	62	-
Simple_N	3	32	123	-
Simple_Queued	9	43	328	-
Simple_Background	7	281	734	-
High_Priority_1	188	228	46	-
High_Priority_N	169	181	70	-
High_Priority_Queued	134	297	112	-
High_Priority_Background	139	723	131	-
High_Priority_Polled_1	0	117	197	60
High_Priority_Polled_N	0	138	274	71
High_Priority_Polled_Queued	0	119	433	69
High_Priority_Polled_Background	0	335	795	199

Different implementations have been shown, with different compromises between performance and level of service. The basic sporadic server implementation must be chosen according to the event-receive operations that are available in the system. The replenishment management policy is chosen according to the timing requirements of the application. Performance metrics have been provided to help the implementor to choose the best implementation for his or her system.

7 References

[1] M. González Harbour and L. Sha: "An Application-level Implementation of the Sporadic Server" Technical Report CMU/SEI-TR-26-91, September 1991.

[2] J.J. Gutiérrez García, and M. González Harbour, "Increasing Schedulability in Distributed Hard Real-Time Systems". Proceedings of the 7th Euromicro Workshop on Real-Time Systems, Odense, Denmark, June 1995, pp. 99-106.

[3] J.J. Gutiérrez García, and M. González Harbour, "Minimizing the Effects of Jitter in Distributed Hard Real-Time systems". Journal of Systems Architecture, 42, Num. 6&7, December 1996.

[4] M.H. Klein, T. Ralya, B. Pollak, R. Obenza, and M. González Harbour. "A Practitioner's Handbook for Real-Time Analysis". Kluwer Academic Pub., 1993.

[5] S.Ramos-Thuel and J.P. Lehoczky, "On-line scheduling of Hard Deadline Aperiodic Tasks in Fixed-Priority Systems", Proceedings of the Real-Time Systems Symposium, December 1993, pp. 160-171.

[6] J. Rumbaugh, "Object-Oriented Modeling and Design", Prentice-Hall, 1991.

[7] B. Sprunt, L. Sha, and J.P. Lehoczky. "Aperiodic Task Scheduling for Hard Real-Time Systems". The Journal of Real-Time Systems, Vol. 1, 1989, pp. 27-60.

[8] K. Tindell, and J. Clark, "Holistic Schedulability Analysis for Distributed Hard Real-Time Systems". Microprocessing & Microprogramming, Vol. 50, Nos.2-3, April 1994, pp. 117-134.

Capturing and Verifying Performance Requirements for Hard Real Time Systems

R. H. Pierce

York Software Engineering Ltd, Bellwin Drive, Flixborough, DN15 8SN, UK

Sandra Ayache, R. Ward

Matra Marconi Space, 31, rue des Cosmonautes, F-31077 Toulouse, France

J. Stevens, Helen Clifton

Matra Marconi Space, FPC 321, PO Box 5, Filton, Bristol BS12 7QW, UK

J. Galle

E2S, Technologiepark 5, B-9052 Zwijnaarde, Belgium

Abstract. This paper describes the results of a project for the European Space Agency to produce guidelines for the development of real time software for onboard spacecraft applications. The project has produced guidance for the software requirements, architectural design, detailed design and implementation phases of the software development process, based on the use of HOORA and HOOD methods. A system of annotations has been devised for capturing performance and other non-functional requirements in HOORA and HOOD, such that existing method support tools are not affected by the presence of the annotations, which can be processed by additional tools. The paper outlines the guidance and the system of annotations.

1. Introduction

This paper describes the aims and results of the *Realisme* project carried out under contract for the European Space Agency, ESTEC, Contract No. 9558/91/NL/JG. The consortium consisted of Matra Marconi Space (France and UK), E2S (Belgium) and York Software Engineering Ltd (UK), with the Department of Computer Science, University of York acting as consultants. Responsibility for the contents of this paper resides with the authors and organisations which prepared it.

Software embedded in spacecraft, as in all other classes of embedded system, has become increasingly important in recent years and is now critical to the success of many missions. Characteristics of spacecraft computer systems include constrained architectures and very limited computing resources, difficulty of corrective maintenance, the need to supervise and control many on-board activities, and the presence of hard timing requirements where timeliness of execution is critical for correct operation of the system.

Over the past few years, much research has been undertaken into design techniques for dependable hard real-time systems. Activities in this area have been sponsored by ESTEC, for example the HRTOSK project [1] and its successor, the ERC32 project [2], to develop tools for hard real-time systems in Ada. At the same time, ESTEC has supported the development of methods such as HOORA for requirements analysis and HOOD for architectural and detailed design. These methods, while addressing software behaviour and structure well, have paid less attention to the expression and verification of non-functional requirements (NFRs), in particular those concerned with performance, which are vital for spacecraft software.

In parallel with this methodological development, the Ada 95 language has been standardised, with many new features which will offer greatly improved support for hard real-time software, and the POSIX standards for real-time kernels have been published. The two primary aims of Realisme were therefore:

- to draw together the results of all this work, providing detailed guidance to ESTEC (and its contractors) on how to develop hard real-time spacecraft software,
- to propose means of augmenting the HOORA and HOOD methods to allow the expression and verification of NFRs.

Annotations are used to provide extension to the standard methods HOORA and HOOD. Annotations are free text comments which are not checked by method support tools, but can be extracted and processed by additional tools. In this way neither the methods themselves nor existing support tools need to be altered.

The philosophy of Realisme was to provide consolidation rather than innovation, and to provide practical guidance of direct use to software engineers.

2. The Realisme Process Model

Software development projects for ESA/ESTEC are carried out to the software development standard PSS-05 (which is planned to be superseded by ECSS E40 in due course). PSS-05 is a well known standard which has been used in a number of fields apart from space systems. PSS-05 identifies a number of distinct specification and design phases, including User Requirements (UR), Software Requirements (SR), Architectural Design and Detailed Design (DD), with their corresponding requirements for documentation and verification. PSS-05 is, like all software development standards, a high level model.

The ESA Promesse project has produced a detailed process model for software development based upon the requirements of PSS-05. Realisme has taken the Promesse model as a starting point and inserted additional activities to specify and verify non-functional requirements. The Realisme process model therefore provides the framework within which the detailed guidance on methods for software specification, design and verification is set.

3. The Case Study

A specific and realistic case study was used by Realisme to demonstrate and validate the results of the project. The example chosen was a High Speed Multiplexer (HSM) system developed by Matra Marconi Space. It is part of the Data Handling Subsystem for the Polar Platform. Its role is to accept the output data from various instruments (using 12 channels). The data are then packetised by the HSM before being inserted into the single data channel to be transmitted to the ground. The HSM sends telemetry data (TM) to the ground. Telecommands (TC) are sent from the ground to the HSM. This is a fairly simple system but has stringent performance requirements. The software requirements and architectural design were re-expressed using the Realisme method guidelines. The examples in this paper are drawn from the case study.

4. Guidance for Software Requirements Analysis

The software requirements analysis phase of a project takes as input the User Requirements Definition (URD) and produces the Software Requirements Definition (SRD). The Realisme guidelines recommend the use of HOORA for this phase, to construct a logical model to support the software requirements analysis process. The aim of the logical model is to represent the application domain in terms of objects so that we can relate them to user and software requirements. HOORA is a method that models systems in an object-oriented way, traces the model elements to user requirements, translates the model information into software requirements, and generates an initial architectural design from the model information.

4.1 The HOORA Method

The HOORA method distinguishes between three closely integrated models (or views): requirements model (RM), static (or object) model (SM), dynamic model (DM).

The *Requirements Model* specifies the user requirements taken from the User Requirements Document (URD), one of the inputs to the analysis phase.

The static model specifies the objects and their operations. It includes definitions of *classes*, their *attributes* and *operations*, and definitions of *relations* (association, specialisation, aggregation) between these classes. Diagrams used in static modelling in HOORA are:

- a Class Relationship Diagram (CRD) shows classes and the relations between them.

- an Instance Relationship Diagram (IRD) shows relations between instances of classes.

The dynamic model specifies the dynamic behaviour (sequencing of operations). It includes *state* models for class behaviour, and models of *transactions* between objects. There is a distinction between operations and transactions. Transactions represent a particular use (or instance) of operations. A transaction identifies both the sender and receiver object, as well as the applicable operation of the receiver object, whereas an operation does not identify the sender object (it can be used by many objects).

In HOORA, dynamic behaviour is modelled in three types of diagrams:

- a Class Interaction Diagram (CID) is used to show interactions (transactions) between classes.

- a State Transition Diagram (STD) is used to describe the possible states and transitions between states for a single state variable of a class.

- a Transaction Trace Diagram (TTD) is used to describe a complex transaction between objects by describing the pattern of simple transactions it is composed of. It gives one scenario for communication between a number of objects. TTDs are essentially equivalent to the Use Case or Event Trace diagrams which appear in other object oriented requirements modelling methods. The Realisme guidelines use TTDs to express real time requirements.

4.2 Classification of Real Time Requirements

A classification of real time requirements is proposed by the Realisme guidelines, to provide a framework for modelling these requirement in HOORA and later in HOOD. Requirements are classified as follows.

Temporal Requirements

A temporal requirement expresses the need to time a certain process or sequence of events in a process. Temporal requirements can be subdivided into three new categories,

- Timeout requirements, where a time limit is placed on an action,
- Throughput requirements, which express the need to carry out a certain number of actions per unit time, for example: *the system should be able to accept a request every 60 milliseconds*,
- Input/output requirements, which state the time allowable between (input and output) events, for example: *the time between receiving a request and giving an answer shall always be less than 60 seconds*.

Resource Requirements

Resource requirements include constraints on processor, disk and memory, as well as any external device that can be accessed. Resource requirements can be subdivided into two new categories: resource availability (for example *the available platform has 4 MB of memory)* and utilisation rate (for example *the processor shall have a maximum 50 % load for the XYZ functions)*.

Quantitative Requirements

A quantitative requirement expresses the need to store or process a given volume of information expressed in suitable units.

4.3 Specification of Real Time Requirements

The transaction trace diagrams in the HOORA logical model are extended with real time requirements, structured according to their type as defined in the previous section. We give one example of such a diagram and the accompanying text annotation.

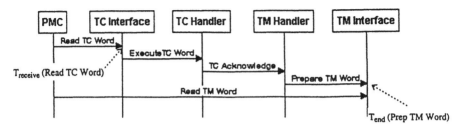

Figure 1: Extended Transaction Trace Diagram

In this example, the PMC (Payload Management Computer) sends telecommands (words) to the HSM, and then the TC and its block of parameters are read. On identification of the end of a TC (block) an appropriate "acknowledge word" is written to the telemetry register to be read by the PMC. The requirement is that this acknowledge word shall be available within 1 millisecond of the receipt of the last word of a TC block.

The TC Interface receives a TC word at $T_{receive}$ (Read TC Word) and the TC Handler executes that word. It identifies the word as the last word of a TC and acknowledges the receipt of the full TC by sending the TC Acknowledge message to the TM Handler. This TM Handler creates a TM word for the acknowledgement, and asks the TM Interface to prepare it as the next TM word to be read by the PMC. Now the PMC can read the acknowledgement at T_{end} (Prep TM Word) from the TM Interface. The RT software requirement is therefore identified by the following annotation:

$DURATION_CONSTRAINT
Transaction TC_Acknowledge
T_{end} (Prep TM Word) - $T_{receive}$ (Read TC Word) < 1 msec

It must be remembered that the system is modelled as a set of objects, *so that we are able to express our requirements.* The distinction between TC Interface and TC Handler, for instance, was required in order to be able to formulate specific RT software requirements. *This is not design.* It merely introduces concepts which are part of the problem domain. We cannot express particular requirements without them.

5. Guidance for Design and Implementation

The guidance for design and implementation introduces the concept of a computational model. A computational model defines the nature of the software components which comprise an application, the design rules or guidelines for using such components, and the approach taken to real-time synchronisation of the internal world model maintained by the application with the external world. By analogy with building architecture, the computational model may be regarded as the "style" or "school" of architecture; the set of design rules and available physical components with which the designer must work, whereas an architectural design represents a particular instance of a design carried out according to those rules.

Differing computational models can be identified which offer suitable support for software systems with differing requirements. The instantiation of a particular computational model for any given software system is performed during design and implementation of the system.

Any suitable computational model is defined in term of:

- the types of components (objects) from which the system will be constructed (e.g. cyclic, sporadic, protected, passive);
- the scheduling paradigm (e.g. RMS, DMS) under which the system is executed and the associated mechanisms;
- the means of communication between components/objects (e.g. mailboxes, entry parameters);
- the means of synchronisation between components/objects (e.g. protected object entries, semaphores);
- if applicable, the means of distribution and inter-node communication (e.g. virtual nodes, remote procedure call);
- the means of providing timing facilities;
- the means of providing asynchronous transfer of control.

The details of such definitions may vary with the particular computational model. A computational model has the following properties: it is abstract, independent of specific design methods and tools, chosen to match system requirements, independent of specific application details, (ideally) supported by analysis techniques.

5.1 Selection of an Appropriate Computational Model

The first and most fundamental choice in the selection of a computational model concerns the use or otherwise of concurrency. Sequential design models of inherently concurrent problems, using for example the traditional cyclic scheduler model, require more effort in design since temporal behaviour needs to be considered in some detail during the design of each object, and are liable to be unstable in the face of quite small coding changes, since execution schedules have to be re-evaluated for every coding change and operations may have to be sub-divided. The problems associated with cyclic scheduling increase with the size of the application and the number of parallel real-world activities which need to be considered.

Concurrency gives simpler and more natural designs, and ones which are more stable against small changes in detailed design and code, since each concurrent activity can be designed in isolation [3]. This is of particular benefit in a large system where many designers are at work. This explains the prevalence of concurrent models for the great majority of real-time systems, the inclusion of concurrency features in Ada, and the large number of proprietary run-time kernels in existence. However, there is a penalty in that more sophisticated analysis techniques are, in general, required to ensure predictability of behaviour and the satisfaction of timing requirements. There is also a penalty in run-time system size and time overheads. Traditionally, therefore, hard real time systems with particularly stringent requirements for dependability (avionics, space software) have relied on sequential designs.

We believe, however, that in the majority of space applications, it is no longer necessary to use sequential designs. In the Realisme guidelines, it is argued that concurrent systems, using suitable computational models and supported by suitable run-time systems, are now appropriate for all forms of spacecraft software. The need for analysability, however, constrains the choice of concurrent computational model.

The computational model chosen has an important influence on how timing requirements are expressed and how they may be verified by analysis. Verification of real time performance requirements (for concurrent systems) can be approached using a range of techniques:

- the HRT approach: this involves use of the *HRT model* described below, and thus constraining the design in such a way that performance requirements can be verified analytically using Deadline Monotonic Scheduling (DMS) theory [4],
- the statistical approach: performance verification is carried out by queuing-theoretic modelling, rather than by guaranteeing the meeting of hard deadlines,
- the empirical approach: verification depends solely on testing.

As an aside, we may summarise the theory of Deadline Monotonic Scheduling briefly by saying that its central principle is that tasks are assigned priorities strictly according to the rule that the task with the shortest deadline (time at which it must complete its action in the current processing cycle) is given the highest priority, and so on. If the worst case execution time of each task is known, and the time each task will spend waiting to communicate with lower tasks is also known, it is possible to show analytically whether all tasks will meet their deadlines. This calculation is known as schedulability analysis.

If it is appropriate, we strongly recommend the HRT model, since it offers the best combination of design convenience and predictability. However, in some circumstances it may not be possible to apply the DMS scheduling theory required by this model, and the statistical approach may have to be adopted. In other cases, simpler models may be required.

5.2 The HRT Model

The characteristics of the HRT model are derived from the need to use DMS techniques to ensure that real time requirements are met. In general, asynchronous communication between objects is preferred for hard real time systems, both on the grounds of efficiency of implementation, and on the grounds of predictability of performance. DMS scheduling theory requires that the time taken in task communication be bounded so that it can be taken into account in schedulability calculations, and this is much easier to demonstrate with asynchronous communication. In addition, a fixed number of tasks is more tractable than a variable number (if a task is not active, it is better to suspend it than to terminate it and start another later). The HRT model takes account of these considerations. Designs using the HRT model can be expressed in HOOD with the Realisme real-time annotations.

The HRT model is therefore characterised as follows.

- there are fixed number of concurrent objects, classified generally as either periodic (*cyclic*) or periodic (*sporadic*). These classifications apply of course to terminal HOOD objects realised as tasks; non-terminal objects cannot be classified in this way since they may contain a mixture of object types,
- asynchronous communication between tasks, using explicit *protected objects* (which offer mutual exclusion of data) and operations to suspend a task and resume it upon the arrival of a stimulus,
- pre-emptive, priority based scheduling with the ability of a task to suspend itself until a given instant in time. Each task must have a unique priority.

Interrupt or polling solutions can both be accommodated within this model. The HRT model is applicable in the following circumstances. there are a fixed number of data sources; data is input at a fixed rate, or if the rate is variable then the variability is predictable such that, even in the worst case, response time requirements can be met for critical activities; hard response times or rate requirements exist in the requirements specification.

These rules imply that there is no contention for resources within the processor which has to be solved by, for example, buffering of data within the protected objects which are used for task communication.

Many real time systems meet these requirements; by contrast, real time systems where there is substantial human operator input are more generally amenable to the statistical or empirical approach. The guidelines also discuss other computational models, including cyclic scheduler approaches and a restricted tasking model, and discuss cases where they may be applicable.

Note that the HRT model is the same computational model as that supported by the HRT-HOOD *method* [5], but HRT-HOOD requires explicit tool support. In the Realisme guidelines, by contrast, the method recommended is HOOD 4 with additional annotations.

5.3 The Architectural Design Process

When the software requirements have been expressed using HOORA, as is assumed in the Realisme process model, a set of principal problem space objects relevant to the application will already have been selected, together with their major operations. These objects form the initial list of candidate objects for the architectural design, and requirements to design traceability will be enhanced if the HOORA object decomposition is preserved as much as possible.

The architectural design process therefore has three primary objectives:

- to insert "solution space" objects to supplement the "problem space objects" which will have been selected by the HOORA model,
- to transform the object structure identified at the HOORA level, if necessary, into a structure more suitable for the chosen computational model and the satisfaction of non functional requirements; among other considerations, this involves defining

threads of control (implemented as active objects) and the apportioning of functions to each thread,

- to refine the design, adding as appropriate data types, use links, data flows, additional operations and annotations, to achieve completeness.

By this means we can devise a software architecture which will achieve both the functional and non-functional requirements.

5.4 Guidance for Detailed Design and Implementation

The guidance considers implementation issues, including the desirable characteristics of real time kernels needed to support the HRT model. An extensive description is given on the POSIX standard. Details are given of how the HRT model concepts of cyclic, sporadic and protected objects can be implemented in POSIX (using the C language) and contrasts this with the equivalent constructs in Ada 95, which are shown to be much more compact in source language terms [6]. The guidance concludes that Ada 95 can be recommended for future space software systems.

Finally, the guidance discusses additional measures such as static code analysis which can be used to gain extra assurance of dependability in highly critical areas. It does not address testing, beyond remarking that test coverage measurement is desirable, since testing is regarded as adequately covered elsewhere.

6. HOOD Annotations

The REALISME guidelines propose two kinds of annotations: performance requirements annotations and performance prediction annotations.

The goal of performance requirements annotations is to identify the elements of a HOOD design which are constrained by performance requirements. These annotations are mainly dedicated to traceability link purposes between performance software requirements (already modelled as annotations to the HOORA model) and design elements. The RT requirements information is attached to the appropriate design objects. The performance requirements annotations are the RT requirements already mentioned in the SR phase, but with additional syntax to annotate them to HOOD design elements.

The goal of performance prediction annotations is to associate, with the HOOD operations impacted by performance requirements, a set of data needed to build performance models (e.g. consumption of CPU resource by the execution of an operation). They are dedicated to performance models building purposes: performance data or performance estimates are attached to the appropriate design objects, in order to be able to predict performance by various means, including DMS schedulability analysis.

Note that the estimates are not RT *requirements*; they are pure attributes, introduced during design, for the purpose of performance prediction and scheduling analysis.

6.1 Performance Prediction Annotations

The Performance Prediction Annotations consist of the following.
HRT Annotations

These annotations express the real-time behaviour of objects. They are mainly concerned with concepts in the HRT computational model (object type (cyclic/sporadic/protected), offset, period, deadline, priority, worst case execution time budget); however certain annotations are also relevant to cyclic scheduling and other models. The priority of a cyclic or sporadic object is of course computed from its deadline.

Resource Oriented Annotations

These annotations describe resource consumption (processing resource, I/O resource, communications resource), primarily for the purpose of estimating execution time (elapsed and CPU time).

Memory Usage Annotations

These provide a means of recording budgets and, if appropriate, actual usage for memory of various classes. These annotations can be used independently of the computational model selected.

Transaction Annotations

These annotations represent transactions involving a number of objects operating in sequence, and provide timing properties for these objects. They provide the ability to state the end to end transaction processing time and compare it with the deadline of the objects which contribute to the transaction. The transaction annotations were first introduced as diagrammatic extensions to HRT-HOOD in a paper by Cornwell and Wellings [7], but for the purposes of Realisme, which avoids the use of non-standard methods, they have been expressed in an equivalent textual form in which each transaction is given a unique name. A transaction is defined as a contiguous flow of data or stimuli between a number of participating objects, frequently but not always between an input and an output operation. The transaction annotations identify the following for each transaction.:

- the operation or object which initiates the transaction, with the arrival rate of data,
- the intermediate operations which handle the transaction,
- the operation which terminates the transaction, with the deadline for the transaction.

Each transaction annotation identifies the data flows between objects which carries the transaction data (note that the data flow names need not be the same for each part of the transaction since the data involved in the transaction may well be transformed at each step). For details of the transaction and other annotations, the reader is referred to the Realisme guidelines [8].

6.2 Annotation Processing

For each of these types of annotations, a syntax is defined to annotate a HOOD design model element with such information. Tools are envisaged which will operate on the annotations, for example:

- a tool to check the syntax and consistency of the annotations, both internal consistency and consistency with the rest of the HOOD design,
- a tool to exchange information with a DMS scheduling tool,
- a worst case execution time analysis tool.

As stated previously, such tools may be independent of the method support tool used.

6.3 Annotation Example

Two example of annotations taken from the HSM case study are given. In the SRD a RT requirement is stated as:

The software shall provide a transaction between class PMC and class TC_Interface referred to as Read_TC_Word. RT software requirement: the software shall be able to accept a telecommand block 60 milliseconds after the previous telecommand block.

In the generated HOOD design, the object TC_Interface contains a performance requirement annotation derived from the HOORA model, referring to a RT throughput software requirement. This is shown here as it would appear in the HOOD ODS.

```
OBJECT TC_Interface is ACTIVE
   IMPLEMENTATION_CONSTRAINTS
   $PERFORMANCE_CONSTRAINTS
      $OPERATION TC_Interface.Read_TC_Word;
      $THROUGHPUT_CONSTRAINT TC1 "the software shall be
      able to accept a telecommand block 60 milliseconds
      after the previous telecommand block"
      DERIVED FROM SR TC_Interface-TA-1-FUNC;
   $END_PERFORMANCE_CONSTRAINT
```

An example of a performance prediction annotation is given below for the TM_Handler object. This declares that this object is of sporadic type and that the operation TC_Acknowledge has a deadline of 60 milliseconds. This is the time when TM_Handler must have finished and be ready to accept a new call to TC_Acknowledge:

```
OBJECT TM_Handler is ACTIVE
   IMPLEMENTATION_CONSTRAINTS
   $HRT_PROPERTIES
      OBJECT_TYPE SPORADIC;
      PRIORITY <>;
      OPERATION TC_Acknowledge;
      DEADLINE 60ms DERIVED FROM ELEMENT Read_TC_Word SR
      TC_Interface-TA-1-FUNC JUSTIFICATION "the software
```

```
        shall be able to accept a telecommand block 60
        milliseconds after the previous telecommand block";
    $END HRT_PROPERTIES
```

Further examples of the transaction and other annotations are given in the guidelines.

7. Conclusions

The Realisme project has succeeding in providing detailed guidelines to assist software engineers to capture real time and other non-functional requirements, and to carry out the design process in a way which ensures that the satisfaction of these requirements is given due prominence. A system of annotations has been defined which allows real time requirements and design information to be added to standard methods without any need for changes to the methods or to supporting tools.

8. Acknowledgements

The authors gratefully acknowledge the assistance of their colleagues during the Realisme project. Particular thanks are due to Professor Alan Burns and Dr. Andy Wellings of York. Rod Allen, Tullio Vardanega and Jorge Amador-Monteverde of ESTEC have also contributed notably to the success of the project.

9. References

[1]   A. Burns, A. J. Wellings, C. M. Bailey and E. Fyfe. "The Olympus attitude and orbital control system", in Ada Sans Frontieres, Proc. 12th Ada-Europe Conference, LNCS 688, pp. 19-35. Springer-Verlag, 1993.

[2]   T. Vardanega, "Tool Support for the Construction of Statically Analysable Hard Real-Time Systems in Ada", Proceedings of the 17th Real-Time Systems Symposium, IEEE, Dec 96.

[3]   C. D. Locke, "Software architecture for hard real-time applications: cyclic executives vs. fixed priority executives," Real-Time Systems Vol. 4 No. 1, pp. 37-53, Real Time Systems (Netherlands), March 1992.

[4]   N. C. Audsley, A. Burns and A. J. Wellings, "Deadline Monotonic Scheduling theory and application", Control Engineering Practice, Vol. 1 No. 1, pp. 71-78, 1993.

[5]   A. Burns, A. J. Wellings, "HRT-HOOD: A Structured Design Method for Hard Real-Time Ada Systems", Elsevier, 313 pages, 1995.

[6]   R. Pierce, "Guidelines and Procedures for Software Design and Coding", Realisme project deliverable D2200.1, York Software Engineering Ltd, UK, 1996.

[7]   P. Cornwell, A. Wellings, "Transaction Specifications for Object-Oriented Real-Time Systems in HRT-HOOD", A. P. Cornwell, A.J. Wellings, Proc. 1995 Ada in Europe, LNCS 1031, pp 365-378. Berlin: .Springer-Verlag, 1996.

[8]   J. Galle, "RT Software Development Guidelines", Realisme project deliverable D3100.1, E2S n.V., Zwijnaarde, Belgium, 1996.

Task Termination in Ada 95

A.J. Wellings[1], A. Burns[1] and O. Pazy[2]

[1] Department of Computer Science, University of York, U.K.
[2] O. Pazy, 48 Beeri St., Tel-Aviv 64233, Israel

Abstract. Ada 83 removed from the programmer the burden of coding potentially complex termination conditions between clients and servers by introducing an 'or terminate' option to the select statement. With the use of indirect communication (emphasised by the provision of protected objects in Ada 95), it is no longer straightforward to obtain program termination. This paper illustrates the problem and shows how the asynchronous select statement and a general-purpose library package can be used to simplify the termination protocols. The advantages and disadvantages of the approach are discussed. The paper then considers the extent to which termination could be supported in Ada. It explores the idea of having a termination option with an entry call.

Keywords: asynchronous communication, termination, Ada 95

1 Introduction

Although there were many perceived difficulties with the Ada 83 (U.S. Department of Defense 1983) tasking model, one of its benefits was that it provided a simple mechanism for application programmers to specify termination conditions. With the use of indirect communication (emphasised by the provision of protected objects in Ada 95(Intermetrics 1995)), it is no longer straightforward to obtain program termination. This paper firstly considers the problem of termination when asynchronous communication is introduced. It then considers the extent to which termination in Ada 95 can be supported without having to resort to *ad hoc* protocols between producers and consumers. Finally we present our conclusions.

2 The Basic Problem

The motivation for having a terminate alternative on the Ada select statement was to provide a simple mechanism with which to terminate server tasks. For example, consider the following Ada program:

```
task type Producer;           task Consumer is
                                 entry Next(...);
task body Producer is         end Consumer;
begin                         task body Consumer is
   ....                       begin
```

```
    loop                          loop
      ...                           select
      Consumer.Next(...);             accept Next(...) do
      ...                               ... end;
      exit when ...;                  or terminate;
    end loop;                       end select;
  end Producer;                   end loop;
  P1, P2 : Producer;            end Consumer;
```

This program will terminate irrespectively of how many Producers are created. The Consumer task simply indicates that it wishes to terminate when there are no more tasks requiring its services. Without the terminate option, it would be necessary to program the Consumer's termination explicitly.

With the above approach, the Producer has to wait for the Consumer to service its request. An alternative paradigm is where the Producer simply issues its request and then continues. The classical solution to this problem is to introduce a bounded buffer between the tasks. To do this in Ada 83 required the introduction of a buffer task and modifications to the Producer and Consumer.

```
    task Buffer is               task body Buffer is
      entry Get(...);              Full : Boolean := False;
      entry Put(...);              Empty : Boolean := True;
    end Buffer;                      ...
                                 begin
    task type Producer;            loop
    task Consumer;                   select
                                       when not Full =>
    task body Producer is              accept Put(...) do
    begin                                ...
      loop                               Full := True;
        ...                              Empty := False;
        Buffer.Put(...);               end;
        exit when ...;               or
      end loop;                       when not Empty =>
    end Producer;                       accept Get(...) do
                                          ...
    task body Consumer is                Full := False;
    begin                                Empty := True;
      loop                             end;
        ...                          or terminate;
        Buffer.Get(...);           end select;
        ...                       end loop;
      end loop;                  end Buffer;
    end Consumer;
    P1, P2 : Producer;
```

This solution introduces a termination problem. When the Producer tasks finish, the Consumer task is left waiting on a closed entry of the Buffer task. Note also that the Buffer task will not terminate because the Consumer task has visibility of the buffer and consequently can call Get. The system is thus deadlocked. We are, therefore, forced to consider ways to terminate the consumer.

In Ada 95, the Buffer task would be replaced by a protected object. However, the problem for the consumer remains.

Programming termination in concurrent systems is non-trivial. Tokens must be passed from producers to consumers to indicate that a producer is about to terminate (this is the approach that is often taken with occam programs (Burns 1988), for example). In Ada, each client could register with the server, and the server could keep track of all its registered clients. Clients would also de-register when they have finished with the server or when they terminate (using Ada's finalisation facility). Servers can then terminate when all their clients no longer need their services. However, it was just these types of *ad hoc* algorithms that Ada 83 was trying to avoid with its termination option on the select statement.

3   Termination in Ada Revisited

In this section we reconsider termination in Ada 95. In particular, we address:

1. whether termination can be implemented by the programmer using the asynchronous transfer of control facility and a general-purpose package,
2. the implications of removing the terminate option of the select statement,
3. the implications of adding a terminate alternative to the entry call facility.

3.1   Programmer-defined termination

The goal of this section is to define a general-purpose mechanism which allows termination between tasks involved in asynchronous communication. In such an approach, the server task usually has to make an entry call to a buffer (which in Ada 95 would be implemented as a protected object) to obtain the clients' requests. For the server to terminate, it must withdraw its request for new services, that is, cancel its entry call. The only way that the task can withdraw its offer of communication is via: 1) a timed entry call, 2) a conditional entry call, or 3) an entry call within an asynchronous select statement The first two approaches introduce polling and therefore will not be considered. We will illustrate how the asynchronous select statement can be used to get server termination. Consider the following package specification:

```
with Ada.Finalization; use Ada.Finalization;
package Termination is
  protected type Terminator is
    entry Wait_Termination;
    procedure Log_Termination;
    procedure Log_Interest;
  private
    Interested : Natural := 0;
```

```
    In_Use : Boolean := False;
  end Terminator;
  type Termination_Aid(T : access Terminator) is new
    Limited_Controlled with null record;

  procedure Initialize(Object : in out Termination_Aid);
  procedure Finalize(Object : in out Termination_Aid);
end Termination;
```

Here we define a protected type that can be used to help program termination. A group of clients and servers have access to an object of type **Terminator** (usually declared by the server). The clients indicate their interest by calling Log_Interest; when they terminate they call Log_Termination. Whenever a server wishes to wait on a protected entry, it uses an asynchronous select statement with the target entry call as the triggering event and a call to the terminator's Wait_Termination as the first statement in the abortable part. The controlled type Termination_Aid is used to facilitate client interaction with the terminator. The primitive operations of the type call the appropriate logging procedures of the **Terminator** object. The body of package **Termination** is:

```
package body Termination is
  protected body Terminator is
    entry Wait_Termination when Interested = 0 and In_Use is
    begin
        null;
    end Wait_Termination;

    procedure Log_Termination is
    begin
      Interested := Interested - 1;
    end Log_Termination;

    procedure Log_Interest is
    begin
      Interested := Interested + 1;
      In_Use := True;
    end Log_Interest;
  end Terminator;

  procedure Initialize(Object : in out Termination_Aid) is
  begin
    Object.T.Log_Interest;
  end Initialize;

  procedure Finalize(Object : in out Termination_Aid) is
  begin
    Object.T.Log_Termination;
  end Finalize;
end Termination;
```

The count Interested keeps track of clients as they are elaborated. The flag In_Use ensures that servers do not prematurely terminate before any of their clients have had a chance to register themselves. Note that instead of keeping a count of the number of clients, it would be possible to keep track of task identifiers and ensure that all tasks logging termination have also logged interest. The code for a typical client is:

```
with Termination; use Termination;
with Server_Interface;
...
  task type Producer;

  task body Producer is
    Term: Termination_Aid(Server_Interface.My_Terminator'Access);
  begin
    loop
      -- produce and place in buffer shared with servers
      Server_Interface.Buffer.Put(..);
      exit when ...;
    end loop;
  end Producer;
```

Each client declares an instance of the controlled object Termination_Aid passing a pointer to the server's terminator object. This ensures that the client registers its interest on creation and informs the terminator when it has finished. The servers have the following structure:

```
with Termination; use Termination;
package Server_Interface is
  My_Terminator : aliased Terminator;
  -- rest of server interface including Buffer declaration
end Server_Interface;

package body Server_Interface is
  -- implementation of interface, Buffer, etc
  task type Consumer;

  task body Consumer is
  begin
    loop
      select
        Buffer.Get(...);
        -- consume
      then abort
        My_Terminator.Wait_Termination;
        exit;
      end select;
    end loop;
  end Consumer;
end Server_Interface;
```

Each server uses the call to the buffer protected entry as a triggering event in an asynchronous select statement. The abortable part contains a call to the terminator entry. Note that the alternative (which at first sight appears more intuitive):

```
select
  My_Terminator.Wait_Termination;
  exit;
then abort
  Buffer.Get(...)
  -- consume
end select;
```

is incorrect. The reason is that it is possible for both the Wait_Termination entry and the Get entry to become open before the start of the select statement (when the last item has been put and the Producer task has terminated). In the former case, the last item will be consumed; in the latter, the last item will be lost.

3.2 Limitations of the Approach

Although the approach given in this section is quite elegant, it does not generalise very easily to a dynamic system. In particular, where clients are created dynamically by other tasks who are not registered as clients, it may be difficult to prove that the server does not terminate prematurely. In this case, all tasks must be made registered clients. However, it is possible to construct examples where premature termination could easily occur; consider the following:

```
with Termination; use Termination;
  ...
  task Nested;

  task body Nested is
    My_Terminator : aliased Terminator;

    task type Producer;
    type P_Producer is access Producer;

    task type Consumer;

    protected Buffer is
      entry Get(...);
      entry Put(...);
    private
      ...
    end Buffer;

    task body Producer is
      Term: Termination_Aid(My_Terminator'Access);
```

```
begin
  ..
  Buffer.Put(...);
  ...
end Producer;

task body Consumer is
begin
  loop
    select
      Buffer.Get(...);
    then abort
      My_Terminator.Wait_Termination;
      exit;
    end select;
  end loop;
end Consumer;

protected body Buffer is separate;

Ap1, Ap2 : P_Producer;
C1: Consumer;
begin
  Ap1 := new Producer;
  delay 5.0; -- or any time consuming computation
  Ap2 := new Producer;
end Nested;
```

With the above example, the Consumer task will potentially terminate prematurely, if task AP1.all terminates before AP2.all is created.

A possible solution to this problem is to make Nested a client of Consumer.

```
task body Nested is
  My_Terminator : aliased Terminator;
  Term: Termination_Aid(My_Terminator'Access);
  ...
```

However, the problem then is how to terminate Nested. Nested cannot terminate until its dependent tasks have terminated. The Consumer is a dependent task which is waiting for Nested to terminate. To remove this deadlock, it is necessary for Nested to call My_Terminator.Log_Termination explicitly as the last statement it executes! Alternatively, the terminator can be nested in an inner block of the Nested task:

```
task body Nested is
  My_Terminator : aliased Terminator;
  ...
begin
  declare
    Term: Termination_Aid(My_Terminator'Access);
```

```
begin
  Ap1 := new Producer;
  delay 5.0;
  Ap2 := new Producer;
end; -- finalisation of Term occurs here
end Nested;
```

None of these solutions is entirely satisfactory.

3.3 Removing termination

Given that Ada 95 does not support the automatic termination of tasks communicating asynchronously, we now briefly consider the extent to which a server task involved in a rendezvous can easily program its own termination using the approach outlined in Section 3.1 and thus remove the need for a termination option from the language completely. The approach would require the following structure for server tasks:

```
select -- NOT VALID Ada
  accept Service_A ...
or
  accept Service_B ...
then abort
  My_Terminator.Wait_Termination;
end select;
```

Of course this is not valid Ada. Interestingly, neither is this:

```
select -- NOT VALID Ada
  My_Terminator.Wait_Termination;
then abort
  select
    accept Service_A ...
  or
    accept Service_B ...
  end select;
end select;
```

As a select statement cannot appear in the abortable part (for ease of implementation).

In summary, it is not possible to use the approach given in Section 3.1 to program termination of the servers in a synchronous systems (using rendezvous) and hence there is a strong motivation to retain the terminate option.

3.4 Entry Call with a Termination Option

An alternative approach to requiring the user to program termination is to require that the language be extended to provide automatic termination. One way to provide this capability is to add a terminate option to the entry call facility.

Consider again the simple producer/consumer program. Consumers would be structured as follows:

```
task type Consumer;

task body Consumer is
begin
  loop
    select
      Buffer.Get(...);
      -- consume
    or terminate; -- NOT VALID Ada
    end select;
  end loop;
end Consumer;
```

The terminate option would be mutually exclusive with the delay, else and then abort options. There are two cases to consider: 1) the Buffer object is a task, and 2) the Buffer object is a protected object. In both of these cases, a task waiting on an entry call with the terminate option will terminate if and only if all tasks which have the same master as the target protected (or task) object are either terminated or similarly waiting on an entry call with a terminate option. If one of these tasks is waiting on a different object than the first one considered, then the same termination check has to be performed for that object too. If the call with terminate is done from within an abortable part (in some dynamically-nested level), then the calling task is assumed to be "non-terminatable" at that point. Of course, producer/client tasks can also terminate in the normal way when they have finished their allotted work (by reaching the end of their body).

Semantic Changes/Difficulties

The proposal made in this section raises some semantic issues that have to be studied further. Below, we enumerate those topics that immediately come to mind together with our initial thoughts about them.

Interaction with user-defined finalisation Before all tasks waiting on an entry call with "terminate" can terminate, the construct that declares the protected object (or an access to the protected type) must itself be completed or have issued an entry call with "terminate". However, after a construct is completed, it must finalize. This finalisation step may include user-defined finalisation routines which may issue further entry calls on the task or the protected object since the latter's entries are still visible at this point. Such entry calls will violate the termination condition which has already been determined; this is, of course, unacceptable. Note, however, that finalization routines must be at the library-level and in most cases they will not see the terminating object.

Extending the notion of masters In order to properly define the set of "all possible tasks", the notion of masters will have to be extended (mainly because access values designating protected objects can be passed around in a partition). Currently, this concept is tightly coupled to tasks and their active nature. Masters are also an essential part of the language model, but still quite subtle. More work is needed to determine if extending the concept of a master is feasible.

Interaction with Asynchronous Transfers of Control For this feature to work, the termination condition defined above must be relatively stable. That is, in order to avoid the need for a complicated protocol, there should be a limited set of well-defined events that can cause the calling task to leave the "call-with-terminate" state. As we have discussed above, two such events are currently recognised: one is when the corresponding entry becomes open (and then the entry call completes and the task continues execution). The other is when the termination condition is reached causing the task to terminate. Note that both of these cases are detectable state changes in the protected object itself (that is, when its lock is held). They are not triggered asynchronously from the outside. As a consequence, the algorithm that is required to commit to termination is fairly straight-forward.

However, an entry call (with terminate) issued by the client, may itself be dynamically nested within an outer abortable part. The code that makes the call may not even be aware of the fact that it is inside such an abortable construct[1]. If the abortable part aborts, thus cancelling the entry call, the calling task may continue executing on a different path. This will make the termination condition transient which will require the synchronisation protocol to be much more complex. Note that the construct in question may be aborted by a totally unrelated task (i.e. a task that is not necessarily in the "possible tasks" set). It may also be triggered by the opening of an entry of an unrelated protected object. This problem does not exist for the selective-accept with terminate construct. The language does not allow accept statements to be nested (dynamically or statically) inside an abortable part. The motivation for this restriction was partly due to similar problems.

There does not seem to be a simple solution to this problem. The implementation cost may be quite significant.

Interaction with the requeue statement Clearly, the semantic meaning of requeuing a task with and without the abort option needs to be defined when an entry has been called with a terminate option. Presumably, requeuing with abort should allow the task to terminate, whereas without abort would remove the termination option. However, further study is needed to determine whether any other interactions exist.

---

[1] Here, we are only concerned with abortable constructs which are not the entire task. No special problem is introduced if the calling task is aborted as a whole.

Usability Issues

In addition to semantic problems introduced above, the result of adding a terminate option to an entry call means that:

- some programs which previously would deadlock would now terminate if the entry is called with a termination option, as illustrated below:

```
task A is                    task B;
  entry One;
end A;

task body A is              task body B is
begin                       begin
  ...                         ...
  select                      select
    when False =>               A.One;
      accept One do           or
        ...                     terminate; -- NOT VALID Ada
      end;                    end select;
  or                          ...
    terminate;                ...
  end select;               end B;
  ...
end A;
```

- a task which previously had Tasking_Error raised, would now wait for termination if it called a completed task with the terminate alternative specified, as illustrated below (the rendezvous never occurs, A terminates):

```
task A is                    task B;
  entry One;
end A;

task body A is              task body B is
begin                       begin
  ...                         ...
  if False then               select
    accept One do               A.One;
      ...                     or
    end;                        terminate; -- NOT VALID Ada
  end if;                     end select;
                              ...
  ...                       end B;
end A;
```

Finally, consider what would happen with the following code:

```
task A is                    task B;
  entry One;
end A;

task body A is              task body B is
```

```
begin                          begin
   . . .                          . . .
   select                         select
      accept One do                 A.One;
         . . .                    or
      end;                          terminate;  -- NOT VALID Ada
   or                             end select;
      terminate;                    . . .
   end select;                   end B;
   . . .
end A;
```

In this situation, the rendezvous would occur and no termination would take place. However, if the accept statement was guarded and the guard evaluated to false, then termination would take place (if all other tasks are terminated or waiting at a select statement with a terminate option open).

4 Conclusion

In this paper we have revisited task termination in Ada 95. We conclude that termination of tasks involved in asynchronous communication is more difficult than for those involved in synchronous communication. Whilst protected objects and the asynchronous select statements can be used to help program asynchronous termination, it may be difficult to prove that premature termination will not occur.

One potential solution to this problem is to add a terminate alternative to the entry call facility. Although this initially appears to be an attractive solution, there are semantic problems which need to be considered further (in particular, the interactions with finalisation and asynchronous transfer of control). Moreover, the addition of such an feature to the language is likely to add a significant cost to the implementation. A similar mechanism already exists for the selective-accept construct, but there it seems more justified since task are inherently a more heavy-weight construct. Protected objects are intended to serve as a light-weight and efficient mechanism, and therefore, every small addition to their implementation cost is much more noticeable. Also, there is a danger that cost will be incurred even if the feature is not used by a program.

References

Burns, A. (1988). *Programming in occam 2*, Addison Wesley.

Intermetrics (1995). Ada 95 reference manual, *ANSI/ISO/IEC-8652:1995*, Intermetrics.

U.S. Department of Defense (1983). Reference manual for the Ada programming language, *ANSI/MIL-STD 1815 A*, U.S. Department of Defense.

Parameter-Induced Aliasing and Related Problems can be Avoided

(Towards a More Abstract View of Variables)

Wolfgang Gellerich and Erhard Ploedereder

Department of Computer Science
University of Stuttgart
D-70565 Stuttgart
Germany
telephone: +49 / 711 / 7816 213; fax: +49 / 711 / 7816 380
gellerich@informatik.uni-stuttgart.de

Abstract. Aliasing is an old but yet unsolved problem, being disadvantegous for most aspects of programming languages. We suggest a new model for variables which avoids aliasing by maintaining the property of always having exactly one access path to a variable. In particular, variables have no address. Based on this model, we develop language rules which can be checked in local context and we suggest programming guidelines to prevent alias effects in Ada 95 programs.

1 Introduction and Overview

Most procedural languages treat variables more or less as symbolic names for memory cells. Thus variables have addresses that can be used to establish an additional access path independent of the variable's name by either applying an address operator or passing the variable as reference parameter. This causes an effect called *aliasing*: differently named variables can overlap in memory.

1.1 Why the Problem is a Problem

Parameter-induced aliasing can occur between a formal reference parameter associated to a variable also being accessed directly, or between two formal reference parameters as in reverse1 (figure 1). An assignment to one variable can then have the unexpected effect of also changing another variable although its name has not been the target of an assignment. The disadvantages of aliasing for most aspects of programming languages are well-documented [Hoa73,Hor79,GJ87]. In particular, aliasing is likely to cause program errors and makes software reliability doubtful. E.g., reverse1(x,x) does not show the intended behaviour: an assignment to B[i] also changes A[i] so that the lower half of the array will be overwritten by values from the upper half. When aliasing occurs between a non-local variable and a formal parameter name as in figure 2, the value of

```
TYPE Vec = ARRAY [1..N] OF REAL;        type Vec is array (1..N) of real;
...                                      ...
PROCEDURE reverse1 (VAR A, B: Vec);     procedure reverse2 (A: in Vec;
VAR i: INTEGER;                                             B: out Vec) is
BEGIN                                    begin
  FOR i:= 1 TO N DO                        for i in A'range loop
    B[i]:= A[N -i +1];                       B(i):= A (A'last -i +1);
  END;                                     end loop;
END reverse1;                            end reverse2;
```

Fig. 1. A procedure with potential aliasing [Ack82] in Modula-2 and Ada

```
A: T;
procedure P(f: in out T) is begin A:= Const2; end P;
...
begin
  A:= Const1;
  P(A);
```

Fig. 2. Aliasing between a non-local variable and a formal parameter

variable A after calling P is Const2 if T is passed by reference, and Const1 in case of passing by copy-in/copy-out.

Aliasing also interferes with data dependence analysis. Some optimising Ada compilers rely on the absence of aliasing [BCS96], an assumption allowed by the language semantics. In other languages, one can not do that: e.g., Fortran 77 follows an approach similar to Ada by disallowing assignments to dynamically aliased variables, but "such assignments are common practice and tolerated by most compilers" [ZC91] which "painstakenly avoid using register optimisation on global variables or call-by-reference formal parameters to ensure that aliased variables behave in the expected fashion" [Coo85]. Here, alias analysis [CK89,For94,MSE95,Ruf95,PS96] may be applied which can be done quite efficiently today. However, a study concerning parallelisation of real-world Fortran code [MW93] revealed that the sets of potentially aliased names determined by compile-time analysis contain 4.4 variables on average. The largest alias set contained 55 variables, while only 39.7% of all parameters were un-aliased. Aliasing thus weakens the precision of data dependence analysis, since few of the potential aliases are actual aliases.

1.2 Where Aliasing is Needed

There are also situations where aliasing is quite natural and even necessary. For example, aliasing can occur when using pointers to represent general graphs or in situations where object-oriented techniques are used to model shared use or access to a real-world object. A general purpose language needs to cover such cases by appropriate constructs. But, aliasing of ordinary variables is something to be avoided. Except for the almost trivial case of explicit renaming, the major source for such aliasing are parameters. We will only address this case.

1.3 Overview

After a short discussion about aliasing and its relation to parameter passing in different programming languages, we will introduce a new model for variables in section 3. Section 4 then states language rules implementing this model in a statically and efficiently checkable way. We will, however, only discuss the effects on basic language constructs. Section 5 addresses the problem of aliasing inside data structures. Section 6 discusses some technical issues of this model. Finally, section 7 translates these rules into Ada 95 programming guidelines that achieve the effects of these rules without extending the language.

2 Aliasing and Parameter Passing

2.1 Terminology

Based on their lifetime, we distinguish several classes of variables: **Static variables** are bound to memory locations during the entire execution of the program. **Semi-dynamic variables** are created upon subprogram activation. Another classification distinguishes where a variable is declared with respect to a certain point of reference: **Global variables** are declared at the outer-most scope level and visible in any nested structures, as long as not hidden by local declarations. **Local variables** are those declared in the same subprogram where the reference occurs. In Ada, static variables are always global and declared at package level. However, languages like Fortran, Algol 68, Lucid, C, and C++ also provide static variables visible inside subprograms only.

2.2 Parameter Passing in Ada

Ada has three formal parameter modes, IN, OUT, and IN OUT. This looks like a rather abstract approach, specifying the direction of data flow rather then describing parameter passing in implementation-related terms only, as most other procedural languages do.

However, the effect of parameter passing is then partially defined in such terms, e.g., by distinguishing between by-reference types and by-copy types. For some types, the Reference Manual does not specify a certain passing method, leaving this decision to the implementor's choice. Creating more than one access path to a variable and thereby depending on the actual passing method is classified as *bounded error* in Ada 95 [Ada95], meaning that the effect of the program is not predictable but will nevertheless lie within certain bounds. For example, reverse2(x,x) has a bounded error. In Ada 83 [Ge83], such programs were declared *erroneous*, implying completely undefined behaviour.

It is easily proven that the absence of such effects is undecidable in general [Jok82] and can therefore not be detected by compilers. This is detrimental to program reliability because "a warning of such "erroneousness" without an effective enforcement mechanism is like shouting in a hurricane" [Bak93]. For example, it is possible to "steal from a limited private account" if the parameter passing mechanism is known [Bak93].

To summarise, Ada pretends providing a high level of abstraction but, for program analysis, its parameter passing rules are actually more annoying than those of languages like Modula: The behaviour of reverse1(x,x) might surprise the programmer, but at least all implementations will produce the same result and the behaviour can be predicted from source code without the need to involve implementation-dependent details.

2.3 Parameter Passing in Other Languages

The Modula-2 version of reverse1 is easily corrected by specifying by-value for the in-going parameter, which actually creates an *initialised local variable*. However, this could be regarded as unacceptable due to the inherent inefficiency when applied to large data items.

C++ [Str92] and Modula-3 [Har92] allow a reference parameter to be specified as *constant*. Although this avoids accidental changes to a parameter that was passed by-reference only to avoid copying, the aliasing problem still persists: reverse1(x,x) would not work correctly in either language.

2.4 A Modified Definition of Aliasing

Usually, the term aliasing describes the situation in which two different names denote overlapping memory areas. While this definition is quite common and easy to understand, it does not precisely cover those cases that are suspect with respect to program understanding and compiler optimisation. The above discussion suggests two modifications:

- Aliasing between two mode IN parameters obviously causes no problems. In the following, we will use *aliasing* only to describe cases where an update might occur via at least one of the names in question.
- When passing parameters by-reference, the access conflict between the aliased names (i.e., actual and formal parameter) occurs immediately. This is not the case when using "Copy-in, Copy-out" parameter passing. Here, the effects of an assignment to the formal parameter on the actual parameter are delayed until the subprogram returns. Thus effects similar to normal aliasing occur upon such return and an additional source of nondeterminism is caused by leaving the order of "copying-out" unspecified. In the following, *aliasing* will include these cases.

3 Variables Without Addresses

It has been stated that the ability to *change* a variable's value is the principal problem in procedural languages and that one should have so-called *single assignment variables* instead [Ack82,KMW84,Ske91,Can92]. Such variables can be bound to a value but that binding then remains immutable during program execution, thus preventing any kind of mutable state. This approach is often considered overly restrictive [Hoa73,KMW84,Yue91,Fin95].

In contrast, our approach is based on the idea of having *only one* access path to a variable, its *name*. Any language construct is then defined in a way guaranteeing not to introduce a second access path. This approach is easily modelled using functions mapping names to values, and it allows multiple assignments to variables.

To derive a set of statically checkable language rules, we imagine address-less variables to consist of a *container* able to hold one value of the variable's data type. We make no assumption about the implementation of containers other than that they are *isolated*, i.e., that there is no overlap between them. Every container has a "name-plate" with *exactly one name*, this being the only way to access the container. Both the value held in the container and the name-plate of the container are mutable over time.

In this model, passing a variable as OUT or IN OUT parameter means to exchange its name plate by the formal parameter's name for the duration of the subprogram execution. IN parameters are pictured as binding the actual parameter's value to the formal parameter's name, thus creating a named constant.

The semantic description can further be simplified by abstracting from containers. Constants as well as variables are names associated with a value yielded by the evaluation of the variable in an expression. This association is formally described by a *value binding function*. Due to space limitations, the details of a formal model are not presented here.

4 Efficiently Checkable Language Rules

We are now going to state rules that a language based on this model would have. While it is obvious how to treat assignments and expressions in this model, subprograms need some attention. The usefulness of subprograms comes from their ability of being parameterised, i.e., different actual arguments can be accessed using the same formal parameter name from within the subprogram's body. However, the introduction of aliases must be avoided and the language rules for doing this must be checkable without program-wide analysis. As a first consequence, applying 'address or 'access to variables cannot be allowed.

4.1 Passing Address-less Variables as Parameter

In terms of the named container model, passing a variable as OUT or IN OUT parameter means to exchange its former name plate by the formal parameter's name. Thus, the old name becomes invisible, making it impossible to access the variable while it is bound to a formal parameter. This consideration leads to our first rule:

R1: A variable (or formal OUT or IN OUT parameter) can not be bound to more than one OUT or IN OUT formal parameter in the same call.

The same view helps in stating rules that prevent aliasing between formal parameters and non-local variables. We will have to distinguish between static and semi-dynamic variables.

4.2 Rules Concerning Semi-Dynamic Variables

Our second rule concerns non-local accesses to semi-dynamic variables:

R2: A semi-dynamic variable (or formal OUT or IN OUT parameter) can either be accessed by local subprograms directly as non-local variable, or it may be passed to local subprograms as IN OUT or OUT parameter, but not both.

To put this into a statically checkable form, any semi-dynamic variable is visible to the body of the subprogram containing its declaration but its scope does not automatically include nested subprograms. By default, a variable is then not visible in such nested subprograms but can be passed to them as OUT or IN OUT parameter. Declaring a variable to be DIRECT makes its name visible in all nested subprograms, thus allowing direct access. However, DIRECT variables can not be passed as OUT or IN OUT parameter to such nested subprograms (see figure 3).

```
procedure P1 is
i: Integer;
j: DIRECT Integer;

  procedure P2 (k: in out Integer) is
    ...        -- i is invisible, j is visible
  end P2;

begin
  P2(i);    -- i can be passed as IN OUT parameter
  P2(j);    -- illegal
end P1;
```

Fig. 3. Using DIRECT

4.3 Rules Concerning Static Variables

Static variables – regardless of whether they are global or not – can not be treated like semi-dynamic variables. Consider a semi-dynamic variable x declared inside P and passed as IN OUT parameter along a call chain. If finally a recursive call to P is made, no aliasing occurs as P's recursive activation has a separate instance of x. However, we have aliasing if x is static.

Using DIRECT for declaring global variables would be too restrictive: Consider a variable i which is imported by a package. If i is declared DIRECT, it can *never* be used as parameter. Otherwise, i can be passed to subprograms, but is now only visible in the initialisation part of packages. In either case, this contradicts the intent of a global variable.

Dividing Scopes into Levels. We split the global name space by associating a *level number* $l(V)$ with every static variable V. This is a positive number chosen by the programmer, acting as a marker associated with that variable. Let 1 be the minimum number used. Next, an *access level* $a(P)$ is chosen for any subprogram P declared at global level. This number is treated as part of the subprogram's signature and is implicitly valid for any of its local subprograms. Using these specifications, an effect similar to that of rule **R2** can be achieved:

R3: The body of a subprogram P can access all static variables V with $l(V) \leq a(P)$ directly. All variables with $l(V) > a(P)$ can be passed to P as OUT or IN OUT parameter.

Figure 4 shows an example, using the symbol @ to specify level numbers.

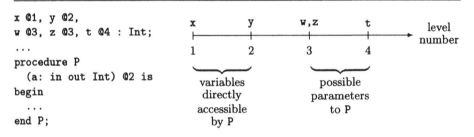

Fig. 4. Using Level Numbers

Correlation with Existing Language Concepts. Two extremes for choosing a subprogram's access level are 0 and the maximum m of all level numbers used. These cases correspond to well-known concepts: the initialisation parts of global packages can be considered as subprograms declared with $a = m$ and thus having access to all global variables but no parameters. Procedures with $a = 0$ are independent of global state as they have no access to global variables, but they may take any variable as parameter and can only call subprograms also having $a = 0$. This is the concept of *pure* subprograms introduced in High Performance Fortran [Koe94] and, using pragma *Pure* for whole packages, in Ada 95.

Interaction with Programming Concepts. To discuss how programs are organised using this model, we will use a classification of applications for packages given by G. BOOCH [Boo87]. From the above it is plain to see that subprograms belonging to *abstract data types* and thus provided by packages not having an internal state would be declared *pure*. The same applies to library packages providing *groups of related program units*, e.g., transcendental functions. Also, it is clear how initialisation parts would be treated.

Packages declaring static variables locally in their body are classified as *abstract state machines* by Booch. Such package have an internal state which is accessible through exported subprograms. Here, the state variables would be declared having $l = 1$ and the subprograms having access level $a = 1$. These subprograms can therefore directly access the package's local variables. Other static variables, that are not intended to implement local state can be passed as parameters to these subprograms.

For the remaining case of variables exported by packages, the programmer must decide which category of subprograms access them directly, and assign level numbers and access levels accordingly. However, such variables should occur rarely since results from software engineering suggest, with respect to coupling and cohesion, to use global variables sparingly.

4.4 Passing Parameters as Parameters

We already stated that rules **R1** and **R2** also apply to formal parameters. To prevent aliasing of static variables in indirectly called subprograms, we must further avoid that a callee changes a global variable that could have been passed to the caller, i.e., the caller must at least see all variables directly accessible to the callee:

R4: A subprogram P can only invoke subprograms Q with $a(\mathtt{Q}) \leq a(\mathtt{P})$.

This rule implies that passing one of P's formal parameters to Q can never cause aliasing of static variables inside Q.

5 Dealing with Natural Aliasing

As discussed in section 1.2, there are cases where aliasing is quite natural. However, we must take care to prevent its propagation.

R5: Rules **R1** and **R2** extend to variables of structured types in that the whole variable and one of its components or two non-disjoint components of the same structured variable can not be passed in the same call.

Passing different components of the same structured variable is legal. However, the disjointness of components can not always be checked statically. Passing two array components A(expr1), A(expr2) is allowed only if *expr1* $\neq$ *expr2*. If this can not be checked at compile time (e.g., using analysis techniques known from parallelising compilers), run-time checks must be used. However, by analysing about 300MB Ada source code, we found that only about 0.2% of all calls pass two components of the same array. Such run-time checks will also be needed if dereferenced pointers are passed.

6 Implementation and Optimisation Issues

In our model, it is safe to optimise passing OUT or IN OUT parameters by choosing between call-by-reference and copy-in-copy-out as an implementation. Due to the absence of parameter-induced aliasing, the result of a program can not depend on this choice [Don77]. Concerning IN parameters, our model does *not* necessarily result in a loss of efficiency due to copying the actual parameter. For example, when calling **reverse2**, it is possible to pass a reference[1] to the callee unless both actual parameters are the same variable. Note that handling the latter case correctly would require a copy in any language. Generally, copying the value of a variable V passed as actual IN parameter to a subprogram P is necessary in the following cases:

A. Variable P is also passed as OUT or IN OUT parameter in the same call.
B. Variable P is also modified directly by the called subprogram.
C. Subprogram P passes its formal IN parameter to other subprograms possibly having access to V.

Case **A** is easily checked in local context with any necessary copy to be made by the caller. In cases **B** and **C**, we can make a locally checkable conservative approximation. A copy can be omitted

- if V is semi-dynamic and not visible to P due to rule **R2**, or
- if V is static and not visible to P because of rule **R3**.

If one of these conditions is fulfilled, variable V must be invisible in any subprogram called from inside P, too. Another alternative is to use the results of inter-procedural side effect analysis for the decision whether a copy is needed. Obviously, this would yield the best results, but the analysis might be expensive unless it is done anyway for other optimisation purposes.

7 Applying the Model to Ada 95

As stated earlier, the restrictions derived from the new model could be used as programming guidelines to prevent errors caused by aliasing in today's Ada programs. However, doing so requires some refinements to the rules stated so far because, in Ada, the choice to pass either a copy or a reference when processing IN parameters is also influenced by the parameter's data type.

Rules **R1** and **R2** need to include IN parameters that are not of a by-copy type. The checks implied by rule **R5** need to include IN parameters of structured types and their components. In cases where the disjointness of components is not obvious, it might be useful to verify the properties of the particular algorithm.

Checking rules **R3** and **R4** requires assigning level numbers to all global variables and subprograms. It might be a lot of work to do this for an existing program. However, pure subprograms and *abstract state machines* should be

---

[1] Even if the actual parameter is an expression, its value will be stored somewhere.

easy to identify and can serve as a starting point, hopefully covering a sizeable percentage of the source code. In short, level numbers "bring some order to the chaos" and facilitate the otherwise very difficult proof of absence of aliasing.

8 Related Work

8.1 The Euclid/Turing Approach

Euclid [HLL⁺77b] and its successor language Turing [HMRJ88] were designed to support formal program verification by making "minimal changes and extensions to Pascal" [HLL⁺77a]. Both languages fail to provide a more abstract view on variables but simply add restrictions to Pascal.

Euclid's rules to prevent parameter-induced aliasing concern the *point of use* of a variable. A procedure P must declare an import list containing all non-local names which are accessed inside the body. If P imports a procedure Q, all names imported by Q must be imported by P, too. Since this is a lot of work for the programmer and, as it is immediately obvious to the compiler which non-local names are accessed by a procedure, import lists where made optional in Turing. Any imported variable may not be passed to that procedure as VAR parameter.

The problem with this approach is that creating import lists requires program-wide analysis with information about possible references to non-local variables propagated along the edges of a call graph. In contrast to that, our model avoids parameter-induced aliasing by specifying the access method at the *point of declaration* of a variable. This can be checked in local context.

It seems that the Euclid rules were regarded to be too restrictive. According to the Turing report, alias prohibition is no longer strictly enforced: "an implementation may extend the language to allow execution of programs violating these restrictions, given that appropriate error messages are issued" [HMRJ88]. There seem to be *no* Turing compilers rejecting programs with aliasing [Cor94].

8.2 Explicit Usage of Copy-In-Copy-Out

It has been contended that using copy-in-copy-out instead of call-by-reference makes parameter-induced aliasing impossible [ML87]. Although this prevents aliasing in its original definition, non-determinism could still arise, since a program's result might depend on the order in which the copy-out steps are performed. Moreover, this approach is inefficient for large data structures.

8.3 Disallowing Global Variables

It has been suggested to avoid aliasing by disallowing global variables which were also criticised for some other undesirable effects [WS73]. This approach was taken in the design of Gypsy [Amb77]. But, readability and writability of source code as well as program efficiency suffers from unnecessarily long parameter lists.

9 Summary and Future Work

Starting with a short review of aliasing, we introduced a new model of variables accessible through their name only. Implemented by a (new) language, this model prevents parameter-induced aliasing by a set of rules which can be checked without program-wide analysis. We also showed how these rules could be used as programming guidelines for Ada 95 programming.

One application of our variable model is the development of a new language in which program execution is not coordinated by control flow but by data dependences only. Here, the absence of aliasing is a critical issue.

We currently implement our language rules by modifying the Gnu Ada 95 compiler GNAT.

References

[Ack82] W.B. Ackerman. Data Flow Languages. *IEEE Computer*, 15(2):14–25, February 1982.

[Ada95] *Ada 95 Reference Manual*. Intermetrics, Inc., 1995. ANSI/ISO/IEC-8652:1995.

[Amb77] A.L. Ambler. GYPSY: A Language for Specification and Implementation of Verifiable Programs. *ACM SIGPLAN Notices*, 12(3):1–10, March 1977.

[Bak93] H.G. Baker. How to Steal from a Limited Private Account – Why Mode IN OUT Parameters for Limited Types *must* be Passed by Reference. *ACM Ada Letters*, XIII(3):91–95, May/June 1993.

[BCS96] T. Birus, C. Cipriani, and D. Sutherland. Interprocedural call optimization. In *Reliable Software Technologies – Ada-Europe 1996*, volume 1088 of *LNCS*, pages 319–329. Springer, 1996.

[Boo87] G. Booch. *Software Engineering with Ada*. The Benjamin/Cummings Publishing Co., 2 edition, 1987.

[Can92] D.C. Cann. Retire Fortran ? A Debate Rekindled. Technical Report UCRL-JC-107018 Rev.2, Lawrence Livermore National Laboratory, 1992.

[CK89] K.D. Cooper and K. Kennedy. Fast Interprocedureal Alias Analysis. In *Sixteenth Annual ACM Symposium on Principles of Programming Languages*, pages 49–59, 1989.

[Coo85] K.D. Cooper. Analyzing aliases of reference formal parameters. In *Conference Record of the Twelfth Annual ACM Symposium on Principles of Programming Languages*, pages 281–290. ACM, 1985.

[Cor94] R. Cordy, 1994. Discussion in newsgroup comp.lang.misc.

[Don77] J.E. Donahue. Locations considered unnecessary. *acta informatica*, 8:221–242, 1977.

[Fin95] R.A. Finkel. *Advanced Programming Language Design*. Addison Wesley, 1995.

[For94] István Forgács. Double iterative framework for flow-sensitive interprocedural data flow analysis. *ACM Transactions on Software Engineering and Methodology*, 3(1):29–55, 1994.

[Ge83] G. Goos and J. Hartmanis (eds). *The Programming Language Ada Reference Manual*. Springer, 1983.

[GJ87]   C. Ghezzi and M. Jazayeri. *Programming Language Concepts*. John Wiley and Sons, 1987.

[Har92]   S.P. Harbison. *Modula-3*. Prentice-Hall, Englewood Cliffs, NJ, 1992.

[HLL⁺77a] J.J. Horning, R.W. Lampson, R.L. London, J.G. Mitchell, and G.J. Popek. Notes on the Design of Euclid. *ACM SIGPLAN Notices*, 12(3):1-77, March 1977.

[HLL⁺77b] J.J. Horning, R.W. Lampson, R.L. London, J.G. Mitchell, and G.J. Popek. Report on the Programming Language Euclid. *ACM SIGPLAN Notices*, 12(2):1-79, February 1977.

[HMRJ88]   R.C. Holt, P.A. Matthews, J.A. Rosselet, and J.R.Cordy. *The Turing Programming Language*. Prentice Hall, 1988.

[Hoa73]   C.A.R. Hoare. Hints on Programming Language Design, 1973. key note address at the ACM SIGACT/SIGPLAN Conference on Principles of Programming Languages; (reprinted in [Hoa89]).

[Hoa89]   C.A.R. Hoare. *Essays in Computing Science*. International Series in Computer Science. Prentice Hall, 1989.

[Hor79]   J.J. Horning. A Case Study in Language Design: Euclid. In G. Goos and J. Hartmanis, editors, *Program Construction*, volume 69 of *Lecture Notes in Computer Science*. Springer, 1979.

[Jok82]   M.O. Jokinen. The Effect of Parameter Passing and Other Implementation Dependent Mechanisms is Undecidable. *ACM SIGPLAN Notices*, 17(9):16-17, September 1982.

[KMW84]   D.J. Kuck, J.R. McGraw, and M.J. Wolfe. A debate: Retire FORTRAN? *Physics Today*, 37(5):66-75, May 1984.

[Koe94]   C.H. Koelbel. *The High Performance Fortran Handbook*. MIT Press, 1994.

[ML87]   M. Marcotty and H. Ledgard. *The World of Programming Languages*. Springer, 1987.

[MSE95]   M.Y. Mohd-Saman and D.J. Evans. Inter-Procedural Analysis for Parallel Computing. *Parallel Computing*, 21:315-338, 1995.

[MW93]   H.G. Mayer and M. Wolfe. Interprocedural Alias Analysis: Implementation and Empirical Results. *Software Practice and Experience*, 23(11):1202-1233, November 1993.

[PS96]   R. Palimaradevi and R.K. Subramanian. Alias analysis for parallelization. In *Proceedings of the ISCA International Conference on Parallel and Distributed Computing Systems 1996*, volume I, pages 292-295. ISCA, 1996.

[Ruf95]   E. Ruf. Context-Insensitive Alias Analysis Reconsidered. In *Proceedings of the SIGPLAN '95 Conference on Programming Language Design and Implementation*, pages 13-22. ACM, 1995.

[Ske91]   S.K. Skedzielewski. Sisal. In B.K. Szymanski, editor, *Parallel Functional Languages and Compilers*, pages 105-157. Addison-Wesley, 1991.

[Str92]   B. Stroustrup. *Die C++ -Programmiersprache*. Addison-Wesley, 2. edition, 1992.

[WS73]   W. Wulf and M. Shaw. Global Variables considered harmful. *ACM SIGPLAN Notices*, 8(2):28-34, February 1973. (summarized in [ML87]).

[Yue91]   C.K. Yuen. Which Model of Programming for Lisp: Sequential, Functional or Mixed? *ACM SIGPLAN Notices*, 26(10):83-92, Oktober 1991.

[ZC91]   H. Zima and B. Chapman. *Supercompilers for Parallel and Vector Computers*. Addison-Wesley, 1991.

Towards an Integration of Syntactic Constructs and Structural Features for Formalised Object-Oriented Methods

K.S. Cheung, K.O. Chow & T.Y. Cheung
Department of Computer Science
City University of Hong Kong
Tat Chee Avenue, Kowloon, Hong Kong

Abstract. An integration of formal syntactic constructs and object-oriented (OO) structural features is essential to a formalised OO method. It requires the formal semantics to be structured according to OO conventions. It also requires the OO features to be completely and consistently interpreted by formal semantics. In this paper, a list of guidelines for achieving the integration is suggested. These guidelines are derived from a review of the existing formalised OO methods under two categories, OO style formal methods and formal style OO methods. The former possess a strong syntactic foundation but lack a complete coverage of OO features. The latter support all OO features but suffer from incomplete or inconsistent semantics. It is suggested that multiple schemas, on a common syntactic foundation with abstracted syntactic constructs that follow OO conventions, should be adopted.

Keywords. Formal method, Object-oriented method, Software specification.

1 Introduction

Formal methods are characterised by the use of precise semantics for software specification and verification but are criticised for lacking structural features. OO methods possess effective structural features with the notions of classification, encapsulation and inheritance but endure ambiguous analysis models. In order to achieve unambiguous and well-structured software specification, formal methods and OO methods are combined to take advantage of the formal syntactic constructs and OO structural features. The issue was first addressed in 1991 [1]. Since then, many formalised OO methods have been proposed and reported in the literature [2, 3, 4, 5].

Syntactic constructs and structural features are elements of a software specification method for denoting system behaviours and managing complexity [6, 7]. They should be integrated so that a system can be specified in compliance with the decomposition of the system [8, 9]. When applying to a formalised OO method, this integration requires the formal semantics to be structured according to OO conventions. It also requires the OO features to be completely and consistently interpreted by formal semantics. However, the existing formalised OO methods have not fully achieved this integration. Some possess a strong syntactic foundation but lack a complete coverage of OO features. The others support all OO features but suffer from incomplete or inconsistent semantics. The purpose of this paper is to explore such integration through a comparative review on the existing formalised OO methods.

2 Existing Formalised OO Methods

There are two general approaches to combining formal methods and OO methods. The first is to adopt OO style specification based on the existing formal methods [10, 11, 12, 13, 14, 15, 16, 17, 18]. The second is to adopt formal style specification based on the existing OO methods [19, 20, 21, 22, 23]. In the following, three methods of either approach are reviewed with emphasis on the syntactic constructs and structural features. A University Library System (ULS) case example is used for illustration.

2.1 OO Style Formal Methods

Formalised OO methods first appeared as OO style formal methods. They include those formal methods extended to accommodate OO features such as Object-Z [10], Z++ [11] and VDM++ [16], and those formal methods re-interpreted in OO conventions such as Hall's approach [12], Shuman & Pitt's approach [13] and Cusack's approach [18]. The Object-Z [10], VDM++ [16] and Hall's approach [12] are selected in our review.

Object-Z

The main extension in Object-Z [10] from the Z method [24] is the introduction of a class schema. Figure 1 shows the class *libuser* in the ULS example. The attributes, *uid*, *quota* and *onloan* are defined as state variables in the state schema. The class constraint is also defined in the state schema. The operations, *borrow* and *return* are defined in the respective operation schemas.

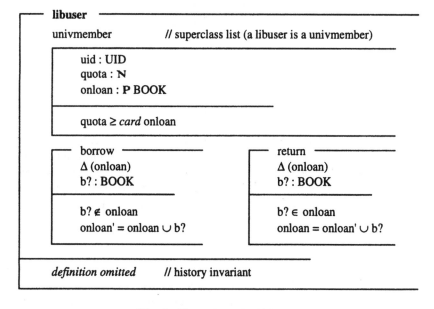

Fig. 1. Class schema in Object-Z.

In Object-Z, encapsulation of attributes and operations is denoted by including the state schema and operation schema into the class schema. Inheritance is also denoted by including the superclass schema into the class schema. However, the class schema as well as the schema inclusion constructs do not cover all OO features. Features such as multiple inheritance, aggregation and object interaction are not denoted.

VDM++

The main extension in VDM++ [16] from the VDM [25] is the introduction of a class specification. Figure 2 shows the class *libuser* in the ULS example. The *is subclass of* statement declares the superclass *univmember* whose features are inherited. The class constraint is defined in the *invar* statement. The attributes, *uid*, *quota* and *onloan* are defined in the *instance variables* statement while the operations, *borrow* and *return* are implicitly defined in the *methodlist* statement.

```
Class libuser
        Is subclass of univmember
        Instance variables
                uid : UID
                quota : N
                onloan : P BOOK

        Invar quota ≥ card onloan
        Methodlist
                borrow (b : BOOK)
                        pre   b ∉ onloan
                        post  onloan = onloan ∪ b
                return (b : BOOK)
                        pre   b ∈ onloan
                        post  onloan = onloan ∪ b
        End libuser
```

Fig. 2. Class specification in VDM++.

In VDM++, encapsulation of attributes and operations is denoted by incorporating relevant instance variables and methods into the class specification. Inheritance is also denoted by the same way. However, there are syntactic restrictions which hinder a complete coverage of OO features. Features such as multiple inheritance, association, object lifecycle and object interaction are not denoted.

Hall's approach

Hall [12] introduced some OO conventions to re-interpret the Z language [24]. These include the identification of individual objects and the expression of states and operations for a class of objects. Using the ULS example, Figures 3 and 4 show the Hall's approach on object identification and class operations respectively.

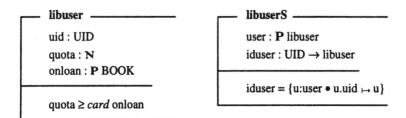

Fig. 3. Hall's approach on object identification.

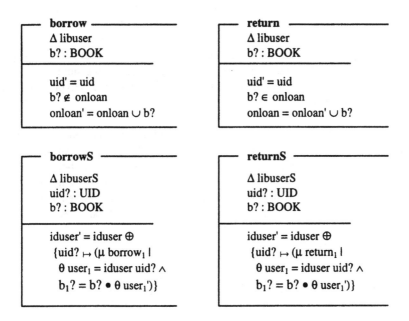

Fig. 4. Hall's approach on class operations.

In Figure 3, the schema *libuser* defines an object while the schema *libuserS* defines a collection of objects. In Figure 4, the schemas, *borrow* and *return* define the operations for an object while the schemas, *borrowS* and *returnS* define the operations for a collection of objects. According to Hall's approach, each object has a unique identifier and a system is defined as a function which relates a set of identifiers to the objects. States and operations of a class are defined by calculating the effects from the states and operations of an object of the class.

Since the Z language is not primarily for OO style specification, it is difficult to adjust its semantics to accommodate OO features without adding new syntactic constructs. Although there are possible conventions for denoting classes and objects, the outcome semantics is rather complicated. Some OO features such as inheritance and object interaction can hardly be re-interpreted in plain Z semantics.

2.2 Formal Style OO Methods

Formal style OO methods came into existence around two years ago. They include those OO methods incorporated with formal syntax such as Syntropy [19] and Fusion [20], and those OO methods separately appended with formal syntax such as Dodani's approach [21], ROOA [22] and Bourdeau & Cheng's approach [23]. The Syntropy [19], Fusion [20] and Dodani's approach [21] are selected in our review.

Syntropy

Syntropy [19] is considered as a second generation OO method which incorporates formal semantics as a part of the analysis models. The analysis models capture two views of a system, type view and state view. The type view denotes the objects and their relationships. The state view denotes the changes of states of an object throughout the object lifecycle. The type view is expressed using notations of the object model of an existing OO method, OMT [26]. The state view is expressed using Harel's statechart notations [27].

In the analysis models, formal semantics is mainly involved in defining constraints, called invariants. These invariants are expressed in predicate logic. An association between two classes is expressed as two functions with constraints on their cardinality numbers. The names of the functions represent the roles of the associated classes. Using the ULS example, the following shows an association between the classes, *libuser* and *book*. It is expressed as two functions, *borrower* and *loanitem*.

$$\text{borrower} : \text{libuser} \rightarrow \textbf{set} \text{ of book}$$
$$\text{loanitem} : \text{book} \rightarrow \text{libuser}$$

States and state transitions are denoted in Harel's statechart notations [27]. The execution of the operations, *borrow* and *return* is defined as follows.

$$\text{borrow (b:BOOK) } [\text{ b} \notin \text{onloan }] / [\text{ onloan'} = \text{onloan} \cup \text{b }]$$
$$\text{return (b:BOOK) } [\text{b} \in \text{onloan }] / [\text{ onloan} = \text{onloan'} \cup \text{b }]$$

In Syntropy, the formal semantics is not complete in itself. The problem is that the formal semantics cannot be readily merged with the informal model notations.

Fusion

Fusion [20] is also considered as a second generation OO method which incorporates formal semantics as a part of the analysis models. There are three analysis models in Fusion, namely, object model, operation model and lifecycle model. The object model denotes objects and their relationships using notations from two existing OO methods, OMT [26] and Booch's method [28]. The operation model defines operations using "semi-formal" structural English. The lifecycle model denotes object interaction using some formal semantics called lifecycle expression.

A lifecycle expression contains two syntactic elements, alphabets and operators. Alphabets denote the occurrence of events. Operators are applied to the occurrence of events or execution of operations There are some precedence orders among the operators. Figure 5 shows a lifecycle expression *loantran* in the ULS example.

---

lifecycle loantran

loantran = borrow .
        (#befdue . return) I (#overdue . fine . return)

fine = *definition omitted*

Fig. 5. Lifecycle model in Fusion.

Although formal semantics in the lifecycle model is self-contained, such formalised lifecycle model is only a part of the overall analysis models.

Dodani's approach

In Dodani's approach [21], formal syntax is separately appended to an existing method, OMT [26]. There are three analysis models in OMT, namely, object model, dynamic model and functional model. It is proposed to adopt an algebraic specification for the object model, Harel's statechart notations [27] for the dynamic model and the Z semantics [24] for the functional model. Using the ULS example, Figure 6 shows the class *libuser* where the operations are algebraically declared.

Class libuser

    constructors   createuser : UID → Boolean
    operations   borrow : BOOK → Boolean
                        return : BOOK → Boolean
    selectors   *definition omitted*
    destructors   *definition omitted*
    axioms   *definition omitted*

Fig. 6. Class specification in Dodani's approach.

The execution of the operations, *borrow* and *return* is defined as follows.

$$\{ b \notin \text{onloan} \} \text{ borrow (b:BOOK) } \{ \text{onloan}' = \text{onloan} \cup b \}$$
$$\{ b \in \text{onloan} \} \text{ return (b:BOOK) } \{ \text{onloan} = \text{onloan}' \cup b \}$$

In Dodani's approach, different types of formal semantics are appended to the analysis models in a piece-meal fashion. Inconsistency in the semantics is resulted.

3 Integration of Syntactic Constructs and Structural Features

Based of a comparison of six formalised OO methods, a list of guidelines for achieving an integration of formal syntactic constructs and OO structural features are derived. The ULS example is re-visited for illustration.

3.1 Comparison of formalised OO methods

In order to achieve the integration, a formalised OO method should satisfy two groups of criteria. The first group of criteria refers to the syntactic constructs. It requires the formal semantics to be structured according to several OO conventions, namely, encapsulation, inheritance, object lifecycle and object interaction [29]. In OO analysis, a system is considered as a collection of interacting objects. Throughout an object lifecycle, there are changes of behaviours of the object. Objects possessing the same attributes and operations are grouped into a class. Classes exhibiting common features are generalised to form an inheritance hierarchy. A formalised OO method should take full advantage of these OO conventions in structuring formal semantics.

The second group of criteria refers to the formal interpretation of OO features. It requires all OO features to be completely and consistently interpreted by formal semantics. The semantics should be mutually agreeable and conformable to a coherent whole so that verification is allowed [30, 31]. Also, the semantics should be abstracted in some forms to avoid unnecessary details. A formalised OO method should take full advantage of this complete, consistent, verifiable and suitably abstracted semantics for interpreting the OO features. Table 1 shows the comparison of six formalised OO methods according to these two groups of criteria.

Criteria for the required integration	OO style formal methods			Formal style OO methods		
	Object-Z	VDM++	Hall's	Syntropy	Fusion	Dodani's
1a. Syntactic constructs for encapsulation	Yes	Yes	Yes	Yes	Yes	Yes
1b. Syntactic constructs for inheritance	Partial	Partial	Partial	Yes	Yes	Yes
1c. Syntactic constructs for object lifecycle	Partial	No	No	Yes	Yes	Yes
1d. Syntactic constructs for object interaction	No	No	No	Yes	Yes	Yes
2a. OO features interpreted by complete semantics	Yes	Yes	Yes	No	No	Yes
2b. OO features interpreted by consistent semantics	Yes	Yes	Yes	Partial	Partial	No
2c. OO features interpreted by verifiable semantics	Yes	Yes	Yes	Partial	Partial	Partial
2d. OO features interpreted by abstracted semantics	Yes	Yes	No	No	Yes	Yes

Table 1. Comparison of six formalised OO methods.

Comparison results on the syntactic constructs (the first group of criteria) In Table 1, the three OO style formal methods satisfy criterion *1a* but do not fully satisfy criteria *1b*, *1c* and *1d*. For criterion *1a*, Object-Z and Hall's approach use a class schema while VDM++ uses a class specification. For criterion *1b*, Object-Z and Hall's approach denote inheritance by inclusion of the superclass schema while VDM++ denotes a superclass by a declarative statement. Although the states and operations of the superclass are inherited, further details such as multiple inheritance and overriding features are not explicitly denoted. For criterion *1c*, object lifecycle is not denoted by VDM++ and Hall's approach. It is partially denoted using history invariant in Object-Z. For criterion *1d*, no syntactic construct is offered in Object-Z, VDM++ and Hall's approach. On the other hand, the three formal style OO methods satisfy all the criteria *1a*, *1b*, *1c* and *1d*. They adopt notations from two existing OO methods, OMT [26] and Booch's method [28] which follow the OO conventions. Harel's statechart notations are also adopted in these methods for denoting the object lifecycle.

Comparison results on the formal interpretation of OO features (the second group of criteria) In Table 1, the three OO style formal methods satisfy nearly all the criteria, *2a*, *2b*, *2c* and *2d*. These methods possess a rich set of unique syntax so criteria *2a*, *2b* and *2c* are satisfied. The Z syntax is used in Object-Z and Hall's approach while the VDM syntax is used in VDM++. Criterion *2d* is satisfied by Object-Z and VDM++ which introduce some constructs for abstracting the class details. There is no construct for abstracting semantics in Hall's approach. On the other hand, the three formal style OO methods do not satisfy most of these criteria. Criterion *2a* is only satisfied by Dodani's approach where formal semantics is appended to all the analysis models. It is not satisfied by Syntropy and Fusion. In Syntropy, formal semantics is adopted in defining constraints only. In Fusion, formal semantics is adopted in the lifecycle model only. For criterion *2b*, some inconsistency exists between the formal and informal semantics in Syntropy and Fusion. In Dodani's approach, different types of semantics are used so inconsistency is resulted. Criterion *2c* is not satisfied by these three methods because verification cannot be performed on the incomplete or inconsistent semantics. For criterion *2d*, only Fusion and Dodani's approach offer some abstracted syntactic constructs, for example, the lifecycle expression in Fusion.

Summarising the comparison results, OO style formal methods possess a strong syntactic foundation but lack a complete coverage of OO features. They are based on some established formal methods such as the Z [24] and VDM [25]. However, there are syntactic restrictions which make the specification not fully OO. For example, encapsulation and inheritance are simply made by schema inclusion in Object-Z and Hall's approach. Since these constructs are primarily designed for structuring the language semantics itself [32] and not for object orientation, the structuring power of OO features cannot be fully utilised. In contrast, formal style OO methods support OO features but suffer from incomplete or inconsistent semantics. These methods are based on the existing OO methods which are tailored for object orientation. All OO features are covered. However, the formal semantics is either partially incorporated into the analysis models such as in Syntropy and Fusion, or appended to the analysis models without a common syntactic foundation such as in Dodani's approach.

3.2 Guidelines for achieving the integration

The comparison results highlight some deficiencies of the existing formalised OO methods. An integration of formal syntactic constructs and OO structural features is hindered. In order to achieve the integration, the following guidelines are suggested.

Multiple schemas Borrowing the ideas from Object-Z and Hall's approach, multiple schemas should be adopted as the formal syntactic constructs. The division of these schemas should tightly follow the OO conventions. Three types of schemas are suggested - class schema, object lifecycle schema and object interaction schema, which conform to encapsulation, inheritance, object lifecycle and object interaction. The object interaction schema is often missed in many formalised OO methods.

Complete formal semantics As a general requirement in software specification, the formal semantics should be complete in itself so that every OO feature can be formally interpreted. The class schema should denote both the encapsulated features and the inherited features. The object lifecycle schema should denote the changes of behaviours of an object throughout the object lifecycle such as states, event traces and operation traces. The object interaction schema should denote different scenarios of an interaction, which include the interacting objects and the message sequences.

Common syntactic foundation The formal semantics should have a common syntactic foundation so that verification on completeness and consistency is allowed [30, 31]. For example, the class details and the object interaction scenarios should be defined using common syntax so that verification on any contradiction between them can be performed. It is suggested to adopt first-order predicate calculus as the common syntactic foundation. The Z method [24] and VDM method [25] can be referenced.

Abstracted Syntactic constructs For the sake of separation of concerns, some abstracted syntactic constructs are recommended in order to hide unnecessary semantic details. For example, in Hall's approach, an operation of a class is defined by calculating the effect from the operation of an object of the class. The outcome semantics is rather complicated. Some abstracted syntactic statements should be used, especially for defining operations of a class, event traces in an object lifecycle and message sequences in an interaction scenario.

3.3 Illustration using the ULS example

Using the ULS example, the semantics based on the guidelines is illustrated in Figures 7, 8 and 9. Multiple schemas have been adopted - a class schema as shown in Figure 7, an object lifecycle schema as shown in Figure 8 and an object interaction schema as shown in Figure 9. Various OO features can be completely interpreted. First-order predicate calculus is used as the common syntactic constructs, for example, in defining operations in Figure 7, event traces in Figure 8 and message sequences in Figure 9. In the figures, abstracted syntax is introduced, for example, the *operations* statement in Figure 7 and the *event traces* statement in Figure 8.

Class of libuser
    Attributes
        uid, quota, onloan
    Operations
        borrow (b : BOOK)
            pre $b \notin$ onloan
            post onloan' = onloan $\cup$ b
        return (b : BOOK)
            pre $b \in$ onloan
            post onloan = onloan' $\cup$ b
  Inv quota $\geq$ *card* onloan

Fig. 7. Suggested class schema.

Lifecycle of libuser
    States
        accountactive
            inv   quota > *card* onloan
        accountsuspend
            inv   quota = *card* onloan
    Event traces
        [loanevent, onduedate, ...]
    Operation traces
        [borrow, return, ...]

Fig. 8. Suggested object lifecycle schema.

Scenario of loantran
    Actors
        libuser, counter
    Scenarios
        normal
            mseq [(libuser, counter, borrow (b)),
                (libuser, counter, return (b))]
        overdue
            mseq [(libuser, counter, borrow (b)),
                (counter, libuser, bookcall (b)),
                (libuser, counter, return (b))]

Fig. 9. Suggested object interaction schema.

4 Conclusion

It is accepted that a combination of formal methods and OO methods would achieve unambiguous and well-structured software specification. An integration of formal syntactic constructs and OO structural features is required. In this paper, four guidelines for achieving the integration are derived from a comparative review of six formalised OO methods. Such guidelines pinpoint the deficiencies of these methods in two aspects, syntactic constructs and structural features. As found in the review, some of these methods possess a strong syntactic foundation but lack a complete coverage of OO features. The others support all OO features but suffer from incomplete or inconsistent semantics. It is suggested that multiple schemas, which tightly follow OO conventions, should be adopted as the formal syntactic constructs. The formal semantics should be complete in itself with a common syntactic foundation. Also, abstracted syntactic constructs should be used to hide unnecessary semantic details. All these would enable a formalised OO method in achieving the required integration of formal syntactic constructs and OO structural features.

5 References

[1]   D. deChampeaux et al, "Formal Techniques for Object-Oriented Software Development", *Proceedings of OOPSLA '91*, pp. 166-170, ACM, 1991.

[2]   S. Stepney et al, "A Survey of Object Orientation in Z", *Software Engineering Journal*, Vol. 7, No. 2, pp. 150-160, 1992.

[3]   S. Stepney et al (eds.), *Object Orientation in Z*, Springer-Verlag, 1992.

[4]   K. Lano & H. Haughton (eds.), *Object-Oriented Specification Case Studies*, Prentice Hall, 1993.

[5]   A. Ruiz Delgado et al, "A Review of Object-Oriented Approaches in Formal Methods", *Computer Journal*, Vol. 38, No. 10, pp. 777-784, 1995.

[6]   T.H. Tse & L. Pong, *An Examination of Requirements Specification Languages*, Technical Report TR-89-09, Department of Computer Science, University of Hong Kong, 1989.

[7]   A. Davis, *Software Requirements: Analysis and Specification*, Prentice Hall, 1990.

[8]   V. Berzins et al, "Abstraction-based Software Development", *Communications of the ACM*, Vol. 29, No. 5, pp. 402-415, 1986.

[9]   P.G. Neumann, "Flaws in Specifications and What to do about them", *Proceedings of the 5th International Workshop on Software Specification and Design*, pp. xi-xv, IEEE, 1989.

[10] D.A. Carrington et al, "Object-Z: An Object-Oriented Extension to Z", in S. Vuong (ed.), *Formal Description Techniques*, Vol. 2, pp. 281-296, North Holland, 1990.

[11] K. Lano, "Z++: An Object-Oriented Extension to Z", *Proceedings of the 5th Annual Z User Meeting*, pp. 151-172, Springer-Verlag, 1991.

[12] J.A. Hall, "Using Z as a Calculus for Object-Oriented System", *Proceedings of VDM '90 (LNCS, Vol. 428)*, pp. 290-318, Springer-Verlag, 1990.

[13] S.A. Shuman et al, "Object-Oriented Process Specification" in C. Rattray (ed.), *Specification and Verification of Concurrent Systems*, pp. 21-70, Springer-Verlag, 1990.

[14] S.L. Meira, "Modular Object-Oriented Z Specifications", *Proceedings of the 5th Annual Z User Meeting*, pp. 173-192, Springer-Verlag, 1991.

[15] A.J. Alencar & J.A. Goguen, "OOZE: An Object-Oriented Z Environment", *Proceedings of ECOOP '91 (LNCS, Vol. 512)*, pp. 180-199, Springer-Verlag, 1991.

[16] E. Durr, "VDM++: A Formal Specification Language for Object-Oriented Designs", *Proceedings of IEEE CompEuro'92*, pp. 214-219, IEEE, 1992.

[17] A. Laorakpong & M. Saeki, "Object-Oriented Formal Specification Development using VDM", *Proceedings of the International Symposium on Object Technologies for Advanced Software (LNCS, Vol. 742)*, pp. 529-543, Springer-Verlag, 1993.

[18] E. Cusack et al, "An Object-Oriented Interpretation of LOTOS", in S. Vuong (ed.), *Formal Description Techniques*, Vol. 2, pp. 211-226, North Holland, 1990.

[19] S. Cook & J. Daniels, *Designing Object Systems: Object-Oriented Modelling with Syntropy*, Prentice Hall, 1994.

[20] D. Coleman et al, *Object-Oriented Development: The Fusion Method*, Prentice Hall, 1994.

[21] M. Dodani, "Semantically Rich Object-Oriented Software Engineering Methodologies", *Report on Object-Oriented Analysis and Design*, Vol. 1, No. 1, pp. 17-21, 1994.

[22] A Moreira & R. Clark, "Rigorous Object-Oriented Analysis", *Proceedings of the International Symposium on Object-Oriented Methodologies and Systems (LNCS, Vol. 858)*, pp. 65-78, Springer-Verlag, 1994.

[23] R.H. Bourdeau & B.H.C. Cheng, "A Formal Semantics for Object Model Diagrams", *IEEE Transactions on Software Engineering*, Vol. 21, No. 10, pp. 799-832, 1995.

[24] J.M. Spivey, *The Z Notation: A Reference Manual*, Prentice Hall, 1989.

[25] C.B. Jones, *Systematic Software Development Using VDM*, Prentice Hall, 1986.

[26] J. Rumbaugh et al, *Object-Oriented Modelling and Design*, Prentice Hall, 1991.

[27] D. Harel, "Statecharts: A Visual Formalism for Complex Systems", *Science of Computer Programming*, Vol. 8, pp. 231-274, 1987.

[28] G. Booch, *Object-Oriented Analysis and Design with Applications*, Benjamin-Cummings, 1994.

[29] P. Coad & E. Yourdon, *Object-Oriented Analysis*, Prentice Hall, 1991.

[30] M. Broy, "Methodological Objectives for Formal Description Techniques", in J. Quemada et al (eds.), *Formal Description Techniques*, Vol. 3, pp. 1-16, Northern Holland, 1991.

[31] J.A. Goguen, "More Thoughts on Specification and Verification", in N. Gehani & A. McGettrick (eds.), *Software Specification Techniques*, pp. 47-52, Addison-Wesley, 1985.

[32] J.C.P. Woodcock, "Structuring Specification in Z", *Software Engineering Journal*, Vol. 4, No. 1, pp. 51-66, 1989.

The Dangers of Inheritance

John English

School of Computing and Mathematical Sciences
University of Brighton, Brighton BN2 4GJ, UK
Email: je@brighton.ac.uk

Object-oriented programming is a powerful programming paradigm which can help to increase program maintainability and code reuse. Based on the notion of inheritance, object-oriented programming allows variations of existing systems to be derived as extensions of it. However, the enthusiasm with which object-oriented programming has been adopted has blinded many people to the very real dangers which can arise from careless use of a paradigm with many subtleties. This paper considers some of these dangers and describes ways in which they can be avoided.

1. Introduction.

The history of programming reveals a succession of crises; as the size of problems at a particular time outstripped the means available to solve them, a paradigm shift occurred which resolved the problems of the time, which in turn allowed the size of the problems that could be solved to grow even larger and precipitate yet another crisis. The mainstream paradigms have successively been based on the use of assembly languages, high-level languages, structured programming, data abstraction and now object-oriented programming.

Object-oriented programming provides mechanisms for resolving many of the difficulties which beset what is now referred to as 'programming in the large'; it provides mechanisms which aid in promoting code reuse and (more importantly) maintainability. The most significant addition to Ada 95 is the addition of object-oriented programming facilities to the data abstraction features of Ada 83. 'Object-oriented' has now been adopted as a buzzword in the programming industry, much as 'structured' became a buzzword when structured programming was in vogue. There is, rightly, a lot of enthusiasm for developing object-oriented systems, just as there was a lot of enthusiasm for developing 'structured' systems during the 1970s and early 1980s.

Structured programming techniques enabled much larger systems to be developed reliably than was previously possible, but they proved ineffective for dealing with the problems of systems maintenance. Object-oriented programming can solve many of these problems, but like previous paradigms it too has its shortcomings. If care is not taken, a number of subtle errors can occur which will not be detectable until run time or until *derivation time*, the time during maintenance when new derived types are added to an existing parent type. As a result, injudicious use of object-oriented programming facilities can actually reduce program reliability and impact systems maintenance if insufficient care is taken. The purpose of this paper is to reveal some of the possible pitfalls which are present in Ada 95.

2. The benefits of inheritance.

Consider a system which is intended to implement an electronic diary. The diary itself can be defined by an abstract data type Diary_Type, which will be a collection of objects of yet another abstract data type Appointment_Type. We can define Appointment_Type as a record containing a date and time together with a description of the appointment:

```
type Appointment_Type is
  record
    Date    : Time_Type;      -- date and time
    Details : String(1..100);  -- description
  end record;
```

It is possible that in the future there will be a maintenance requirement which involves adding a type Meeting_Type which combines an ordinary appointment with other details such as a room number, a list of attendees, and so on. In Ada 83 [1] this would involve redefining Appointment_Type as a **variant record** with variants to describe plain appointments, meetings, and any other variants that may be required:

```
type Appointment_Kind is (Appointment, Meeting);

type Appointment_Type (Kind : Appointment_Kind) is
  record
    Date    : Time_Type;
    Details : String(1..100);
    case Kind is
      when Appointment =>
        null;
      when Meeting =>
        Room : Room_Type;
    end case;
  end record;
```

This means that the declarations of Appointment_Kind and Appointment_Type need to be changed every time a new variant is identified, and changes must be made to all the places in the code which have to distinguish between different kinds of appointment. This is a major effort, which will involving changing, rebuilding and retesting large amounts of existing code. Some existing code which previously worked correctly might have had bugs introduced by the changes, so this is an expensive proposition.

Ada 95 [5] introduces the notion of *tagged types* to overcome this, just as other object-oriented languages use *classes*:

```
type Appointment_Type is
   tagged record
     Date    : Time_Type;
     Details : String(1..100);
   end record;
```

New types can be *derived* from this which extend the existing type:

```
type Meeting_Type is new Appointment_Type with
   record
     Room : Room_Type;
   end record;
```

Any operations on Appointment_Type which are declared in the same package specification will be *primitive operations* of Appointment_Type, and will be *inherited* by any derived types. Derived types can also *override* the inherited operations to provide specialised behaviour. Consider the following primitive operations for Appointment_Type:

```
procedure Appointment (Date    : in Time_Type;
                       Details : in String;
                       Result  : out Appointment_Type);
function Date    (Appt : Appointment_Type) return Time_Type;
function Details (Appt : Appointment_Type) return String;
procedure Put    (Appt : in Appointment_Type);
                         -- display appointment
```

These operations will all be inherited by Meeting_Type (with Appointment_Type parameters being replaced by Meeting_Type parameters). The functions Date and Details will work unchanged, but the procedure Put above is likely to need to be overridden to display the details of a meeting in an appropriate way, and extra primitives (such as a function Room to extract the Room component of a meeting) will need to be added.

The important feature which gives object-oriented programming languages their power is what Ada 95 refers to as *dispatching* of primitive operations. Each tagged type has an associated *class-wide* type (e.g. Appointment_Type'Class for Appointment_Type) which includes the type itself and all types derived from it, so that an Appointment_Type'Class variable can actually contain an Appointment_Type value, a Meeting_Type value, or a value of any other type derived from Appointment_Type. If a primitive operation is used with a class-wide parameter, the actual type of the parameter is used to select the correct version of the operation. Thus, a call to Put with an Appointment_Type'Class value will call the

Appointment_Type version of Put if the value is actually an Appointment_Type, the Meeting_Type version of Put if the value is actually a Meeting_Type, and so on. By making Diary_Type a collection of Appointment_Type'Class values, new types of appointment can be added to an existing system without disturbing any existing code, and this will eliminate the need to rebuild and retest existing code. This allows great savings to be made during the maintenance phase of a system's lifetime.

3. The dangers of inheritance.

3.1 Calling primitives from other primitives.

In Ada 95, when a primitive operation is inherited its signature is identical to that of the inherited operation except that all mention of the parent type's name is systematically replaced by that of the derived type ([6], 3.4(18)). Thus, using the appointments-and-meetings example above, Meeting_Type will inherit a Put operation whose signature will look like this:

```
procedure Put (Appt : in Meeting_Type);
```

Suppose that Put is then overridden by Meeting_Type so as to extend its semantics (by displaying the room number in addition to the other details). Calling Put for a class-wide value will dispatch to the appropriate version of Put for the actual type. Now suppose that Put is called from another primitive operation:

```
procedure Other_Primitive (Appt : in Appointment_Type) is
begin
   ...
   Put (Appt);
   ...
end Other_Primitive;
```

Meeting_Type will inherit Other_Primitive, but the version of Put which will be called from inside Other_Primitive will always be the Appointment_Type version, rather than the overridden Meeting_Type version as one might expect. This is because inside Other_Primitive, Appt is not a class-wide type so dispatching does not occur. The inherited operation might be imagined to be defined like this:

```
procedure Other_Primitive (Appt : in Meeting_Type) is
begin
   ...
   Put (Appt);      -- what type is Appt here?
   ...
end Other_Primitive;
```

The interpretation of Appt in the call to Put is still as a value of type Appointment_Type; the body of the procedure is the one that was defined for

Appointment_Type, so Appt is still treated as an Appointment_Type value within the procedure body. The resulting behaviour is as though an implicit type conversion from Meeting_Type to Appointment_Type has occurred; the procedure signature has been modified but the body has not, so the signature no longer matches the corresponding body. Ada specifically avoids allowing implicit type conversions because of the problems they can cause, so this is quite surprising! The solution is to remember to convert the value to the class-wide type before calling other primitives:

```
procedure Other_Primitive (Appt : in Appointment_Type) is
begin
   ...
   Put (Appointment_Type'Class(Appt));
   ...
end Other_Primitive;
```

Obviously, this is easy to overlook, and can give rise to some very puzzling behaviour. As noted above, the problem will only become apparent at *derivation time* when a new type is derived which overloads Put, but the problem is not a problem with the derived type itself (although that is how it might appear to be) but with the code for the parent type (whose source might not be available at derivation time).

3.2 Errors in specifying overridden operations.

It is well known that typographical errors in most languages can result in erroneous programs compiling correctly. For example, C and C++ are notorious for the risk of using '=' (the assignment operator) instead of '==' (the equality operator) in the condition of a loop or *if* statement; a missing semicolon at the end of an Algol 60 or Coral 66 comment would result in the next statement being taken to be part of the comment; and in Fortran, mistyping a comma could convert a loop heading into an assignment. Ada 83 was carefully designed so that simple typographical errors like these would not result in error-free compilations; the remaining risk is that objects with very similar names might be confused, but unless the objects have overlapping scopes and compatible types this will only result in a compile-time error.

However, a problem arises in Ada 95 when overriding primitive operations of tagged types. The signature of the overriding operation must match the signature of the inherited operation exactly, or what will happen will be that a new primitive operation will have been added without affecting the inherited operation. For example, the type Controlled defined in the standard package Ada.Finalization provides a primitive operation called Finalize:

```
procedure Finalize (Object : in out Controlled);
```

It would be easy for a British programmer to spell this as 'Finalise' instead of 'Finalize', so that a type derived from Controlled might end up with two primitives: one called 'Finalize' which is inherited from Controlled, and one called 'Finalise' which is new to the derived type. However, the risk is not confined to this situation;

any typographical error in the name of an overriding declaration will have the same result. The effect will be a program which compiles correctly but is semantically incorrect, and it will be possible to achieve this effect with no more effort than is required in a language like C.

Furthermore, in the case of Finalize, the operation is invoked automatically when an object of a type derived from Controlled is destroyed. Since it would normally do nothing visible (typically being responsible for deallocating dynamic storage allocated by the object) it might be difficult to discover that the supposedly overriding operation Finalise is never being called.

One way that Ada 95 could have overcome this problem is to require overriding declarations to explicitly state that this is what they are, for example as is done in Object Pascal [2]; the compiler could then detect the case of an overriding declaration that does not have a corresponding primitive inherited from the parent type. Similarly, overriding declarations that were *not* marked as such could be flagged at compile time.

A solution not requiring any language changes would be for the compiler to list all new and overridden primitives of each tagged type that is declared; another solution would be to use a *class browser* which can be used to explore inheritance hierarchies and the primitives provided at each level in a hierarchy. Unfortunately compiler facilities and tools such as this are rarely available as yet, so that error detection is only possible through source code inspection, although even when they *are* available errors can only be detected by inspection of the output they produce; a language modification would have the advantage that a compile-time error could be generated.

Class browsers are also invaluable for reasons other than those given above. A derived type does not explicitly list the operations it inherits, so without looking at the parent type (and the grandparent type, and so on) it is impossible to know what the complete set of available operations for the derived type actually is. This is particularly important for deep inheritance hierarchies, as for example occur with GUI frameworks (e.g. Borland's C++ OWL library [3] for Microsoft Windows, or Microsoft's own MFC [7]). Without being able to see what operations a particular type provides, there is always a risk of reinventing the wheel at lower levels in the inheritance hierarchy.

3.3 Inherited constructors

Unlike some languages (e.g. C++), an Ada 95 tagged type inherits all the primitive operations of its parent type. In the case of *constructor* operations (like the procedure Appointment for Appointment_Type) this can be very dangerous. The specification of the procedure that Meeting_Type inherits will look like this:

```
procedure Appointment (Date    : in Time_Type;
                        Details : in String;
                        Result  : out Meeting_Type);
```

The result of calling this procedure will be that the Meeting_Type result will be created in exactly the same way as it was when the result was an Appointment_Type; the room number won't have been set up. Defining another procedure which includes a parameter for the room number won't override this because the parameter list will be different. This is a serious problem because it provides a way to construct Meeting_Type objects incorrectly. One solution is to override Appointment so that it provides a default value for the room number; another possibility is to raise an exception if Appointment is called to create a meeting:

```
procedure Appointment (Date    : in Time_Type;
                       Details : in String;
                       Result  : out Meeting_Type) is
begin
   -- This procedure should never be called
   raise Program_Error;
end Appointment;
```

This is unsatisfactory because it involves declaring an unnecessary procedure which should never be called; it is also unsatisfactory because if Appointment is accidentally called to initialise a meeting, detection of the error will happen at run time instead of at compile time.

In the case of non-limited types the constructor can be declared as a function rather than as a procedure:

```
function Appointment (Date    : Time_Type;
                      Details : String)
         return Appointment_Type;
```

If a function is a primitive operation of a tagged type and it returns a result of that type, any derived types inherit it as an *abstract operation*, i.e. a function for which no implementation exists. Since Meeting_Type is an extension of Appointment_Type, returning an Appointment_Type result and pretending it's a Meeting_Type will be unsatisfactory as the room number will not have been set up. Inherited abstract operations must be explicitly overridden:

```
function Appointment (Date    : Time_Type;
                      Details : String) return Meeting_Type;
```

Again, it might be possible to set the room number to a default value, but the most sensible definition will probably be one that raises an exception as a similar function for meetings will probably be needed which includes an extra parameter for the room number.

If you use a function the compiler will be able to detect the problem; if you use a procedure the compiler is unable to help. For this reason it is necessary to exercise great care with primitive procedures which have an *out* or *in out* parameter of the type in question.

Another solution is to declare Appointment in a separate package so that it isn't a primitive operation of Appointment_Type and so will not be inherited by Meeting_Type. One way to do this is to use an internal package within the package that declares Appointment_Type:

```
package Appointments is
   type Appointment_Type is tagged private;

   -- Internal package containing constructor function:
   package Create is
      function Appointment (Date    : Time_Type;
                            Details : String)
                return Appointment_Type;
   end Create;
   ...
end Appointments;
```

Appointment is now declared in a different package from Appointment_Type; this means that it will not be a primitive operation of Appointment_Type. The constructor can be called using the name Create.Appointment.

An alternative possibility is to construct all objects dynamically and use constructor functions which return access values. Since functions like this don't return a value of the type itself, they will not be primitive operations of the type and so will not be inherited. However, this then raises the problem of disposing of the dynamic object at the end of its lifetime.

3.4 Explicit constructor calls.

In C++, constructors are automatically called when objects are created. In Ada 95, the nearest approach to this is the primitive operation Initialize for controlled types (types derived from the types Controlled or Limited_Controlled which are defined in Ada.Finalization, as described above). Unlike a C++ constructor, Initialize takes no parameters other than the object to be initialized, so it is usually necessary to provide a separate constructor, as Appointment was for Appointment_Type. The danger here is that it is possible to forget to call the constructor, and it is necessary to write the primitive operations in such a way that uninitialised objects are detected and reported, although again this will defer error detection from compile time to run rime.

Initialize and Finalize are typically useful for dynamic memory allocation and deallocation. For example, it is possible to make private types completely opaque by hiding the implementation details in the package body:

```
package P is
   type T is tagged private;
   ...
```

```
private
   type T_Implementation;      --  defined in the package body
   type Implementation_Access is access T_Implementation;

   type T is new Controlled with
      record
         Implementation : Implementation_Access;
      end record;
   procedure Initialize (Object : in out T);
   procedure Finalize   (Object : in out T);
end P;
```

The package body will contain the full declaration of T_Implementation; Initialize can allocate a T_Implementation object and set up the Implementation component and Finalize can deallocate it.

A possible danger arises when deriving from a controlled type. If the type extension itself needs to be controlled, the Initialize procedure for the derived type will need to call the parent type's version of Initialize to initialise the components inherited from the parent type, and similarly for Finalize:

```
package P.Q is
   type T2 is new P.T with private;
   ...
private
   type T2_Implementation; -- defined in the package body
   type Implementation_Access is access T2_Implementation;

   type T2 is new P.T with
      record
         Implementation : Implementation_Access;
      end record;
   procedure Initialize (Object : in out T2);
   procedure Finalize   (Object : in out T2);
end P.Q;
```

The same technique is used here to hide the implementation of T2's extra components. Initialize and Finalize will not only have to allocate and deallocate the T2_Implementation component of T2, but will also need to call the versions of Initialize and Finalize defined for the parent type T, and there is of course a risk that this step could be forgotten. As noted above, omitting a call to the parent version of Finalize will result in memory leaks which might well remain undetected until the system is in use at full stretch in a production environment.

This is a sharp contrast to other languages such as C++. In C++ constructors have a special status: they are not inheritable, they are called automatically, they will call parent constructors automatically, and they can have parameters. Because Ada 95 does not treat constructors specially, the programmer becomes responsible for ensuring correct usage.

One possible solution to this problem is to define T2_Implementation as a controlled type, and then use a component of this type to extend T:

```
package P.Q is
   type T2 is new P.T with private;
   ...
private
   type T2_Real_Implementation;      -- defined in the body
   type Real_Implementation_Access is
                 access T2_Real_Implementation;

   type T2_Implementation is new Controlled with
     record
        Real_Implementation : Real_Implementation_Access;
     end record;

   procedure Initialize (Object : in out T2_Implementation);
   procedure Finalize   (Object : in out T2_Implementation);

   type T2 is new P.T with
     record
        Implementation : T2_Implementation;
     end record;
end P.Q;
```

Now when a T2 object is created , the version of Initialize for T2_Implementation will be called to initialise its Implementation component, and the version of Initialize inherited from T will then be called to initialise the T2 object as a whole ([6], 7.6(12)). Similarly when a T2 object is destroyed, Finalize will be called for the object as a whole as well and then for its Implementation component. However, note that this is done in the opposite order to C++ [4], which calls base class constructors before the constructor for a derived class (and vice versa for destructors). If the order of events is important, this technique might not be appropriate (for example, a window might be derived from a controlled type, and it might be necessary for Finalize to clear the window from the screen before the parent type's Finalize destroys the underlying data structures).

4. Conclusions.

Object-oriented programming is an essential part of every modern programmer's toolkit. As section 2 of this paper showed, there are many tangible benefits which arise from an object-oriented outlook, and at present there is no rival paradigm which can promise the same level of benefits in terms of maintainabilty, reusability and extensibility. Because of this, it cannot be ignored by any serious programmer. However, the price that currently has to be paid for the benefits is that:

- we have returned to the situation where single-character typographical errors can result in erroneous programs that still compile correctly;
- the detection of some errors has been deferred from compile time to run time; and
- the detection of other errors has been deferred still further to *derivation time*, by which time it is possible that the source code containing the bug is not available for repair.

Careful coding practices can alleviate the burden; similarly, increased compiler support and tools such as class browsers can help, but as yet these are rarely available. However, until the next language review, they are the best available solution, and for object-oriented programming to be successful, we urgently need better tools.

In the meantime, the problems discussed above need to be carefully avoided if the potential benefits of object-oriented programming are to be realised, and it is to be hoped that the description of these difficulties given in this paper will help to raise awareness of the possible problems.

References.

[1] ANSI/MIL-STD-1815A. *Reference Manual for the Ada Programming Language* (1983)
[2] Borland International Inc. *Object Pascal Language Guide* (1996)
[3] Borland International Inc. *Object Windows for C++ Programmer's Guide* (1993)
[4] Ellis, M. and Stroustrup, B. *The C++ Annotated Reference Manual* (Addison Wesley 1990)
[5] Intermetrics Inc. *Ada 95 Rationale* (1995)
[6] Intermetrics Inc. *Ada 95 Reference Manual* (1995)
[7] Microsoft Corporation, *Visual C++ Class Library Reference* (1993)

CCO-MARS'96

Integrating HOOD, Ada, and XInAda

in a Full Ada Operational Software Project

Philippe Pichon

CISI
Space Engineering Division
13 rue Villet

Z.I. du Palays

31400 Toulouse
France

email: ccoconf@ perseus.cisi.cnes.fr
phone: +34 (0) 5.61.17.66.66 - fax: +34 (0) 5.61.17.66.96

Abstract. The development of the "CCO MARS'96" system for the French space agency, CNES, has proved a very enriching experience concerning the integration of HOOD, Ada, and XInAda in an operational project. The two main points of interest are one in the area of Man Machine Interfaces (MMIs), and the other in the development cycle of an operational product using HOOD and Ada technology. Developing a full Ada MMI using XInAda and Ada's tasking features turned to be a successful challenge that yielded important guidelines for the future design of such software applications. The MMI and its interface to the rest of the software were modeled using the HOOD method. A homogeneous design for the entire product was thus achieved as HOOD was the method chosen to cover the whole development cycle. As a consequence of this technical integration, large intrinsic development security and confidence were obtained even though glitches made the overall process tedious; but the lessons learned from the mishaps are now invaluable.

Keywords. Operational, MMI, XInAda, HOOD, Ada, parallel I/Os.

1 Introduction

This paper begins with a brief overview of the project itself and the present day situation of the CCO software. It then goes on to describe the specific features of the development of the application. This entails explaining how the HOOD method was applied to the life cycle of the project, in particular with respect to the Graphical User Interface part (GUI). The description of the design of the MMI with HOOD and of the representation of its links with the rest of the application software introduces a section concerning the implementation of the GUI using XInAda (the all-Ada implementation of the X/Motif graphical MMI libraries). Finally, the section on the lessons learned outlines the key issues that arose during the project concerning this technology in terms of advantages and drawbacks as perceived by the development team. The conclusion hints at future improvements deemed worth investigating with a view to better put into practice the gained experience.

2 The CCO-Mars'96

2.1 The CCO and The Mission to Mars

The MARS'96 project is an international mission to Mars coordinated by the Russians which is part of a more global program aimed at observing the Red Planet. To this purpose the space probe hosts two scientific platforms each managing several experiments, two penetrators, two small soft-landing stations, and an orbital module. The transfer phase to Mars is expected to last a year; and the mission itself another year.

Considering the importance of the French participation in the mission, CNES was asked by the Russians to take the responsibility of the French part of the ground segment of the mission (CMSF). Within CMSF, COM (Centre des Operations Mars) is in charge of handling the data exchanged between the Russian mission and control center (CMM) and the French entities. CCO's (Centre de Coordination des Operations) role as part of COM is to act as an interface receiving, controlling and dispatching the data flow between CMM and the different French sub-systems. These comprise the scientific laboratories taking part in the space probe's payload, the interplanetary navigation center, and the mission data processing center.

2.2 Present Day Situation

The space probe was launched this last November the 16th 1996, and the CCO had then already been operated daily for a month to process launch and early flight activities data. Unfortunately, the launch procedure went amiss and the space probe failed to separate from the fourth stage of the Proton vehicle. The mission has for the time being been put off; and the CCO is being packed away with the hope in mind of bringing it back up for a possible re-scheduling of the mission beginning 2001.

2.3 Description of the CCO

2.3.1 Functional Description of the CCO

The main functions of the CCO in terms of services are:

- management of operational data: this consists in checking, archiving and dispatching the operations data files. These contain informations concerning the resources requested by the laboratories for their experiments and those finally allocated by the mission control center together with the definition of the working intervals of each experiment. The operations plan, which helps the operators organize their daily and weekly tasks, is drawn up from the indications in these files.
- label control and dispatching of navigation data: the navigation data files' headers are checked by the CCO which then starts validation, qualification and archiving tasks on the remote CNI (Centre de Navigation Interplanétaire) computer. The CCO application archives both the control report it produces along with the validation and qualification reports the CNI sends back.
- label insertion and dispatching of binary real-time telemetry data: TMTR (TéléMesure Temps Réel) data is dumped from the space probe during what are called real-time telemetry sessions. CMM sends the set of associated files to the CCO which checks them for expected but missing files, present but not expected ones and unknown ones. For each experiment, the related telemetry files are parsed to build a header characterizing the main telemetry data file to which it is added. The valid experiment files are then forwarded to the corresponding laboratory. The

CCO keeps a history of the processed files and the control report of the associated session.

- label control and dispatching of binary off-line telemetry data: TMTD (TéléMesure Temps Différé) data is real-time telemetry data fed back to CMM to be processed over again. The returned files have their headers (produced by TMTR processing) checked for coherence with the file itself. The validated files are passed on to the corresponding laboratory. The CCO also builds up an archive of the files processed along with their control report.

2.3.2 Operating the CCO

The CCO is operated by two specially trained users via a user-friendly man-machine interface (MMI):

- the routine operator
- the operations manager

The routine operator is in charge of activating and monitoring the different data processing tasks in accordance with the operations plan. He also has access to support services such as:

- the application's logbook to which the different tasks report both their activity progress and any warnings or error messages.
- a data browser based on an off-the-shelf Motif object that helps going around file directory trees. It enabled the user to display any of the files in the environment ranging from ordinary ASCII data files or application configuration files to binary telemetry files.
- a catalog look-up facility that guides the user through the catalogs towards the archived control reports, processed file history and so on he wants to look up.

In addition, the operations manager also has access to:

- an archive and clean-up function
- a system window.

2.3.3 The CCO seen from a Software Point of View

The CCO reads the data files from directories corresponding to their type and origin which can either be the Russian mission control center, the interplanetary navigation center at CNES, or the different scientific laboratories. Processing includes controlling the structure of the filenames and of the file headers, updating a local archive and dispatching the processed files according to their types. The processing required by a file differs from one type to another (some files are binary data files, others plain ASCII).

The different functions of the CCO can all be activated simultaneously -within compatibility restrictions- so that the different types of processing can be run in parallel. This is necessary to be able to take into account all the types of data that are present at the time of the session but this sometimes means a heavy load of I/Os.

The system-level interface specifications were so unfinalised that a processing definition file was defined on the basis of an extended PVL (Parameter Value Language) syntax in order to keep up easily with file and filename structure evolutions without source code modifications. The scope of elements liable to change and the extent of the possible updates made this issue quite complex.

It goes without saying that Ada was used as the programming language for the application, but it must be stressed that the entire MMI is also coded in Ada, using the XInAda graphical library.

Systems calls are scarce but proved inevitable and are confined in two dedicated objects.

2.4 Project Profile

2.4.1 Time Scale

The development cycle of the CCO system project spans from the 1st of January 1996 to the 12th of July 1996.

This was a very reduced time scale for such a project development in proportion to the workload. Meeting the deadline was a key issue as any shift in the schedule meant disrupting the ground segment operational software validation phase which already had its back to the wall of the launch date. Rescheduling the launch meant waiting until the end of 1998 since launch windows periodicity is 25 months... And one should remember that the mission had already been called at one time Mars'94...

2.4.2 Team

The average team size was 4 people, most of who, it must be noted, were rather inexperienced with HOOD, Ada and least of all XInAda. Support by a HOOD expert was planned and was effective at the start of the project and for the preliminary design phase. Another HOOD/Ada expert joined the team at a later stage.

All in all, the global effort amounts to 27 man*months.

2.4.3 Code Volume

The total volume of code that was produced (85500 lines) can break down as follows:
- 30400 lines were generated automatically using the MMI generator TeleUse'Ada for the GUI,
- 8200 lines were made up of re-used software components,
- the remaining 46900 lines were developed, 8000 of which for the MMI.

2.4.4 Development Environment

The development environment comprised:
- an Alsys Ada 83 compiler 6.2; and a VADSmp 3.0 compiler for the target generation at CNES,
- the Unix Solaris 2.4 operating system,
- Stood 3.0 to implement HOOD,
- TeleUse'Ada 3.0.2 as GUI generator,
- XInAda 3.0/1.5 as the X/Motif library implementation.

3 The Development Cycle and HOOD

3.1 Introduction

The development cycle followed on the project was a classical V-cycle adapted for the MMI part which underwent a prototyping phase.

The engineering method used was object based: it was decided right from the start of the project to go right through with HOOD. Hence, Stood, TNI's (Techniques Nouvelles d'Information - the company developing and distributing Stood) tool implementing the method, supported the whole development cycle, from the preliminary design phase, through coding and tests (an object's unitary test procedures are included in the object itself), to integration and finally validation. Guaranty and maintenance modifications would still, and would have continued to be, supported by HOOD and Stood.

3.2 Architectural Design

The architectural design phase included an author/reader cycle that was put into practice by setting up two such loops: the one that was internal to CISI involved the CISI HOOD expert assigned to the project, and the other, with CNES, involved both the CNES HOOD expert and the CNES project technical leader. Each cycle entailed cross-reading a design output, discussing the reader's remarks and then taking into account the feedback. The customer cycle was interspersed with the internal CISI cycle so that a meeting with CNES started the next iteration of an internal CISI one. The output resulting from updating the design with the CISI reader's feedback was then passed over to CNES in order to start the next external cycle.

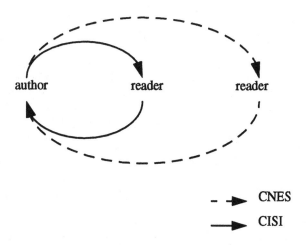

Fig. 1. Author/reader cycle

Neither HOOD experts belonged to the project and were thus unawares of technical details. They not only guided the development team in using HOOD, but their 'neutral' understanding of the design also was an eye-opener on certain technical aspects. The CNES project leader's role in the cycle also obviously was to ensure that the design met the requirements.

For the architectural design review (ARD), pre-terminal (second last) decomposition level was achieved. The code was generated for the first time at this stage and all the package specifications missed being totally compile-error free by only a couple of days. Had the state of the package interfaces allowed it, a prototype of the application would have been envisaged as a demonstration at the ARD but this proved too stringent a task in the context although it only was a near miss.

3.3 Detailed Design

Hence, the first task of the detailed design phase consisted in making the package specifications compile and only thereafter in refining the HOOD hierarchy. Due to lack of experience, some 'pseudo-code' was written to describe provided and internal operations whereas it would have been preferable to produce Ada code directly in order to gain time and clarity in the later coding phase.

A keypoint had been planned as the end of the detailed design phase milestone.

3.4 Coding

The team went into coding as a natural continuation of the detailed design phase. Patches to the Stood generated code became necessary at this point to get around some of HOOD's limitations. Indeed, some initialization requiring that a configuration file be read needed to be done at elaboration time. The *begin/end* section of a package body was used to this end although HOOD disallows it. At a later stage, it became apparent that a *storage_size* clause was necessary for the tasks of the application. This clause can only apply to task types which are not provided for by HOOD. So, another patch procedure joined the previous one.

3.5 Testing

Concerning the unitary tests, CNES had strongly recommended to include in each object an operation covering the tests of all its operations, so that an object could be exported with the means to test it. This proved rather cumbersome and somewhat unrealistic in that the input data files to the objects also had to go along with the testing operation. Also, there being no requirements to maintain the unitary tests, having to constantly update these operations for compilation purposes in later stages of the project became rather annoying. As of today, no objects have yet been exported to other projects so that the effectiveness of such arrangements has yet to been shown.

As far as actual trouble shooting goes, the team made the most of the compiler's *history* feature that traces all raised exceptions even when handled and the debugger was only used to a a very limited extent and restricted to particularly dire cases.

Nothing much need be reported on the integration and validation phases as far as using HOOD and Ada for the development of the application goes. They ran smoothly because Ada and HOOD were used. The problems that really cropped up were linked with XInAda.

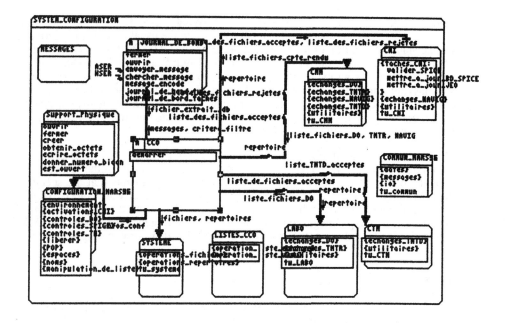

Fig. 2. HOOD system level design of the CCO

3.6 Configuration Control

On the CCO system, configuration control encompasses more than the usual source files in that the whole HOOD design and TeleUSE'Ada input files are subjected to it. For the moment, although the entire design and code are delivered to CNES, the code is the only input to the generation procedure. Moreover, Stood does not yet provide for a means of tracing the objects of configuration management. TNI is currently working on it. Although automatic code extraction is not yet available either, CISI has worked on an approach to include in the generation procedure such 'batch' code generation from the HOOD design. It had been foreseen to implement this functionality on the project. It had further been envisaged that CNES acquired TeleUSE'Ada to generate the MMI specific code directly from TeleUSE'Ada's input definition files. The question of automating this last aspect, however, was not, at the time, a current issue. Hence, configuration control would have gradually shifted from the source code to the actual design itself.

4 The Man Machine Interface

4.1 TeleUse'Ada

Most MMIs are now built using a graphical interface generator. TeleUSE'Ada was chosen for its ability to produce Ada, with an interface to the XInAda library which implements the X/Motif libraries entirely in Ada.

TeleUse'Ada has a WISIWIG (What I See Is What I Get) type of interface which makes access to the tool easy and simple. Apart from the usual functionality providing for the static description of the screens making up the GUI, TeleUse offers a language of its own to describe the dynamics of the final interface. This D-language, as it is called, implements an event programming technique that does not however support Ada tasking and Ada's exception mechanism (these features are however perfectly legal by XInAda standards and were thoroughly used throughout the MMI). The final GUI requires the XInAda package *Tu_Runtime* to execute the Ada code resulting from the automatic transcoding of the D-language to Ada.

In the TeleUse'Ada environment, Application Interface Mapping (AIM) files define the binding between the TeleUse'Ada generated code and the rest of the software components, be they MMI-application objects (software components that are specific to the MMI but outside the X/Motif world) or pure application software objects. This feature is very handy splitting the development of the MMI from the rest of the application itself, pending integration of the TeleUse'Ada generated code, the MMI-application code and the actual application code. Realistic prototyping is thus easily achieved quite early in the project.

4.2 XInAda

XInAda implements the set of X/Motif libraries (*Xm*, *Xt*, *Xlib*) in Ada. However, some of the C-Motif operations are not supported by XInAda, which a C-Motif expert at first finds slightly awkward; but reciprocally, XInAda offers some interesting added functionality. These differences are due to inevitable, but sought after, language specificities (variable argument count in C, tasking and exceptions in Ada). Hence, despite thin documentation, someone familiar with the C-Motif world finds his way around in XInAda as corresponding operation names are easily derivable from one another, except for the *Xt* library which for implementation reasons differ to a larger extent. The drawback is only moderate because direct interfaces with this library are usually quite limited. Binding with XInAda also requires the C '*nsl*' and '*socket*' libraries.

An important feature of XInAda is the *work procedure* mechanism that enables communication of tasks with the MMI's mainloop. It enables a call-back procedure to make an asynchronous rendez-vous with a task entry so that the mainloop is not locked on call-backs requiring long processing time. The mainloop is then warned of the task's entry completion by the work procedure called by the task itself when it is done with its activity.

Both TeleUse'Ada and XInAda are fully object oriented, fitting in smoothly with a general HOOD approach.

4.3 The Application, the GUI, HOOD and TeleUse'Ada: the Development Dycle

The development cycle of the GUI was slightly different from the one used for the rest of the application because its design underwent a prototyping phase. Two prototypes were produced: one for the architectural design review, and one half way through detailed design. The development cycle of the GUI then caught up with the classical cycle of MMI development within the cycle of the remainder of the project. The presence of the end users at the demonstrations of the prototypes, early in the development process, reduced the not so unusual final convergence iterations towards their satisfaction.

Guidelines to developing MMIs usually suggest an approach in three stages. To start with, a static description of the GUI sets up the looks of the screens highlighting the software's required functionalities. Next, the implementation of the dynamic behavior shows how the screens interact and how they react either to a user-event, such as a mouse or keyboard action, or to the MMI-application. Finally the last stage of the pure GUI development cycle consists in defining the application interface mapping (AIM) scheme.

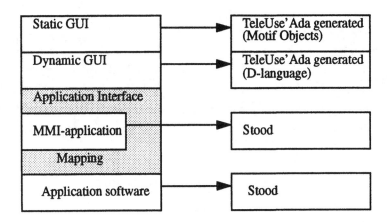

Fig. 3. Levels of utilization of TeleUse'Ada and Stood

The GUI's static aspects of the CCO system were formalized using TeleUse'Ada: this entailed both the description of the screens with the tool and the generation of the corresponding Ada code. In addition, describing the screens as HOOD objects also proved useful identifying and formalizing the MMI call-backs. The HOOD design of the MMI also modeled software components specific to the MMI but outside the X/Motif world. The final code for these objects was produced using Stood, and applying the HOOD method fully and right to the end.

HOOD also helped formalize the relationships between the screens or sets of screens to start describing the dynamics of the GUI: the actual dynamic behavior was then implemented using TeleUse'Ada's D-language, later automatically transcoded into Ada.

As a general rule, making use of the formal description possibility of HOOD proved handy achieving steady interfaces between the MMI components and the rest of the software's components.

Figure 4 shows the MMI HOOD hierarchy as it stood at the end of the project. It mainly represents the screens, their relationships and interfaces. Only the three objects X_CCO, IHM_CCO, and Xu have a real HOOD identity; the first two interface the GUI with the actual application software and Xu is an extension to the XInAda library isolated for reusability purposes. The other objects model Motif screens and their operations, the associated call-backs. In fact, these objects only represent the screens generated with TeleUse'Ada. No operations are really called in their HOOD implementation: this is done first in the D-language and then in the generated Ada code produced to implement the dynamics of the GUI.

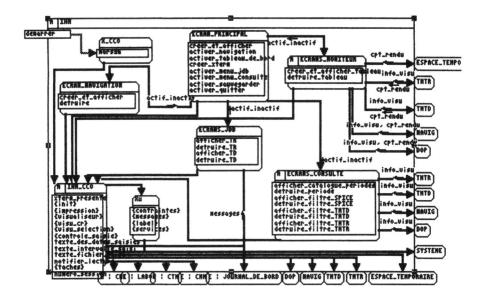

Fig. 4. HOOD representation of the MMI

5 Compiler And Compiler

Product delivery and generation follow strict procedures with CNES. CISI delivers the objects necessary for the generation of the executable file, the application data files and the generation procedure. The end operational executable object is generated by CNES's configuration management department.

The target compiler is Rational VADS. But because of poor data links with the CNES network, the entire development of the CCO used CISI's configurations which meant using the Alsys compiler the company has.

Once the application was validated, the HOOD design and its extracted code together with the TeleUSE'Ada generated MMI code were transferred on the CNES configuration for validation with the VADS environment (compiler and XInAda libraries).

Apart from minor syntax glitches that arose at compile time, more surprising differences showed up between the two environments at execution time. These were of two different nature:

- One concerned the processing performance. Indeed, there was a factor of up to fourteen between the times taken to execute the same task, in the same environment. It turned out to be the way the I/Os were implemented by the compilers and because the software compiled on the target environment did not meet the performance requirements - and there was no way of getting a compiler patch on this aspect - the low level application package in charge of the I/Os unfortunately had to be re-written using C interface pragmas so that it became a disguised C-module.

- The other was linked with the scheduling of the tasks. Indeed, when the user started a particular task - the one with an extremely high number of I/Os - the remainder of the application was locked until the task's termination. Because Unix suspends its processes during I/Os, the actual Ada scheduler was also refrained from giving time to other tasks. As a consequence, on the target compiler that implements all its tasks on the same Unix process there was no possible parallel tasking. However, the other, mapping Ada tasks on Solaris System threads had them running independently and simultaneous processing was possible. The solution to the problem was an extension to the target compiler that precisely mapped its tasks on system threads.

6 The Experience

The experience gained by the project team is manifold.

One aspect concerns the use of HOOD, Stood and Ada in an operational environment. Another reflects the surprising behavioral differences between the Alsys generated application and the VADS generated application. And finally developing a full Ada MMI turned out to be quite a challenge.

6.1 HOOD

6.1.1 Development Cycle

The project found it very difficult to determine the level of design to be achieved for each milestone of the development schedule. Whereas it is necessary to provide for formal reviews in such projects (let alone to assure the customer the design meets his needs), this is difficult to match with an intrinsically continuous engineering process such as HOOD. The project nonetheless came up with definitions, deemed satisfactory to this day, of the production output required for each review or milestone.

Preliminary design is said to be achieved when all the objects have been identified and their provided interfaces (types and operations) described. This work, as part of an author/reader or double author/reader cycle as in our case, protracts the preliminary design phase for a period somewhat longer than usually planned. This has to be taken into account in future such operational projects that are also demanding in terms of associated documentation.

Detailed design phase ends when all the operations - provided and internal - have been found and described.

It is unnecessary to write pseudo-code during the design phases. Code is produced right from the beginning. Any comment one would be tempted to insert can often be replaced by a clearly and explicitly named operation. Invaluable coding time is indeed saved in such a way.

6.1.2 Methodology

The method, with which the team that was largely unfamiliar, was found to be easily accessible to inexperienced developers. Moreover, it generated a certain level of confidence with regards integration and interface coherence in the output components because of the strong formalization proposed.

From a project manager's point of view, the identification of objects provides an easy means of allotting tasks to team members at any stage in the development process of the system.

However, the author-reader cycle may give rise to unduly long discussions over the design since there are always many designs that meet the functional requirements. When it comes to a question of point of view, the client-provider clash unpleasantly lies lurking not far. This is particularly frustrating for the designer which often ends up yielding to king Customer's insistence.

The object oriented side of HOOD has yet to prove its full efficiency in terms of maintenance since the project has not yet been subjected to major updates.

6.2 Ada

The use of Ada reduced unitary testing time because the language's strong syntax and semantics result in severe compilation constraints that are a warranty of coherence in the code.Using Ada throughout the whole application means the project turned up with several re-usable objects, including the MMI.

The compilers's HISTORY feature used in conjunction with Ada's exception mechanism enabled the team to practically do away with the debugger. Compile and bind times, however, remain rather long.

6.3 Man Machine Interface

Using HOOD, Ada and XInAda to develop the MMI has several advantages. The overall design of the application is simpler and more homogeneous since there is only one design method used (HOOD) and one language used. The advantages of Ada, such as the exception mechanism, strong typing, interface security and the general associated quality assurance can thus also benefit the GUI. Multi-tasking also enables to generate a mono-process application which is easier to manage in terms of installation. It also has the advantage of simplifying software communications within the application and limiting the number of internal interface files.

6.4 Tools

6.4.1 Stood

Although Stood's completeness in implementing the HOOD design method is unquestionable, it showed one major drawback in this tight schedule context. Indeed, code generation can be a very time consuming operation. The team quickly turned to modifying directly the Ada source. No matter how risky this was recognized to be (possible loss of updates), it allowed to cut short code-correcting cycles. This could be avoided by a 'reverse coding' capability of the tool.

6.4.2 Ada Compilers

The compiler's HISTORY feature used in conjunction with Ada's exception mechanism enabled the team to practically do away with the debugger. Compile and bind times, however, remain rather long.

The main issue, as brought up in section 5, was the differences in compiler behaviour. This was particularly unexpected, including by the HOOD/Ada experts, from a strongly normalized language.

6.4.3 TeleUse'Ada and XInAda

TeleUse'Ada's own interface is very easy and efficient to use which makes it simple and comfortable to describe a GUI. This means that prototypes can be exhibited at a very early stage of the project, much to the customer's satisfaction. The D-language is an interesting feature that reduces the amount of code to produce manually so that the dynamics of the GUI can be rapidly tested.

Despite XInAda's obvious immaturity, it enabled the production of an application totally in Ada. Using it on the project really helped getting it closer to a tried product.

7 Conclusion

Meeting the deadline was in fact quite tedious but for reasons not always linked with the technology used: XInAda's immaturity, compiler differences, but also underestimations and lack of experience. The experience is however rich and braced us up to go ahead with developing future operational software using full Ada technology.

Code-Data Consistency in Ada

Vincent M. Celier
Drasko Sotirovski
Christopher J. Thompson

Hughes Aircraft of Canada
13951 Bridgeport Road
Richmond, B.C. V6V 1J6
Canada
tel: (604) 2313205
fax: (604) 2785625
(vmcelier, dmsotirovski, cjthompson)@ccgate.hac.com

Abstract. This paper describes the difficulties that the authors have experienced in maintaining existential consistency between Ada code and the various persistent storages that the code depends on. It identifies certain patterns in the existential relationship between the code and data, and describes how Ada's expressive power and ASIS (Ada Semantic Interface Specification) have been used to overcome these difficulties.

Keywords. Ada, Ada Semantic Interface Specification, Air Traffic Control

Introduction

One common expectation from the user's perspective of a software product — be it simple software components like stacks, lists or queues, popular desktop spreadsheets and text editors, operating systems or complex real-time control systems — it is an implicit expectation of flexibility. The software product is expected to easily adapt its behavior, capacity, or performance to suit the needs of a particular user, site, or installation. The Canadian Automatic Air Traffic System (CAATS) being built by Hughes Aircraft of Canada is no exception: one and the same software is required to support a dozen sites different in size, traffic patterns, operational procedures, etc.

Software adaptability is often a functional requirement: CAATS is, for example, required to adapt to the actual structure of airways, airspace partitioning between different controllers, etc. However, software adaptability is as often a designers' response to unknown or unstable phenomena: the actual text of an error message to be presented to the user or the actual size of an array is often better not to hardcode into the system. CAATS experienced some difficulties in managing this latter category of adaptability and this paper describes the nature of these difficulties and how CAATS is using Ada [1] and ASIS (Ada Semantic Interface Specification) [2] to overcome them.

The unique property of this kind of adaptability is that elements of the source code define the requirement for the existence of a corresponding data item in some persistent storage. This paper explores a technique for maintaining this existential relationship between the source code and data items in other persistent storage.

The Model Problem

To explore some of the difficulties and chosen solutions, we start with the following model problem. Correct sizing of various buffers and arrays is often difficult to predict and, therefore, software designers often opt to make the software flexible relative to the actual sizing: the actual value is stored in a persistent storage and used at elaboration time or at start-up. CAATS supports a notion of system parameters through the following (simplified) Ada design:

```
package System_Parameters is

    procedure Save_All_Collections;
    procedure Load_All_Collections;

end System_Parameters;

generic
    Name: in String;
    type Parameter is (<>);
package System_Parameters.Collection is

    generic
        type Value is (<>);
    package Discrete_Kind is
        procedure Define    (The_Parameter: in Parameter;
                             With_Value:    in Value);
        function  Value_Of (The_Parameter: in Parameter) return Value;
    end Discrete_Kind;
    ...
end System_Parameters.Collection;
```

A "System Parameter Collection" is a set of "system parameters". Each system parameter is identified by a value of the generic parameter discrete type Parameter. A system parameter can represent a discrete value or a real value. Here we only present the discrete case, but there could be similar generic packages such as Floating_Point_Kind and Fixed_Point_Kind.

To define "offline" the different collections of system parameters, one calls the procedure Define of an instantiation of Xxxx_Kind for each parameter in each instantiation of Collection, then calls the procedure Save_All_Collections. This stores all system parameters collections in some persistent form such as in a file.

To get "online" the current value of a system parameter one uses the function Value_Of for the parameter in the corresponding instantiation Xxxx_Kind of the instantiation of its Collection. Load_All_Collections must have been called before any call to a function Value_Of; one option is to call it in the body of package System_Parameters.

The actual sizing of various buffers can now be left unspecified until elaboration or later. One can define the sizing to be a system parameter:

```
type Number is range 0 .. 10_000;
type My_Parameter is (Number_Of_X, Size_Of_Y, ...);
package My_Collection is new
            System_Parameters.Collection
                (Name       => "My_Collection",
                 Parameter => My_Parameter);
package My_Number_Parameter is new
            My_Collection.Discrete_Kind (Number);
```

Before running the subject application, the required values can be defined and saved offline:

```
My_Number_Parameter.Define (Number_Of_X,   25);
My_Number_Parameter.Define (Size_Of_Y,    4711);
...
System_Parameters.Save_All_Collections;
```

And the code will use them online for sizing purposes during initialization:

```
type Array_Of_X is array (Number range <>) of Number;
...
System_Parameters.Load_All_Collections;
...
declare
  X_Storage_Size: constant Number :=
      My_Number_Parameter.Value_Of (Number_Of_X);
  X_Storage: Array_Of_X (1 .. X_Storage_Size);
begin
  ...
```

The implementation of the package System_Parameters relies on a persistent storage: each and every system parameter that the software will ask for has to be in it. Consequently, there is now an existential relationship between declarations in the source code and items in a persistent storage.

The First Difficulty: Depending on other unknown system parameters

Designers are relieved by the fact that they don't have to make the sizing decisions up front. Nor to invent their own mechanism for configuring the software [4] [5]. Soon everyone is busy designing his own class(es) and setting up a number of system parameters to be used for sizing purposes. Writing the code goes smoothly but running it is not as easy:

- To run a test program, one has to prepare not only the values of his own system parameters but **all system parameters from the closure** of the unit being tested. In other words, **code-data consistency** has to be ensured: the persistent storage must contain the system parameters that the Ada code being executed depends on.

  First of all, for many parameters further away in the closure, the designer often has no idea what they are used for and what values to set.

  Second, because the system parameters are result of the design process, every release of the software tends to slightly change the set of parameters.

From the development point of view, each designer is interested in proving proper behavior of his/her code. This includes proving the appropriate behavior of the code for **any** set of values of the parameters that the code depends on. However, the very same designer is virtually never interested in the configuration data used in other classes her code depends on **as long as they behave** as specified. Hence, the problem can be resolved by means of:

Default Behavior

To ease the development process, if values for some system parameters are not found in the persistent storage, each class should use a default set of values found in the code:

```
package System_Parameters is

   type Data is private;

   generic
     type Value is (<>);
   function Data_Of (The_Value: in Value) return Data;

   procedure Save_All_Collections;
   procedure Load_All_Collections;

end System_Parameters;
```

The type Data encapsulates any system parameter of any discrete or real type. For any type of system parameter, a function Data_Of must be instantiated. This instantiation can be used in several collections.

```
with System_Parameters;
generic
  Name: in String;
  type Parameter is (<>);
  type Default_Value is array (Parameter) of System_Parameters.Data;
  Default: in Default_Value;
package System_Parameters.Collection is
   ...
   procedure Define    (The_Parameter: in Parameter;
                        With_Value:    in System_Parameters.Data);
   ...
   generic
     type Value is (<>);
   function Value_Of (The_Parameter: in Parameter) return Value;
   ...
end System_Parameters.Collection;
```

Generic package Collection now has a generic parameter array Default that contains the default values of the system parameters of the collection. If the collection is not saved in the persistent storage, then its value is contained by default in the array Default.

This provides means for the designer to declare default values for each of the system parameters required by the implementation. (It should be noted here that although the designer felt uncomfortable in setting the final value of the system parameter, we found that designers have very little problems in setting up reasonable default values.)

Using the same example as before, the implementation of a class sets up default values

```
type Number is range 0 .. 10_000;
type My_Parameter is (Number_Of_X, Size_Of_Y, ...);
type Default_Value is array (My_Parameter)
                            of System_Parameters.Data;
function Data is new System_Parameters.Data_Of (Value => Number);
Default: constant Default_Value := (Number_Of_X => Data (  25),
                                    Size_Of_Y  => Data (4711),
                                    ...);
package My_Collection is new
        System_Parameters.Collection
            (Name            => "My_Collection",
             Parameter       => My_Parameter,
             Default_Value => Default_Value,
             Default         => Default);
function Get_Value is new My_Collection.Value_Of (Value => Number);
...
System_Parameter.Load_All_Collections;
declare
   X_Storage_Size: constant Number := Get_Value (Number_Of_X);
```

As the above code fragments show, the implementation of System_Parameters is refined: if the persistent storage does not specify a value for, say, Number_Of_X, the default value is assumed.

By providing default values for all system parameters, the designer removes the need for the clients to even know about them — for as long as the default behavior suits their needs.

The Second Difficulty: Gathering all system parameters for integration

Once equipped with default behavior, data dependencies between classes become equivalent to the Ada dependencies between compilation units and designers are busily refining their code and producing new system parameters and new releases of the software. At some point, however, all that software has to be integrated into a single system. And, in iterative software development [6], integration is not a singular activity at the end of the software development cycle but a continuous process: the software developed steadily flows into integration. The same problem reappears:

- To integrate the system, one has to prepare values for **all system parameters contained in the system**.

    First of all, the default values of many system parameters do not meet the needs of the integrated system and many of them will have to be tuned to balance system performance and resource utilization.

    Second, different integration tests may require different sets of system parameters. (For example, the maximum load test is likely to require its own set of system parameters.)

    Finally, once the system has been delivered, many of the system parameters will yet have to be tuned to meet the needs of the particular site or user.

And so, the same problem of **code-data consistency**, postponed by means of default values, strikes again. And we ask ourselves: wouldn't it be nice if the consistency rules of Ada can be extended to the persistent storage so that it is guaranteed that the persistent storage contains all required system parameters?

ASIS Comes in Handy

Ada based systems offer an ideal opportunity for automating collection of data that originate from the code — ASIS. Unlike any other language, Ada provides through ASIS a means for constructing a multitude of tools for collecting information contained in the code. In our example, all system parameters contained in the released code can be collected together with their default values.

In our example, ASIS is used to find all instances of System_Parameters collections, the enumeration of parameters in the collection and their default values.

Because integration is a continuous activity on CAATS, ASIS tools will not only collect the required information from the code but also compare it with the footprint of the previous integration and issue difference reports. E.g. a report should be issued that lists all system parameters that have disappeared from the code since previous integration as well as all new system parameters introduced into the released Ada code. These reports provide insight for the integrators into the nature and scope of the changes and a starting point for understanding how to tune the system. (Figure 1)

In some cases, if system parameters are changed often or the end-user is allowed to change the system parameters, fancier and more friendly front-ends need to be built. However, the pattern remains the same, ASIS based tools are built to extract the

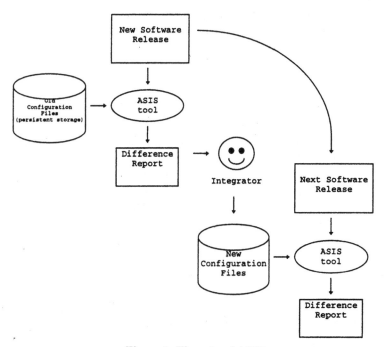

Figure 1: The role of ASIS

necessary information from the Ada code and transform it into the format that the more elaborate front-end requires. For example, the information collected from the Ada code can be transformed into SQL format that many user friendly tools can manipulate.

In CAATS, we keep most of our data in a relational database. From the database we produced offline "fast load files" that are used online by the deployed software. Because we are quite confident that the fast load files produced represent exactly what is in the database, our tools for data-code consistency checks the code against the database. To access the database, we use SAMeDL [7], both for the production of the fast load files and for the data-code consistency checking. To access the code, we use ASIS in an environment that has visibility on all the developed code.

In the database, each collection is identified by its name: it should be the same name as the generic parameter Name of the corresponding instantiation of Collection. Each system parameter in a collection is identified by its name. All generic parameter Parameter are enumerated types. The name of system parameter in the database is the identifier of the corresponding type Parameter.

Here are the different steps of a tool that checks the system parameter collections:

- From the database, using SAMeDL generated subprograms, load into memory all system parameters of all collections.
- Using ASIS, open the Ada environment context.
- Identify the library unit System_Parameters.Collection.
- Find all library units that are "direct dependents" of System_Parameters.Collection.
- For each dependent library unit:
  - Iterating on its elements, find the instantiation of System_Parameters.Collection.
  - Get the value of the actual parameter Name of the instantiation: this is the name of the collection: if the collection is in the database, mark it as found; if it is not, report that the collection is not in the database, and continue with the next library unit.
  - Get the identifiers of the generic parameter Parameter. For each of them, if it is the name of a system parameter in the database, mark it as found. If it is not in the database, report this fact.
  - If there are any system parameters in the database that is left unmarked, report them.
- If there is any collections in the database that is left unmarked, report them.
- Close the Ada environment context.

It is envisioned that such a tool will make use of ASIS in a standard fashion as described in [3]. The CAATS system currently uses a System Parameter mechanism similar to the simplified one described in this paper. In the over 400K SLOCS currently integrated, there are over two hundred system parameters in use and we expect to have more than twice that many by the end of the project.

Conclusion

The development of the CAATS system has seen the following pattern again and again:

- Ada design in support of behavior adaptable through configuration data

- requires default behavior during software development and

- ASIS tools to maintain code-data consistency during system integration and maintenance.

Other examples that we believe are common for many systems include the following:

- CAATS software is capable of detecting a number of erroneous <u>system events</u> (e.g. storage problems, disk availability or some other problems) that need to be reported to the maintenance personnel. The actual text of the message is adaptable and the fast load file requires that each and every event that the system can detect is provided with appropriate text. During development a default text can be used for as long as the developers can understand the message being issued. Before delivery, ASIS tools are used to ensure that fast load files with text messages for the end-user are in fact consistent with the actual set of events that the software can report.

- When a user request cannot be accomplished, CAATS application software returns a <u>semantic response</u>, a description of what went wrong and why. Different semantic responses have to be presented to the user as different text messages. Again, during development, a default textual representation will suffice as long as the developers can understand it. And again, late in the integration phase, configuration data that describe each and every semantic response that the system can return has to be prepared for the end-user.

In the past, CAATS has made use of a variety of ad-hoc development tools to help manage this kind of configuration data. It is only through the experiences of iterative software development and working to keep the system integrated at all times, that we have discovered the need for such tools. Our current focus is on enhancing the "integration toolset" to exploit the capabilities offered by ASIS.

References

[1] ISO/IEC 8652:1995, Information Technology - Programming Languages, their environments and system software interfaces - Programming Language Ada.

[2] Association for Computing Machinery (ACM) Special Interest Group in Ada (SIGAda) ASISWG/ISO/IEC JTC 1 SC 22/WG 9 ASISRG, ASIS WOrking Draft, Version 2.0.j, 1 November 1996, available World Wide Web site at => hppt://www.acm.org/ sigada/WG/asiswg

[3] Architecture of ASIS - A tool to Support Code Analysis of Complex Systems, Colket, et el. ACM Ada Letters, Volume XVII, Jan/Feb 1997

[4] Philippe Kruchten & Christopher Thompson, "An Object-Oriented, Distributed Architecture for Large Scale Ada Systems," Proceedings of the TRI-Ada '94 Conference, Baltimore, November 6-11, 1994, ACM

[5] Ch. J. Thompson and V. Celier, "DVM: an object-oriented framework for building large distributed Ada systems," Proc. of Tri-Ada'95, Anaheim, Ca., Nov. 1995, pp.

[6] Philippe Kruchten, Christopher J. Thompson, "Iterative Software Development for Large Ada Programs," Alfred Strohmeier (Ed.), Reliable Software Technologies - Ada-Europe'96: proceedings, Lecture Notes in Computer Science, vol 1088, Springer, Ada-Europe International Conference on Reliable SoftwareTechnologies Montreux, Switzerland, June 10-14 1996, ISBN 3-540-61317-X

[7] ISO/IEC 12227:1994, Information Technology - Programming languages, their environments and system software interfaces - SQL/Ada Module Description Language SAMeDL

Supporting Ada 95 Passive Partitions in a Distributed Environment

Frank Mueller

Humboldt-Universität zu Berlin, Institut für Informatik, 10099 Berlin (Germany)
e-mail: mueller@informatik.hu-berlin.de   phone: (+49) (30) 20181-276

Abstract. Ada 95 passive partitions, containing passive library units, provide the means to distribute data within a network of workstations. This paper shows how passive partitions can be implemented *via* distributed shared virtual memory (DSM). DSM provides the logical view of a portion of memory shared between physically distributed workstations within a network. In this paper, we relate design issues and operational characteristics of DSM systems to the semantics of shared passive library units as specified in the Ada 95 distributed system annex. We designed and implemented such a DSM system, operating at the granularity of pages, in a portable fashion over POSIX threads. The DSM system establishes its own communication services and is completely independent of any Ada runtime system support. Protected objects are supported *via* a novel prioritized protocol for distributed mutual exclusion. We integrated the DSM system with the Gnu Ada Translator (Gnat) and its environment to support active partitions. The DSM system integration required minimal changes to the Gnat environment and remains completely transparent to the user and the Ada runtime system. This is the first implementation of shared passive library units within an Ada 95 compilation environment, to our knowledge. The DSM support can provide considerable performance advantages over alternative approaches with repeated remote accesses, since with DSM only the first access to remote data results in communication overhead while consecutive accesses may take the same time as local memory accesses. Using the DSM paradigm, distributed applications can be designed to access distributed shared data efficiently. Furthermore, the shared memory model inherent to the Ada language can be used without modifications in a distributed environment.

1   Introduction

Distributed systems are gaining in popularity because they provide a cost-effective means to exploit the existing processing power of networks of workstations. Nonetheless, there are a number of problems associated with the transition to distributed systems, which often limit the performance gains.

One problem is caused by the communication medium between processing nodes (workstations), which often creates a bottleneck. Recent advances increase the throughput of communications by at least an order of magnitude (*e.g.*, FDDI,

FastEther, ATM), which improves the situation to some extent. However, access to data on remote nodes will always be slower than access to local data. Thus, limiting the number of remote accesses will always be a design goal of distributed systems.

Another problem is rooted in the absence of a global state and the absence of an easily understood programming model to address this issue. As a result, distributed algorithms are often hard to understand and require explicit communication directives (*e.g.* message passing). Simple solutions often employ a centralized approach, where a single server provides a global state to its clients, but the server may create a bottleneck again.

An alternative solution is provided by *distributed virtual shared memory (DSM)* [21, 22]. DSM provides the logical view of a portion of an address space, which is shared between physically distributed processing nodes, *i.e.* a global state. Address references can be distinguished between local memory accesses and DSM accesses, *i.e.* an architecture with non-uniform memory access (NUMA) is created. However, the well-understood paradigm of concurrent programming can be used without any changes, since the communication between nodes is transparent to the programmer.

The distributed systems annex of Ada 95 [8] supports the abstraction of global data shared between processing nodes *via shared passive library units* associated with a certain node (called a *passive partition*). Passive partitions can be supported in various way. For example, message passing or remote procedure calls (RPC) could be employed to fetch data of passive libraries from a certain node each time it is accessed. A much more efficient alternative is provided by implementing passive partitions *via* DSM. Here, only the first data access results in communication overhead to obtain ownership of the data. While a node owns the data, consecutive accesses are as fast as local memory accesses. This paper describes how the Ada 95 model of passive partitions can be mapped onto the DSM model.

2 The DSM Model

DSM can be implemented in hardware or in software. This paper focuses on the latter since it is aimed at existing networks of workstations. A major distinction between different DSM systems is given by the granularity of shared data. Sharing can be accomplished at the word level, the page level, at the scope of objects or within tuples. This paper focuses on page sharing because accesses can be monitored at this level *via* operating system and hardware support available in most systems. Figure 1 depicts such a system with a varying number of CPUs per node (single processor or shared-memory multi-processors) connected by an arbitrary communication medium. A portion of each node's addressing space is reserved for DSM data. While only a subset of all DSM pages may be accessible at a node at a given time (as depicted by the darker shading), this local DSM view is transparent to the user. To the user, the DSM portion of the addressing space seems as a globally consistent, shared data area. For simplicity, it is assumed for now that read and write accesses are not distinguished and that se-

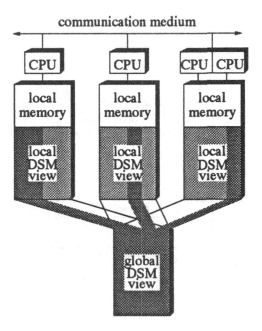

Fig. 1. Schematic View of a DSM System

quential consistency [14] is preserved, *i.e.* memory accesses are globally ordered and a page is owned by one and only one node at a time. These assumptions will be lifted later.

The operational model can be described as follows. Initially, each DSM page is owned by a single designated node. A page table is initialized on each node with the initial owner for each page. If a node accesses data within a page that it owns (darker shading in Figure 1), the data is readily available and the access has the same characteristics as a local memory access. Conversely, if an access references a page that the node does not own (lighter shading in Figure 1), the access is deferred and a remote page request is issued to the owner of the page. When the page is received from the remote node, the access is finally granted.

This exchange of pages is depicted in Figure 2. The pages currently not owned by a node are protected, *i.e.* an access to the page causes a memory fault, for example on node 1. The memory fault is reported to a worker, who determines the (probable) owner of the page and sends a request to the remote owner (node 2). This request is received by the communication server of node 2, where the local page table is consulted. If the node does not own the page anymore, the request is forwarded to its probable owner (node 3). If the communication server on node 3 determines that it still owns the page, it delegates a worker to act upon the page request. The worker invalidates (protects) the page on node 3 and sends the page content directly to the requesting node 1. The communication server of the requesting node 1 then delegates a (possibly different) worker to act upon the sent page. The worker validates the page on node 1 and enables access to the page. Had there been more intermediate nodes, the original page request would have been forwarded along a chain of probable owners. But in the end, the request would be handled by the actual owner (node 3 in the example) as described before.

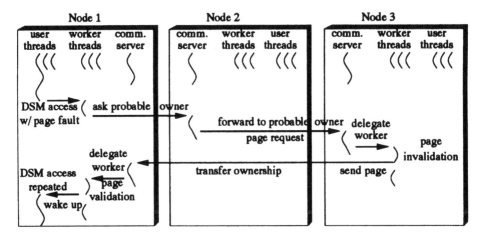

Fig. 2. Operational Model for Page Fault Handling

This model has been be implemented in an environment where nodes are represented by processes. The processes can be distributed arbitrarily on different workstations, possibly also with multiple processes on one workstations. Within each process, different threads of control may be created by an application on the user level while system-level threads include workers and the communication server. Worker threads are delegated to act upon page faults that occurred within a user thread. Among other requests, worker threads also handle page invalidations if the communication server receives a page request for a page that the current node owns. Generally, workers handle any requests that may involve more time-consuming actions. Similarly, the communication server is implemented as a separate thread of control. Its main purpose is to serve as a gate for incoming messages, handle less time-consuming messages right away and delegate more time-consuming requests to workers. This specialization of assigned tasks provides better responsiveness than a monolithic single server model since an I/O-bound or communication-intensive thread blocks until the I/O has been performed while other threads may continue to run.

3 Ada 95 Shared Passive Library Units

The distributed systems annex of the Ada 95 LRM [8] distinguishes between *active* partitions, which are equivalent to a regular Ada 95 program with one or more threads of control (environment task plus user-defined tasks), and *passive* partitions without a thread of control. A distributed program comprises a set of partitions, which can be mapped onto processing nodes (for active partitions) or storage nodes (for passive partitions).

A passive partition contains a set of *shared passive library units*, which are restricted on their references such that they can neither contain a remote access to data within active partitions nor require a thread of control. It furthermore defines shared passive library units as a means for "managing global data between active partitions".

A passive library unit is preelaborated and can be syntactically specified by the pragma Shared_Passive[(library_unit_name)]; . Additional legality rules restrict such a library to essentially the declaration of constants, types, data, and protected types without entries.

4 Mapping Passive Partitions onto DSM

By mapping the Ada 95 model onto the DSM model, the data declared within a shared passive library unit can be represented as the DSM data residing on (possibly protected) pages. The initial owner of a page is the passive partition that the shared passive library belongs to. The DSM system threads (workers and communication server) become an integral part of the runtime system.

4.1 Multiple Writer Protocol

A DSM with a single owner consistency protocol guarantees that at most one active partition may access the data of a passive library at a time. We call this model the single-reader/single-writer (SRSW) protocol. Alternatively, a multi-reader/single-writer (MRSW) protocol may be used in conjunction with data declarations within passive partitions. MRSW provides either read access to the same DSM page (and hence the associated data) of more than one node at a time or write access for exactly one node. Multiple readers form a so-called *copy set* that is represented as a tree of nodes rooted in the first reader. Consider the left picture of example in Figure 3. As a node R requests read access, it may receive a copy of the page from any node in the copy set (say node C). Node R is subsequently inserted into the copy set by node C, *i.e.* node R becomes a child of node C (right picture of Figure 3).

When a node W requests write access, it contacts the root node T of the copy set (*via* a chain of probable owners), also depicted on the right side of Figure 3. Node T then sends a request to invalidate the page (represented as dashed lines) to all its immediate children. Each node C in the copy set propagates this request to its children, invalidates the page, awaits the children's acknowledgment (unless it is a leaf) and sends an acknowledgment to its parent (dotted lines). When T receives an acknowledgment, all copies of the page have been invalidated. Thus, T may now transfer ownership of the page to node W, the requesting writer. The MRSW protocol provides more potential for parallelism than the SRSW

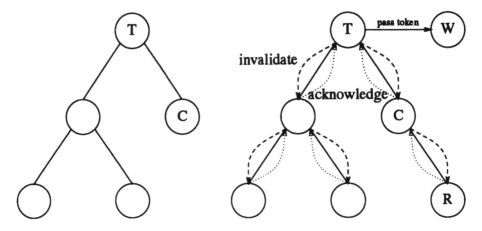

Fig. 3. Example for Multiple Reader Protocol

protocol at the expense of additional communication to invalidate a page. We may give the user the option to choose the protocol for data declaration with a default of the MRSW protocol (see [17] for more details).

4.2 Protected Objects

The protocols discussed so far can be used in conjunction with regular data declarations within passive partitions. However, a sequence of accesses to some data (*e.g.* a read followed by an increment and a write) may not be consistent without synchronization since other active partitions may access the data in between. To guarantee mutually exclusive access, the data should be encapsulated in a protected object. Since protected types within shared libraries are limited to protected procedures and functions within the body, *i.e.* protected entries are not allowed, the protection can be realized by simple mutual exclusion as opposed to the more general "eggshell model" required for protected entries [7, 4]. However, a protocol for *distributed* mutual exclusion has to be provided since protected objects within the passive partition may be accessed from different nodes (active partitions).

A simple protocol for distributed mutual exclusion could be implemented on top of the SRSW protocol. A POSIX mutex object is declared as DSM data (see POSIX threads for details [23]). *Local* mutual exclusion *via* pthread_mutex_lock results in an attempt to lock this mutex. The access may trigger a page request through the SRSW protocol before the local lock may succeed. However, this simple protocol is implementation-dependent on the POSIX threads library since the internal structure of the mutex object is transparent and may contain references to the local Pthreads kernel. In general, this approach is non-portable, in particular for heterogeneous environments.

An improved protocol still utilizes the SRSW protocol but implements local mutual exclusion as an indivisible operation (*e.g.*, *via* test-and-set) on a DSM data object. The access may also trigger a page request but the approach is portable, even for heterogeneous environments. Unfortunately, this protocol may not fully utilize potential parallelism since multiple readers (protected functions) could not access the protected object at the same time.

When the MRSW protocol is used in conjunction with an indivisible operation on DSM data, multiple concurrent readers could be permitted. But the MRSW protocol may admit new readers even after a write attempt has been issued for a protected object. In other words, accesses may not be granted in the same order that they occurred. This violates the Ada semantics of protected objects. Furthermore, accesses to a protected object may be issued at different priority levels. Clearly, a more sophisticated protocol is required.

We have designed a prioritized token-passing protocol for distributed mutual exclusion to address these issues [18]. The unprioritized version is a modified MRSW protocol where requests are served FIFO. Thus, multiple readers are only admitted for adjacent requests, i.e. if no write request was issued between the two read requests. The prioritized version tags probable owner chains with the priority level of former requests. This allows future requests to be forwarded along different chains depending on their priority. A request at the highest priority propagates straight to the actual owner (via some intermediate nodes). A low priority request travels to the last node L requesting access at the same priority or the next higher priority. The request is then stored in this node L. Thus, a distributed FIFO queue of requests is formed and mutual exclusion is granted for members of this queue in the prioritized order. Furthermore, the the protocol requires that additional information is stored along probable owners for "high" priority requests to avoid race conditions. However, the algorithmic details are beyond the scope of this paper (see [18]).

The data for a protected object is passed along with the token for mutual exclusion so that access faults and page transfers are not needed. Instead, the data is validated when the token arrives and invalidated when the token is passed on. A protected procedure requires an exclusive write lock within the token protocol. Simultaneous invocations of protected functions, on the other hand, can exploit their potential parallelism through concurrent read locks. Thus, the prioritized token protocol exhibits the required semantic behavior in terms of the Ada language combined with the benefits of parallel executions.

5 Integration into the Gnat Environment

The Gnu Ada Translator (Gnat) [24] supports the distributed systems annex of Ada 95 via the distributed system annex environment (DSAE), which is available separate from Gnat. DSAE consists of a tool Gnatdist [11] and a library Garlic [12]. Gnatdist is responsible for configuring the partitions of a distributed Ada 95 program. It supports the mapping of partitions onto nodes and drives the compilation and linking of the different components into one program per partition, i.e. it supports the post-compilation semantics of the distributed systems annex. Garlic is a library, which provides the interface between the network and the distributed application. A central synchronizer server handles partition identification and requires that each node register with this server upon elaboration. The library also supports remote subprogram calls that correspond to the pragma Remote_Call_Interface[(library_unit_name)]; and synchronizes the termination of the distributed nodes. However, DSAE does not support shared passive library units.

DSAE and the mapping of passive partitions onto DSM can be combined in one system as depicted in Figure 4. The DSM system provides its own runtime library built on top of POSIX threads [23, 19]. The DSM system can be readily integrated since the Gnu Ada Runtime Library (GNARL) also relies on POSIX threads and does not require any modifications for DSM inclusion (except for DSM initialization). Once the DSM runtime system is initialized, it spawns a pool of workers and a communication server on each node to support a DSM system efficiently in a decentralized fashion. In contrast, DSAE still relies on a centralized synchronization server, which may create a bottleneck. Nonetheless, the Garlic library is used for partition handling, i.e. distributed creation and termination.

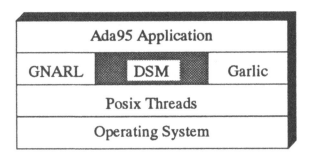

Fig. 4. Layering of Runtime-System Components

Currently, all passive library units reside on one node upon program start and are distributed upon request, i.e. whenever a page fault occurs on a remote node. However, the Gnatdist tool could be enhanced to support the distribution of passive library units onto arbitrary nodes. This would require the generation of a mapping table between host names and page addresses corresponding to the data of the passive library units. Minor modifications of the linking process should be added to include passive library units and the DSM library. Furthermore, the Gnat compiler currently ignores the pragma Shared_Passive[(library_unit_name)]; and needs to be enhanced to check for semantic restrictions on library dependences. The code generator needs to emit different code for protected objects within passive libraries. Instead of calling mutual exclusion routines of the Ada runtime system, mutual exclusion primitives of the DSM system need to be invoked to provide mutually exclusive access on a distributed level. Protected functions of a passive partition acquire a distributed read lock while protected procedures acquire a write lock according to the prioritized token-based protocol for distributed mutual exclusion described in the last section.

6 Future Work

Current work includes the implementation of the protocol for prioritized token-based distributed mutual exclusion. Furthermore, support for Ada 95 passive libraries on heterogeneous distributed environments is being added in a portable way. So far, heterogeneous support within our environment has been realized for C programs, only. Heterogeneous system support requires modifications to the Gnatdist tool to support data conversion between different architectural formats. A number of improvements are being worked on in the DSM runtime system to improve throughput by reducing the amount of required communication, including the support of different coherence protocols and the distinction between read and write accesses. These issues are fully transparent to the user and the Ada 95 system, including the DSAE subsystem.

7 Related Work

DSM systems have been an increasingly popular area of research. Several overviews compare different systems [21, 22]. Software implementations of DSM, such as discussed in our paper, can be distinguished by their reliance on modifications of the operating system, source language, compiler, and runtime system. We focus strictly on runtime system modifications, since we are most concerned with a portable implementation of an existing language construct (Ada 95 shared passive library units). These systems handle data sharing at the page level using page protection mechanisms as described in our work. TreadMarks is a page-based system supporting different consistency protocols and multiple writers [2]. Midway also supports multiple consistency protocols, which can be changed dynamically [5]. Filaments employs a set of lightweight worker threads (similar to our worker threads) to act upon remote processing requests quickly, using adaptive schemes to dynamically reconfigure data placement [15]. The consistency models of these system require explicit synchronization points within a program. Our approach uses a stronger consistency model without explicit synchronization points, which avoids modifications to the compiler and facilitates the integration into existing Ada environments. Other DSM systems handle data at the level of objects (*e.g.* Orca [3]), tuples (*e.g.* Linda [1]), or at variable sizes (*e.g.* Munin [6]).

Midway's entry consistency associates DSM data with locks and transfers the data when locks are passed between nodes [5]. This model is resembled by our handling of protected objects within passive partitions. However, we use a *prioritized* protocol for distributed mutual exclusion while their protocol resembles the much simpler SRSW protocol adapted for mutual exclusion. Mutual exclusion along the lines of the SRSW protocol was first described by Naimi *et. al.* [20]. The MRSW protocol resembles the decentralized dynamic manager algorithm by Li and Hudak [13]. Notice that Li and Hudak's algorithm reduced to writers only is equivalent to the token-based algorithm by Naimi *at. al.*.

A software component to support DSM for Ada was proposed by Kermarrec and Pautet [9]. Their implementation consists of primitive operations to manipulate the distributed shared data, such as peek, poke, copy, alloc, and free. Also, an outline for a generic shared memory manager is given, which can be instantiated for different data types to address the strong typing of the Ada language. An automata describes the transitions between DSM operations. However, the paper does not give enough detail to relate primitive operations to the handling of data pages. It is not quite clear to which extent the proposed system has been implemented or how it might be integrated with an existing Ada compiler.

The DSM variant of a tuple space, as implemented in Linda, has been discussed in the context of Ada. The design issues and interface specification have been discussed for implementing Linda over Ada 83 [10] and Ada 95 [16]. The latter work has also been extended to discuss how Ada 95 passive packages could be supported by such a Linda system [25]. A preliminary library has been developed but the authors admit that the layering over Linda is likely to induce a considerable performance overhead. They suggest an intermediate compilation step to transform passive library units into Linda-like Ada packages to support heterogeneous systems in the future. An integration in the Gnat environment would require changes at the compiler or pre-processor level. In contrast, our DSM system can be readily integrated into Gnat and can be extended to heterogeneous systems almost without compiler modifications. (The only modification would be to require a uniform data alignment for different architectures, which can be easily integrated into the back-end of the compiler.) Otherwise, simple modifications to the Gnatdist tool suffice.

8 Conclusion

We have shown how Ada 95 passive library units can be implemented via distributed shared virtual memory. A DSM system operating at the granularity of pages can be implemented in a portable fashion with an independent communication subsystem. Protected objects can be supported by our prioritized protocol for distributed mutual exclusion. A sample DSM system has been designed and implemented over POSIX threads. It has been integrated into the environment of the Gnu Ada Translator. Due to the independent design of the DSM system, including its own communication layer, the system integration requires minimal changes to the Gnat environment. To the user as well as the Ada runtime system, the DSM system remains entirely transparent. This is the first implementation of shared passive library units within an Ada 95 compilation environment, to our knowledge. The resulting system experiences a communication overhead for the first access to shared data not present on the current node since that data has to be requested from a remote partition. Once the ownership of the DSM data has been transfered to the current node, consecutive accesses take the same time as local memory accesses. Thus, for multiple, consecutive accesses the communication overhead only has to be paid once for data accesses within passive partitions implemented via DSM, where a message-passing or RPC implementation would have to pay the communication overhead for each data reference. Using the DSM paradigm, distributed applications can be designed to access distributed shared data efficiently by avoiding (or at least reducing) simultaneous / interleaved access to this data from different partitions. Furthermore, the shared memory model inherent to the Ada language can be used without modifications in a distributed environment.

References

1. S. Ahuja, N. Carriero, and D. Gelernter. Linda and friends. *IEEE Computer*, 19(8), May 1986.
2. Cristiana Amza, Alan L. Cox, Sandhya Dwarkadas, Pete Keleher, Honghui Lu, Ramakrishnan Rajamony, Weimin Yu, and Willy Zwaenepoel. Treadmarks: Shared memory computing on networks of workstations. *IEEE Computer*, February 1996.
3. H. Bal and A. Tanenbaum. Distributed programming with shared data. In *International Conference on Computer Languages*, pages 82–91, 1988.
4. J. G. P. Barnes. *Programming in Ada 95*. Addison-Wesley, 1996.
5. B. Bershad, M. Zekauskas, and W. Sawdon. The midway distributed shared memory system. In *COMPCON Conference Proceedings*, pages 528–537, 1993.
6. J. Carter, J. Bennet, and W. Zwaenepoel. Implementation and performance of munin. In *Symposium on Operating Systems Principles*, pages 152–164, 1991.
7. E.W. Giering, Frank Mueller, and T.P. Baker. Implementing Ada 9x features using POSIX threads: Design issues. In *TRI-Ada '93 Proceedings*, pages 214–228. ACM, September 1993.
8. ISO/IEC. *ISO/IEC 8652L 1995 (E), Information Technology – Programming Languages – Ada*, February 1995.
9. Y. Kermarrec and L. Pautet. A distributed shared virtual memory for Ada 83 and Ada 9x applications. In *TRI-Ada*, pages 242–251, 1993.
10. Y. Kermarrec and L. Pautet. Ada-linda: A powerful paradigm for programming distributed Ada applications. In *TRI-Ada*, pages 438–445, 1994.
11. Y. Kermarrec and L. Pautet. Gnatdist: A configuration language for distributed Ada 95. In *TRI-Ada*, 1996.
12. Y. Kermarrec, L. Pautet, and S. Tardieu. Garlic: Generic Ada reusable library for interpartition communication. In *TRI-Ada*, pages 263–269, 1995.
13. K. Li and P. Hudak. Memory coherence in shared virtual memory systems. *ACM Transactions of Computer Systems*, 7(4):321–359, November 1989.
14. J. L. Lo and S. J. Eggers. Improving balanced scheduling with compiler optimizations that increase instruction-level parallelism. In *ACM SIGPLAN Conference on Programming Language Design and Implementation*, June 1995.
15. D. K. Lowenthal, V. W. Freeh, and G. R. Andrews. Using fine-grain threads and run-time decision making in parallel computing. *Journal of Parallel and Distributed Computing*, August 1996.
16. K. Lundqvist and G. Wall. Using object oriented methods in Ada 95 to implement linda. In *Ada Europe*, 1996.
17. F. Mueller. Distributed shared-memory threads: DSM-threads. In *Workshop on Parallel and Distributed Runtime Systems*, April 1997.
18. F. Mueller. Prioritized token-based mutual exclusion for distributed systems. In *Workshop on Parallel and Distributed Real-Time Systems*, April 1997.

19. Frank Mueller. A library implementation of POSIX threads under UNIX. In *Proceedings of the USENIX Conference*, pages 29–41, January 1993.

20. M. Naimi, M. Trehel, and A. Arnold. A log(N) distributed mutual exclusion algorithm based on path reversal. *JPDC: Journal of Parallel and Distributed Computing*, 34(1):1–13, April 1996.

21. B. Nitzberg and V. Lo. Distributed shared memory: A survey of issues and algorithms. *IEEE Computer*, 24(8):52–60, August 1991.

22. J. Protic, M. Tomasevic, and V. Milutinovic. Distributed shared memory: Concepts and systems. *IEEE Parallel and Distributed Technology*, pages 63–79, Summer 1996.

23. Technical Committee on Operating Systems and Application Environments of the IEEE. *Portable Operating System Interface (POSIX)—Part 1: System Application Program Interface (API)*, 1996. ANSI/IEEE Std 1003.1, 1995 Edition, including 1003.1c: Amendment 2: Threads Extension [C Language].

24. New York University. The Gnu NYU Ada Translator (GNAT). Available by anonymous FTP from cs.nyu.edu.

25. G. Wall and K. Lundqvist. Shared packages through linda. In *Ada Europe*, 1996.

An Ada Library to Program Fault-Tolerant Distributed Applications *

F. Guerra, J. Miranda, A. Alvarez and S. Arévalo

University of Las Palmas de Gran Canaria and Technical University of Madrid
*fguerra@cic.teleco.ulpgc.es, jmiranda@cma.ulpgc.es,
aalvarez@dit.upm.es, sarevalo@fi.upm.es*

Abstract. This paper describes a library written in Ada which facilitates the construction of fault-tolerant distributed applications based on the active replication paradigm [18]. The library, called Group_IO [10], offers a simple interface to the implementation of reliable, atomic, causal, and uniform multicast. The work on Group_IO has been motivated by our experience with Isis [3] and similar reliable multicast frameworks. The library allows also client–server interactions where the client may be a group—this interaction is not supported by ISIS— and relies on an own consensus protocol [8, 9] to implement the uniform broadcast protocols. Group_IO is the base on which the programming language Drago [2, 15, 16] has been implemented, however it does not require Drago for its use.

Keywords: Distributed Systems, Fault-Tolerant Systems, Ada, Isis.

1 Introduction

The increasing dependence of modern society on computer systems calls for increasing degrees of reliability which become very expensive to implement with traditional hardware and software techniques. In particular, the use of ad-hoc replicated hardware to mask out failures requires special components with costs much higher than the ones of standard, mass produced hardware. As a result, the use of modern solutions in which the tolerance to hardware failures is obtained by means of specialized software running on top of standard, inexpensive hardware, is attracting a considerable degree of attention. However, the construction of this specialized software is a rather complex task, and so the need for software libraries that support these new programming paradigms arises.

The basic approach to fault-tolerance using standard hardware components is the use of distributed systems with hardware and software replication. The two main software techniques used there are the primary-backup approach, and the active replication paradigm [19]. Compared with the primary-backup approach, the active replication technique offers the additional advantage that it

* *This work has been partially funded by the Spanish Research Council (CICYT), contract numbers TIC94-0162-C02-01 and TIC96-0614.*

allows for continuous service in the presence of failures. That is, the system can continue giving service without the need to interrupt for any length of time to be reconfigured or in any way recover it after a failure.

In order to build programs with active replication and minimal additional effort from the programmer, there is a need for transparent mechanisms to handle the communication when a group of replicas receives a service request or requests an external service [13]. In particular, for every single message sent to a group of process replicas, the underlying system should transparently ensure that the message is replicated and a copy of it sent to each replica of the process—this is known as "1-to-n" communication. When all interaction among processes takes the form of message exchanges, all replicas of the same process must receive the same messages, even in the presence of (partial) failures—this is known as "all-or-none" communication—and in the same order. Symmetrically, (replicated) messages sent by the replicas themselves shall be filtered so that only a single copy of each replicated message is actually issued to the rest of the system—this is known as "n-to-1" communication.

The problem of "1-to-n" communication has been discussed at length in numerous publications, where is has received the name of reliable broadcast [4] [17] [14]. By contrast, references to "n-to-1" communication cannot be easily found.

It has been proven that uniform reliable—atomic—and totally ordered broadcast is equivalent to distributed consensus [11]. In the consensus protocol, a number of processes start each one proposing a possibly different value, and at the end of the protocol all (correct) processes end up agreeing on the same value, even if some of them happen to fail during the execution of the protocol itself. To see how both mechanisms are equivalent, one only needs to consider a (sequence of) consensus where the values to agree upon are the actual messages the different processes wish to broadcast, and to understand the agreement to select a particular message as the delivery[2] of that message in all the processes involved in that consensus. In addition, when one process finds that its message has not been selected in a consensus, it just stubbornly insists on proposing the same message until it eventually gets selected. As a result, all processes involved in the (sequence of) consensus end up receiving the same messages and in the same (total) order.

The work on Group_IO has been motivated by our experience with Isis, with similar reliable multicast frameworks, and with the development of different consensus protocols. By contrast, systems such as PVM [6] and MPI [7] had no influence on Group_IO as they only provide a basic broadcast service, without features like causality, order or atomicity, which are needed to program replicas in the fault-tolerant active replication model.

After this brief introduction, in the next two sections we present a short description of ISIS and Drago, respectively. We then have a section on the interface

---

[2] For other than the basic broadcast, *delivery* of messages is an event different from *reception*; the distinction is needed in order to enforce the required message order, in spite of the actual transmission times.

offered by Group_IO, followed by another section with some programming examples. Three more sections then discuss implementation aspects of Group_IO, and its relation with Ada 95 and Drago. The paper closes with some conclusions, and with references to related work.

2 ISIS

ISIS [3] is a toolkit that goes a long way in the active replication line just described and which has been the original inspiration for Group_IO. In ISIS programmers can define groups of processes and then refer to them by a single name. Communication with a group of processes is by means of (different versions of) *reliable*[3] *broadcast*[4], which can be used to implement replicated (as well as *cooperative*[5]) process groups.

However, from our experience with ISIS the system has three major drawbacks. First, ISIS broadcast is not *uniform*, that is, there is no guarantee that non-failed processes receive a message which has anyhow been received by a process failing subsequently to the reception of that message. And the problem with this approach is that if the failed process has taken any actions after receiving that message and before failing, its remaining replicas will be out of sync with it. As a consequence, it is close to impossible to implement active process replication in ISIS along the lines described above.

The second problem with ISIS is that it does not support full n-to-1 communication[6]. Last but not least, ISIS provides no linguistic support. In fact, ISIS is just a collection of libraries written in C, and as such its use leads to code which is both complex and error-prone.

3 Drago

Drago[16] is an experimental language developed as an extension of Ada for the construction of fault-tolerant distributed applications. The hardware assumptions are a distributed system with no memory shared among the different nodes, a reliable communication network with no partitions, and *fail-silent* nodes. (That is nodes, which once failed are never heard from again by the rest of the system.)

The language is the result of an effort to impose discipline and give linguistic support to the main concepts of ISIS[3], as well as to experiment with the group

---

[3] What ISIS calls *reliable* is actually called *atomic* by other authors to reflect its "all-or-none" property.

[4] Actually, a kind of *multicast* remote procedure call, but we will use here the term *broadcast* to follow ISIS convention.

[5] Member processes of a cooperative group usually do not perform exactly the same function, and make use of this fact to "cooperate" in the provision of one or more services.

[6] In particular, when a replicated process group issues a call to another process, be it a single process or a group, as many calls as group members are issued.

communication paradigm. To help build fault-tolerant distributed applications, Drago explicitly supports two process group paradigms, *replicated process groups* and *cooperative process groups*. Replicated process groups allow for the programming of fault-tolerance applications according to the active replication model[18], while cooperative process groups permit programmers to express parallelism and so increase throughput.

A process group in Drago is actually a collection of *agents*, which is the way processes are called in the language. Agents are rather similar in appearance to Ada tasks (they have an internal state not directly accessible from outside the agent, an independent flow of control, and special operations named *entries*) although they are the unit of distribution in Drago and so perform a role similar to Ada 95 active partitions and Ada 83 programs. Each agent resides in a single node of the network, although several agents may reside in the same node. A Drago program is composed of a number of agents residing at a number of nodes.

Aside from distribution, the main difference they have with Ada tasks is that calls to its entries are automatically ordered by the underlying Drago global runtime message system to enforce reliable, causal, uniform coordination among the agents of the same group. This is actually the essence of Drago, and what makes it most useful.

4 Group_IO Interface

Group_IO is a library built as a generic Ada package that provides operations and types to perform distributed client-server interactions among Ada programs organized as groups according to the active replication model. In this model clients—either a single Ada program or a group of them—issue requests to servers made up of groups of Ada program replicas—running in different network nodes—and then wait for replies. Group_IO transparently masks out possible failures of nodes running the Ada program replicas.

Group_IO provides a generic interface that expects the user to define the maximum size of requests and replies, the retransmition time, and other parameters that depend on the particular system and distributed application at hand. Basic types provided by a generic instance of Group_IO are:

```
subtype T_Data is STRING (1 .. Max_Length_Data);
subtype T_Name is STRING (1 .. Max_Length_Name);
type T_Group_Id is private;
type T_Request_Id is private;
```

All the information contained in the requests and replies sent through the network are strings of type *T_Data*. It is the responsibility of user programs to know how to use the messages delivered and to perform type conversion when needed. Group names are strings of type *T_Name*. Group_IO also provides two types to declare handlers for groups and requests, respectively: *T_Group_Id* and *T_Request_Id*.

The way to use Group_IO depends on whether the user software behaves as a client, a server, or a replica.

Client interface:

- Before a client requests a service to a server group, it must start with a call to join that group as a client:

```
procedure Join_Group_Client (Grp_Name : in  T_Name;
                             Grp      : out T_Group_Id);
```

  Join_Group_Client creates the data structures and tasks associated with the client role and returns a group handler (*Grp*.) The exception *Inactive_Group* is raised in case there is no group named Grp_Name.
- After a user program has obtained a group handler *Grp*, it can send a request to the associated group:

```
procedure Send_Request (Grp  : in  T_Group_Id;
                        Mess : in  T_Data;
                        Req  : out T_Request_Id);
```

  Send_Request blocks the caller only until the request arrives to all live members of server group *Grp*, and then it returns the request handler *Req*. The exception *Inactive_Group* is raised if the caller is not a client of group *Grp* or when no members of the group *Grp* are alive anymore.
- The number of replies is not fixed because members of a group may fail. A user program can get the number of pending replies—each group member gives its own reply—with the function:

```
function Replies_Number (Req : T_Request_Id) return Natural;
```

  The exception *Invalid_Handler* is raised when *Req* is an invalid request handler.
- After *Send_Request* returns the request handler, the user program can retrieve the replies received—all members of the server group reply—one by one:

```
procedure Receive_Reply(Req  : in out T_Request_Id;
                        Mess : out     T_Data);
```

  The exception *Invalid_Handler* is raised when Req is an invalid request handler; the exception *No_Replies* is raised when all replies from live members have already been delivered.
- A user program only gets the number of replies it wishes. In particular, it can use a reply before getting the next one, and this will be the usual case in which the first reply to arrive will be used and all the rest will be discarded. User programs can indicate that they do not wish to receive any more of the replies belonging to a certain request calling the procedure:

```
procedure Close_Request(Req : in out T_Request_Id);
```

  Close_Request either marks the handler *Req* as invalid or raises the exception *Invalid_Handler* if it is already invalid before the call.

Server interface:

- All server members must first join the group:

```
procedure Join_Group_Server(Grp_Name : in    T_Name)
                            Grp      : out  T_Group_Id);
```

Join_Group_Server creates the data structures and tasks associated with the server role and returns a group handler. The exception *Inactive_Group* is raised if there is no group named *Grp_Name*.
- Every member of the server group can get the next request made to the group:

```
procedure Receive_Request(Grp  : in  T_Group_Id;
                          Req  : out T_Request_Id;
                          Mess : out T_Data);
```

Receive_Request returns the handler *Req* associated with the request *Mess*. This handler is used later to send the associated reply. The exception *Inactive_Group* is raised when the user code calling *Receive_Request* is not a member of server group *Grp*.
- Servers send its replies associated to a request with the procedure:

```
procedure Send_Reply(Req  : in out T_Request_Id;
                     Mess : in     T_Data);
```

After the reply is sent, the handler becomes invalid—every group member can only send a single reply. The exception *Invalid_Handler* is raised when the handler *Req* is invalid.

Replicated client interface: To implement a fault-tolerant service by means of a group of replicas we should only use the server interface. However, when this group of replicas needs to request a service—the group of replicas can be client of any other group—it is necessary to add to the client interface some operations where the client's group of replicas is referenced.

- Every replica must still call first *Join_Group_Server* as before. However, before the group of replicas issues a request, every replica must execute the next procedure, passing the replica group handler *Replica_Grp* and the name of the server group *Grp_Name* as parameters:

```
procedure Join_Group_Client(Replica_Grp : in  T_Group_Id;
                            Grp_Name    : in  T_Name;
                            Grp         : out T_Group_Id);
```

Join_Group_Client creates the data structures and tasks associated with the replicated client role and returns a group handler. The exception *Inactive_Group* is raised when the caller is not a member of the group *Replica_Grp* or when there is no group named *Grp_Name*.

– When a replica sends a request to a server group, it must also pass the handler associated with the group of replicas.

```
procedure Send_Request(Replica_Grp : in  T_Group_Id;
                       Server_Grp  : in  T_Group_Id;
                       Mess        : in  T_Data;
                       Req         : out T_Request_Id);
```

Again, *Send_Request* blocks the caller only until the request arrives to all live members of server group *Grp*, and then returns the request handler *Req*. The exception *Inactive_Group* is raised when the caller is not a member of group *Replica_Grp*, the replica group is not a client of group *Grp*, or all members of group *Grp* have already failed.

– It is crucial that all the replicas have the same code, perform the same actions, and go through the same sequence of states, and in the same order. Group_IO delivers the same sequence of requests—server role—and replies— client role—to all replicas. However, it is necessary to call the next procedure to find out the kind of the next message delivered because requests and replies are delivered by different procedures[7].

```
type T_Operation_Id is  (Replica_Request, Replica_Reply, Final_Reply);

procedure Next_Operation(Replica_Grp : in  T_Group_Id;
                         Req         : out T_Request_Id;
                         Operation   : out T_Operation_Id);
```

Next_Operation returns the handler *Req* associated to the next request (or reply) and the kind of operation—*Operation* is equal to *Replica_Request* or *Replica_Reply*. This handler is also returned when there are no more replies associated with a request—*Operation* is equal to *Final_Reply*, and so does not need to call *Replies_Number* repeatedly. The exception *Inactive_Group* is raised when the caller is not a member of the group *Replica_Grp*.

5 Programming with Group_IO

Every user program must create its own instance of Group_IO, passing generic actual parameters defining its system and distributed application. For example:

```
with Group_IO;
package My_Group_IO is
        new Group_IO(Max_Length_Mess       => 128,
                     Max_Groups            => 5,
                     Max_Members_Per_Group => 15,
                     Max_Asinc             => 4);
```

My_Group_IO is an instance that defines the maximum length of a request or reply message; the maximum number of groups; the maximum number of

---

[7] This is particularly important for those cases in which the programming language used includes non-deterministic constructs, as is the case with Ada tasks; all non-determinism must then be resolved in the same way for all process replicas.

members per group; and the maximum number of requests that can be pending to be delivered to any server group member. Additional parameters of Group_IO take the default formal parameter values. Let's see some examples of use of *My_Group_IO*:

- **Server**. A server has a loop where it gets the requests, performs the service, and sends the associated reply.

```
with My_Group_IO;
use My_Group_IO;

procedure Server is
   Grp_Id    : T_Group_Id;
   Req_Id    : T_Request_Id;
   Req_Mess,
   Ans_Mess  : T_Data;
begin
   Join_Group_Server("G1", Grp_Id);            -- It is member of group G1
   loop
     Receive_Request(Grp_Id, Req_Id, Req_Mess); -- The next request is delivered
     -- ...                                      -- THE SERVICE IS PERFORMED
     -- ...                                      -- THE REPLY IS PLACED IN Ans_Mess
     Send_Reply(Req_Id, Ans_Mess);              -- The reply is sent
   end loop;
end Server;
```

- **Client**. This example presents the code associated with a client that sends a request and waits for all replies.

```
with My_Group_IO;
use My_Group_IO;

procedure Client is
   Grp_Id    : T_Group_Id;
   Req_Id    : T_Request_Id;
   Req_Mess,
   Ans_Mess  : T_Data;
begin
   Join_Group_Client("G1", Grp_Id);            -- It is client of group G1
   -- ...                                       -- THE REQUEST IS PLACED IN Req_Mess
   Send_Request(Grp_Id, Req_Mess, Req_Id);     -- The request is sent
   While Replies_Number(Req_Id)>0 loop         -- While there are replies
        Receive_Reply(Req_Id, Ans_Mess);       --     The next reply is delivered
        -- ...                                  --     THE REPLY CAN BE USED
   end loop;                                    -- end
   Close_Request(Req_Id);                       -- The handler is marked as invalid
end Client;
```

- **Replicated client**. Let's now see the code of a group of replicas which is simultaneously server and client of other groups.

```
with My_Group_IO;
use My_Group_IO;

procedure Client_Server_Replica is
   Replica_Grp_Id, Server_Grp_Id        : T_Group_Id;
   Req_Id                               : T_Request_Id;
   Replica_Req_Mess, Req_Mess, Ans_Mess : T_Data;
   OP                                   : T_Operation_Id;
begin
```

```
Join_Group_Server("G1", Replica_Grp_Id);        -- It is member of replicas group G1
Join_Group_Client(Replica_Grp_Id,               -- The group G1 is a client of
               "G2",                             -- group G2
               Server_Grp_Id);
-- ...                                           -- THE REQUEST IS PLACED IN
                                                 -- Replica_Req_Mess
Send_Request(Replica_Grp_Id, Server_Grp_Id,
             Replica_Req_Mess, Req_Id);          -- The request is sent
loop
    Next_Operation(Replica_Grp_Id, Req_Id, OP);-- The next event is received
    case OP is
       when Replica_Request =>
             Receive_Request(Replica_Grp_Id,     -- A Request is delivered
                             Req_Id,
                             Req_Mess);
             -- ...                              -- THE SERVICE IS PERFORMED
             -- ...                              -- THE REPLY IS PLACED IN Ans_Mess
             Send_Reply(Req_Id, Ans_Mess);       -- The reply is sent

       when Replica_Reply   =>
             Receive_Reply(Req_Id,               -- The next reply is delivered
                           Ans_Mess);
             -- ...                              -- THE REPLY CAN BE USED

       when Final_Reply     =>
             Close_Request (Req_Id);             -- The handler is invalid
    end case;
  end loop;
end Client_Server_Replica;
```

Next_Operation is also used when the group of replicas is just a client of various server groups because it must know the request handler associated with every delivered reply.

6   Group_IO Implementation

Group_IO is currently implemented over an Ethernet with Sun Sparc stations and uses Paradise [5] as its basic communication service—Paradise only blocks the task issuing an IO operation and not the whole Ada process. The protocols implemented in Group_IO assume a distributed hardware system with no memory shared among the different nodes, a reliable communication network with no partitions, and *fail-silent* hardware nodes; namely, when one of the nodes fails the rest of the system never hears from it again.

Each user program can be seen as a logical machine in the distributed system. Several logical machines may execute on the same physical machine, but each needs its own instance of Group_IO— see figure 1.

The Group_IO body is composed of three levels: Medium Access Level, Group Protocol Level, and User Operation Level. The Medium Access Level uses Paradise to get access to Berkeley sockets. The Group Protocol level uses the services of Medium Access Level to implement the multicast protocols [10] and provides the services required by the User Operation Level. Finally, the User Operation Level implements the user program interface.

Each Group_IO instance has common information used by all the three levels. For every group the user program belongs to, either as a client or as a server,

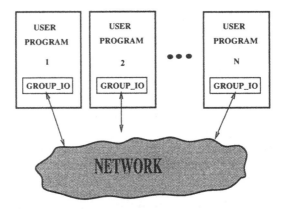

Fig. 1. User programs connected by Group_IO.

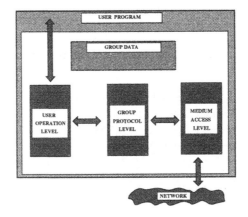

Fig. 2. Internal levels of Group_IO.

this information describes:

- Name of the group.
- Identity of the user program to communicate with the group.
- Role(s) of the program within the used group: client, server, or replica.
- View of the group (number of members and linear order of each one.)
- Pointers to the tasks that execute the different role(s) the user program has within the group.

There are two task types in the Group Protocol Level: the type T_Client executes the role associated with a client and the type T_Member defines the role associated with a server that is member of a group. As an example, the user program with the Group_IO instance shown in figure 3, is both a client of group A and a member of group B. Furthermore, this program communicates also with the rest of members of group B because t is also a client of this group—the members of group B may cooperate to give the requested services, this is known as intragroup interaction.

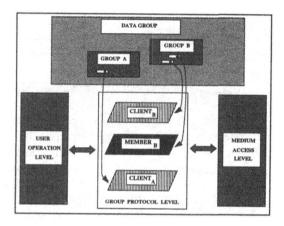

Fig. 3. Example of Group Protocol Level

Currently the groups configuration is static and it is specified by means of two files:

– *Logic_Names.Dat* defines the names associated with every user program, the Internet address (IP) of the machine where the program executes, and the port address (UDP) through which the program communicates. Each line of this file has the following format:

```
PROCESS_NAME, INTERNET_ADDR, PORT_NUMBER
```

– *Groups_Configuration.Dat* defines the names of the groups and the members of every group according to the next syntax:

```
GROUP_NAME := PROCESS_NAME {,PROCESS_NAME};
```

7   Group_IO and Ada 95

Group_IO has been implemented in Ada 83 and has been used with Ada 83 programs. We believe that some features of Ada 95 can be used to improve the implementation of Group_IO, protected objects in particular. What is not clear to us is whether we can take advantage of the distributed partition paradigm instead of a socket library. However, we don't see any problems for Ada 95 programs to make use of the Group_IO library.

A different issue is how distributed programs built with Ada and Group_IO (let's call them Group_IO programs) compare with distributed programs built with Ada 95 distributed active partitions.

One important difference between Group_IO programs and active partitions is that the first accept services explicitly issuing a *receive request* as part of their flow of control, while the second export *passive* subprograms declared in their RCI package specifications. This difference makes the first kind of programs deterministic in its behavior, while the behavior of the second ones is dependent on the runtime system. As we will see below, determinism is essential in the active replication model.

The main difference between Group_IO programs and the distributed programming model of Ada 95 is that Group_IO provides direct support for the active replication model in order to build fault-tolerant applications. Where Ada 95 provides a single remote call, Group_IO transparently gives programmers multiple *send_requests* to all the programs of a replicated group. And more important, the multiple *send_requests* are automatically coordinated so that all programs of the same group are guaranteed to receive the same *requests*, and in the same (causally consistent) order, even in the presence of hardware node failures midway in the sequence of calls. And because replicated Group_IO programs have a deterministic behavior all members of the same group go through the same sequence of internal states, and so give exactly the same replies to all incoming calls. This way live members of a group can mask out transparently the possible failure of other group members, something that cannot be obtained in Ada 95 without a considerable effort from the part of programmers.

On the question of what is the relation between Group_IO and the Distributed Systems Annex of Ada 95 and, in particular, on whether Group_IO can be integrated into the PCS to implement transparent replication of active partitions in Ada95, the answer is yes (with one natural caveat.)

There would be no need to change the specification of System.RPC, nor the compiler or the language itself, only rewrite the implementation of System.RPC so that it calls Group_IO when needed, that is, when the actual remote call is directed towards a procedure of a replicated partition. Whether a certain partition is replicated or not would be decided at configuration time (after compile time and before link time) and that information could be stored in a configuration file, from where the code of System.RPC would retrieve it at run-time.

It is clear nevertheless, that replicated partitions in no case could be serving more than one request at the same time. This is a restriction required not by Group_IO but by the replicated state-machine model, in orden to guarantee replica determinism.

8   Group_IO and Drago

The language Drago uses Group_IO as its communication subsystem and so supports the same group mechanisms as Group_IO. This similarity allows Ada and Drago programs to interoperate in a straightforward manner. For example, we can have one or several fault-tolerant services implemented in Drago executing in a distributed system, and then compile and run "Ada-with-Group_IO" clients that use those services in a manner analogous to the one described in section 5 above. The only thing the clients need to know are the logical names of the Drago groups that implement those services—and those names are within the configuration files. In this way the Drago code may be as complex as the application requires while the interface to the Ada clients can be kept quite simple.

9 Conclusions

This paper has described a reliable multicast library written in Ada, Group_IO, that can be used to easily build fault-tolerant distributed applications, themselves also written in Ada. The programming paradigm supported is the active replication state-machine model.

The current implementation of Group_IO runs on a SUN/OS network with the SUN-Ada compiler, and provides reliable atomic broadcast using an original consensus protocol[1][8][9]. All the communications are based on standard TCP/IP protocols and use the PARADISE[5] library of UNIX kernel calls.

The implementation is rather crude as far as efficiency goes—mainly due to the use of TCP/IP protocols—and no measures of performance have yet been taken. The configuration and load work is currently performed by hand with a minimal support from the file system, basically a configuration file kept at all participating nodes. We are reimplementing Group_IO on top of GNAT with Linux, and investigating how to handle dynamic groups where members enter and leave groups at run-time.

The interface proposed is the result of an effort to impose discipline and give an Ada binding to the main concepts of ISIS [3]. This interface also permits client-server interactions where the client may be a group—this interaction is not supported by ISIS—and it has been designed and implemented to support the code generation for the Drago language [2, 15, 16].

At any rate, the funcionality of Group_IO does not relate much to Ada 95 nor Ada 83, but to the future of Ada instead, i.e. Ada 0X. It is likely that by the time of the new revision of Ada, aspects such as fault-tolerance by replication and reliable broadcast will have to be considered into the new standard. And so the interest of the Ada community to start experimenting with these techniques.

10 Acknowledgments

We wish to thank the members of the Distributed Systems Seminar in the Technical University of Madrid for their help in clarifying the ideas contained in this paper.

References

1. Arévalo, S. and Gehani N. H. 1989. Replica Consensus in Fault Tolerant Concurrent C. Technical Report AT&T Bell Laboratories, Murray Hill, New Jersey 07974.

2. Arévalo, S., Álvarez, A., Miranda, J. and Guerra, F.: A Fault-tolerant Programming Language Based on Distributed Consensus, *Cabernet'94 Workshop*, Dublin (March 1994)

3. Birman, K., R. Cooper, T. Joseph, K. Marzullo, M. Makpangou, K. Kane, F. Schmuck, and M. Wood. *The Isis System Manual. Version 2.1.* September 1990.

4. Chang, J. M. and Maxemchuck, N. 1984. Reliable Broadcast Protocols. *ACM Trans. on Computer Systems*, 2(3), pages 251–273.

5. Courtel, N., *PARADISE: Package of Asynchronous Real-Time Ada Drivers for Interconnected Systems Exchange, version 3.2.* GNU (January 1993).

6. Geist, A. et al.: *PVM: Parallel Virtual Machine; A User's Guide and Tutorial for Networked Parallel Computing.* The MIT Press, Cambridge, Mass. (1994)

7. Gropp, W., Lusk, E., and Skjellum, A.: *Using MPI: Portable Parallel Programming with the Message-Passing Interface.* The MIT Press, Cambridge, Mass. (1994)

8. Guerra, F., Arévalo, S., Álvarez, A., and Miranda, J. A Distributed Consensus Protocol with a Coordinator. *IFIP International Conference on Decentralized and Distributed Systems ICDDS'93.* Palma de Mallorca (Spain). September 1993.

9. Guerra, F., Arévalo, S., Álvarez, A., and Miranda, J. A Quick Distributed Consensus Protocol. *Microprocessing and Microprogramming 39* (1993) pp.111–114.

10. Guerra, F. 1995. *Efficient Consensus Protocols for Distributed Systems.* Doctoral Dissertation. Technical University of Madrid. (In Spanish.)

11. Hadzilacos V. and Toueg, S. 1993. Fault-tolerant broadcasts and related problems. In Sape Mullender, editor, *Distributed Systems*, chapter 5, pages 97–145. Addison-Wesley.

12. Intermetrics, Inc. 1995. *Ada 95 Language Reference Manual.* Intermetrics, Inc., Cambridge, Mass. (January).

13. Liang, L., Chanson, S.T., and Neufeld, G.W.: Process Groups and Group Communications: Classification and Requirements. *IEEE Computer.* (February 1990)

14. Malki, D., Amir, Y., Dolev, D., and Kramer, S. 1994. The Transis approach to high available cluster communication. Technical Report CS-94-14, Institute of Computer Science, The Hebrew University of Jerusalem, 1994.

15. Miranda, J. 1994. *Drago: A Language to Program Fault-tolerant and Cooperative Distributed Applications.* Doctoral Dissertation. Technical University of Madrid. (In Spanish.)

16. Miranda, J., Alvarez, A., Arévalo, S. and Guerra, F. Drago: An Ada Extension to Program Fault-Tolerant Distributed Applications. Proceedings of the *Reliable Software Technologies—Ada-Europe96 Conference*, LNCS 1088, Springer Verlag.

17. Moser, L., Amir, Y., Melliar-Smith, P., and Agarwal, D. 1994. Extended Virtual Synchrony. In *IEEE 14th Intl. Distributed Computing Systems*, pages 56–67, June.

18. Schneider, F.B. Implementing Fault-tolerant Services Using the State Machine Approach: A Tutorial. *ACM Computing Surveys*, 22(4), December 1990.

19. Guerraoui, R. and Schiper, A. Fault-Tolerance by Replication in Distributed Systems. Proceedings of the *Reliable Software Technologies—Ada-Europe96 Conference*, LNCS 1088, Springer Verlag.

T-SMART - Task-Safe, Minimal Ada Realtime Toolset

Brian Dobbing and Marc Richard-Foy

Aonix, Partridge House, Newtown Road, Henley-on-Thames, Oxon RG9 1EN
United Kingdom.
email : brian@alsys.co.uk   richard-foy@fr.thomsoft.com
telephone : +44 1491 579090; fax : +44 1491 571866

Abstract. This paper describes T-SMART, an Ada executive and toolset for the production of safety critical and hard real time applications. T-SMART consists of three integrated parts:

- Ada83 executive audited to DO-178B for use in safety-critical systems

- Traditional Ada compilation system tools eg. Compiler and Debugger

- Tools to support verification, eg. schedulability and coverage analysis.

The existing toolset is compatible with the revision of the Ada language (Ada95) in order to ease the transition when the Ada95 safety-critical market is established. Although such toolsets are not uncommon, the significant differentiator is that the runtime executive has undergone the most stringent independent auditing to DO-178B standard, making it suitable for formal certification. Use of this toolset in actual safety-critical applications lays to rest the view that Ada tasking cannot be used in this market sector, and so provides valuable input to the evolution of the Ada95 Safety Annex H.

Keywords. Certification, Software Reliability, Ada83, Ada 95.

1 Introduction

The use of software has grown dramatically over the last decade with the availability of low-cost, high-performance hardware. It is clear that the safety of human life and property often depends directly or indirectly upon the correctness and deterministic properties of software. In this context, there is an increasing awareness that strict control is needed in order to reduce the risk of errors in the ever more complex applications which are required to be *Safety Critical* (that is, critical to human life) or *Hard Real Time* (that is, where the meeting of certain deadlines is critical to the survival of the system).

The avionics industry has pioneered specific standards for the development, testing and certification of safety critical software, for example via [DO-178B], and many other industries are now following suit in the growing recognition of the legal and ethical obligations on companies and their officers to ensure that systems do not violate safety regulations.

The Ada83 programming language [ADA83] has established itself as the natural choice for the development of safety critical and hard real time systems, and this has been re-inforced in the recent revision of the language [ADA95] with the addition of a special-needs *Safety and Security* annex ("Annex H") dedicated to supporting the emerging safety standards, although the existing definition of this annex precludes the use of tasking *"... Max_Tasks is 0. The last three restrictions are checked prior to program execution."* [ADA95 H.4(2)]. Furthermore, Ada95 also has a special-needs *Real-Time* annex which builds on valuable foundation work at the Software Engineering Institute, Carnegie Mellon University, in the realization of deterministic task scheduling such as Rate Monotonic Analysis in Ada, eg. [GOOD88]. The Ada95 Real-Time annex provides specific language semantics and additional pre-defined packages to simplify the construction of Ada tasking programs suitable for schedulability analysis which, in Ada83, must be achieved via a combination of enforced coding style plus vendor-supplied extensions.

2 C-SMART(Certifiable SMall Ada Run-Time)

Ada is of course a general-purpose language and as such, contains several non-deterministic features which are not suitable for safety critical or hard real time systems. Such a system needs to be totally bounded in execution time and memory usage in order to achieve the necessary static verification as part of the certification process. In addition, since the runtime system itself is an inherent component of the live application, verification of correctness and the required level of auditing must apply to this also.

In the early 1990s Aonix (then called Alsys) identified a core set of runtime facilities which provides a deterministic foundation for safety critical applications written in Ada83, and embodied these in its C-SMART executive. (The latest version is described in [CSMART96]). The Ada subset supported by C-SMART corresponds closely to the recommendations developed by Aeronautical Radio, Inc. (ARINC) and Boeing for the use of Ada in commercial avionics systems, and published in the standard [BCAG91]. C-SMART underwent rigorous independent auditing on behalf of the US Federal Aviation Administration to ensure its worthiness as a certifiable component of subsequent formally-certified safety critical applications, for example the power generation system, brakes system, steering control system, and global position system of the Boeing B777 aircraft. Subsequently, the C-SMART subset definition was a valuable input to the development of the Ada95 Safety and Security Annex H.

In addition to exclusion of non-deterministic aspects of dynamic memory management and dynamic exception handling, the Ada subset defined by C-SMART also excludes all Ada tasking, although interrupt handling is supported. This is mainly due to the non-deterministic timing nature of the major tasking constructs such as the *rendezvous* and the *delay* statement, coupled with the difficulty in achieving the necessary degree of static verification and coverage testing of the complex run-time system algorithms which implement the full semantics. Thus, C-SMART-based applications must use multi-programming of sequential Ada programs to achieve concurrency, controlled by for example a custom hard-coded cyclic executive to guarantee that each program completes its processing within the deadline time. This will also be the case for Ada95 programs using the Annex H subset.

3 Exploitation of Scheduling Theory

Schedulability algorithms which prove that a set of independent periodic tasks meet their critical deadlines (or not) have been available for over twenty years, based on the concept of Rate Monotonic Scheduling [LIU73]. These foundations were built upon at the Software Engineering Institute et al, as illustrated by [KLEIN93] to add support for:

- Aperiodic (as well as periodic) tasks [SPRUNT89]
- Synchronization and communication between tasks [SHA90]
- Dynamic mode change [TIND92]
- Task deadlines occurring before the end of the task period [AUD91]
- Task deadlines occurring after the end of the task period [LEH90]

These advances include use of the *Priority Ceiling Protocol* to bound the blocking time on mutually-exclusive access to shared resources, plus emulation of this protocol within the Ada83 programming language [GOOD88]. This emulation is directly supported in the Ada95 Real-Time Annex ("Priority Ceiling Locking" [ADA95 D.3]). The determinism and verification offered by this scheduling theory opened the way for the inclusion of a restricted form of Ada tasking into the safety-critical subset, thereby allowing developers of critical software to dispense with troublesome cyclic executives and use instead the power of Ada tasking without concern about its inherent pre-emptive scheduling model.

Because of the successful experience and quality of C-SMART in real-life certified applications, Aonix was chosen in two independent projects whose aims were to extend the C-SMART concept, by adding support for the restricted set of Ada83 tasking constructs defined by the latest schedulability analysis theory in a way which is wholly compatible with the Ada95 Real-Time annex, thereby simplifying the transition path. The projects are:

- Safe Ada Executive

This project was initiated and financed by the French Armament Board, and led to the development of an Ada83 executive targeting the Motorola MC68040 and Power PC 604, which was independently audited based on the recommendations in DO-178B.

- 32-bit Microprocessor and Computer System Development

This project was initiated and financed by the European Space Agency (ESA), and led to the development of an Ada83 executive targeting a custom Sparc processor. The executive has been developed and verified under the guidelines of the formal ESA standard [PSS91].

These developments have prompted the evolution of the *T-SMART* certifiable executive and toolset to provide a commercial-off-the-shelf (COTS) solution targeting a wide range of processors, for safety-critical and hard-real-time applications, including those with rigorous certification requirements.

4 T-SMART

4.1 T-SMART Executive

The T-SMART executive is a super-set of C-SMART, re-using the independently-audited executive, and adding the following subset of the Ada tasking model:

- All tasks must be declared at *library-level*, ie. the outermost scope of the program. Thus there are no nested tasks and so no task dependency
- Task termination is not supported, ie. the task bodies must contain an infinite loop, and the **abort** statement is not supported
- The **delay** statement is not supported. Instead, an absolute-time based delay procedure must be called by periodic tasks, compatible with the Ada95 **delay until** statement
- Package Calendar is not supported. Instead, a predefined package which is a subset of package Ada.Real_Time in Ada95 Real Time Annex D.8 is supplied to provide an interface onto the underlying system clock (with the corresponding range and precision), together with a set of arithmetic, logical and conversion operations on clock time and ticks.
- Full Ada rendezvous is not supported. All task synchronization and communication must be via *synchronizing* tasks whose semantics correspond to Ada95 *protected objects* with *priority ceiling locking*, and whose syntactic structure corresponds to the classic *passive* task abstraction in Ada83.
- Tasking attributes T'Callable and T'Terminated are not supported since tasks cannot become abnormal or terminate. The entry attribute E'Count is not supported to simplify auditing of the runtime system.

The factors which were used to define the T-SMART subset were based on:

- Making the run-time system wholly deterministic and as small and simple (in terms of decision points) as possible, in order to undergo the rigorous DO-178B independent auditing to ensure certifiability.

- Supporting the necessary tasking constructs for fully expressing periodic and a-periodic application tasks, together with their synchronization and communication, as defined by the family of scheduling theories above.

- Ensuring that the run-time routines were tightly time-bounded to minimize the overhead for schedulability analysis.

4.2 T-SMART Toolset

In addition to the executive, the T-SMART toolset is composed of two further parts:

- A standard Ada compilation system enhanced with the extensions needed to support the Ada subset

- A specialized set of tools specifically aimed at the requirements imposed by certification and schedulability analysis

4.2.1 Compilation System Enhancements

The changes within the Ada compilation system are mainly within the compiler itself. In particular, in order to minimize the runtime overhead associated with the use of synchronizing tasks, it is highly desirable to support the *passive task optimization* whereby the compiler transforms the task into a set of mutually-exclusive *protected subprograms* using equivalent semantics to the Ada95 protected object. This optimization removes the memory requirements for a runtime stack and task control block for each synchronizing task, and also eliminates the runtime overhead of context switch as part of the execution of each protected subprogram.

Another highly desirable compiler change is compile-time enforcement of the supported Ada subset, in preference to runtime detection of violations. In addition to the obvious benefit of early error reporting of both explicit and implicit violation of the restrictions, the runtime system is simplified by not having to contain many "dummy" subprograms whose statement part consists of merely a **raise** Program_Error. Also this approach is compatible with Ada95 **pragma** Restrictions ([ADA95 13.12]) to simplify future transition paths.

Code which raises exceptions in the runtime system when an unsupported feature is used, known as *deactivated* code (not *dead* code), is not excluded from certification considerations. DO-178B states that the "software planning process should describe how the deactivated code will be defined, verified and handled to achieve system safety objectives." [DO-178B section 4.2(h)]. Coverage testing of this deactivated code is also required by DO-178B: "... additional test cases and test procedures (should be) developed to satisfy the required coverage objectives." [DO-178B section 6.4.4.3(h)].

A compiler that enforces a subset to satisfy safety requirements needs to be carefully crafted. The compilation algorithms should not be changed to implement a particular subset, thereby preserving the value of its maturity and testing, including ACVC validation. This is an important means of raising the trust in the correctness of the toolset being used. Instead, the changes to generate the subset compiler are confined to reporting on violations of the subset.

4.2.2 Specialised Tools

The additional tools which may be available in a T-SMART implementation to support certification and schedulability analysis include:

- Condition code and Coverage Analysis tool (AdaCover)
- Schedulability Analyzer and Scheduler Simulation tool (PerfoRMAx)
- Static Worst Case Execution Time Estimation tool (AdaWCET)
- Dynamic Scheduler Tracing tool (AdaSchedule)

These tools should be almost totally re-useable in any future Ada95 implementation.

Coverage Analysis (AdaCover)

Under the DO-178B guidelines, it is necessary to perform coverage analysis to show that all the object code (both the application program part and the Ada runtime system) has been executed, including all possible outcomes of conditions, by the verification tests. The entire runtime system is subjected to coverage analysis as part of its auditing process. For the user application code, the tool AdaCover is provided to assist in formal certification.

AdaCover is in two logical parts:

1. A target-resident monitor which records the execution of every instruction in the program, including the results of every decision point
2. A host-resident tool which annotates the compiler-generated assembly code listings with the results of stage 1, thereby providing the user with a report of coverage at either the object code or source code level, for the set of executed verification tests

Schedulability Analysis (PerfoRMAx)

The PerfoRMAx tool embodies classic schedulability analyzer and scheduler simulation functionality. Given a definition of the actions performed by the tasks in the application in terms of their priority, execution time, period and interaction with shared resources, plus certain runtime system overhead times, the tool performs analysis of the schedulability of the task set based on a user-selectable scheduling theory, for example Rate Monotonic Analysis (RMA).

The tool is also able to provide a graphical view of the processor load based on a static simulation of the scheduling of the tasks by the runtime system, thereby giving clear indication of potential regions of unschedulability. If such regions exist, the tool outputs messages highlighting the cause of the unschedulability together with suggestions for corrective action.

Worst Case Execution Timing (AdaWCET)

Part of the input to the schedulability analysis process is the execution time data for each individual task action. In order to achieve confidence that the task set is schedulable under worst case conditions, it is therefore necessary to obtain the worst case execution times for each of the actions by the tasks, and in particular those with hard deadlines.

The AdaWCET functionality has been added to the Ada compiler and binder to determine these worst case timings based on the code generation process. Certain user-level tuning parameters are available to ensure that static timings can be computed without excessive pessimism in dynamic contexts, for example when the maximum number of iterations of a loop is not statically known.

The result of enabling the AdaWCET functionality in the Ada binder is the production of statically-computed estimates of the worst case execution times for the periodic actions, a-periodic responses, and protected operations of the program for entry into PerfoRMAx.

AdaWCET performs static timing analysis on Ada code which matches one of a set of templates:

- A *resource synchronizing* task which matches the passive task template and contains only unguarded accept alternatives (equivalent to protected subprograms in Ada95)
- An *event synchronizing* task which matches the passive task template and contains one guarded accept alternative (equivalent to a protected entry in Ada95) and one unguarded alternative
- A *cyclic* task whose body includes an infinite loop starting or finishing with an absolute delay statement
- A *software sporadic* task whose body includes an infinite loop starting with an entry call to a guarded accept statement in an event synchronizing task
- An *interrupt sporadic* task whose body includes an infinite loop starting with an accept statement for an interrupt entry

The execution of the cyclic and sporadic tasks is allowed to contain any number of calls to resource synchronizing tasks.

From the timing perspective, AdaWCET does not include any *blocking* times for shared access to synchronizing tasks; these are added during schedulability analysis based on the usage profile. Likewise AdaWCET disregards runtime system overheads for actions such as entry/exit from a synchronizing task, context switch, delay queue/ready queue management, interrupt handling; these are also taken into account during the analysis.

Scheduler Tracing (AdaSchedule)

The main functionality provided by AdaSchedule is to generate *actual* execution times for the actions of the tasks in the program. This functionality complements the data generated by AdaWCET, which is a statically-computed worst case time. This data is valuable when AdaWCET is not supported for a particular host/target T-SMART implementation, in order to be able to generate accurate timings for input to the schedulability analysis process. It can also be used to refine AdaWCET data when the static calculation has produced a result which is excessively pessimistic, for example when the worst case timing path is executed only in error or exception contexts which need to be excluded from the schedulability analysis.

AdaSchedule is constructed in a similar manner to AdaCover:

1. A target-resident component records *scheduling events* together with a time-stamp of their occurrence
2. A host-resident tool interprets the results of part 1 and converts the scheduling events and their times into actual timings of the specific actions of each task. These timings are in a format suitable for direct input into PerfoRMAx.

The degree of intrusiveness of the event recording has been minimised by use of an in-memory buffer and by recording as little data as possible.

4.3 Transition to Ada95

The Safety Critical Annex H in Ada95 consists of two kinds of directives:

- A set of requirements on the Ada program development tools to generate deterministic and reviewable object code
- A set of language restrictions designed to eliminate non-deterministic Ada constructs.

These language restrictions are at a similar level to those imposed by C-SMART, but crucially exclude tasking and protected objects. Thus, unless and until this annex evolves in the same direction as T-SMART, it will not be possible to validate the T-SMART executive with Annex H.

The intended approach is to make use of Ada95 **pragma** Restrictions ([ADA95 13.12]) by defining an implementation-defined restriction *T-SMART* which implies adherence to the corresponding subset. The existence of this pragma in the source code results in checks for adherence to the subset plus, if successful, use of the T-SMART executive at run-time.

In other respects, the transition of applications to Ada95 will merely consist of replacing the corresponding Ada83-extension constructs with their equivalent in Ada95, eg. passive tasks with protected objects. Other new Ada95 constructs which become available for use are restricted to those which have no run-time impact, for example child units. The *indirection-oriented* style of Ada95 embodied in support for dynamic dispatching and use of general access types pointing to objects and subprograms will be excluded due to its inherent non-determinism and lack of static analysis capability.

5 Conclusion

T-SMART offers a complete COTS solution for concurrent safety-critical applications which require formal certification, and for real-time applications which require schedulability analysis to verify hard deadlines. The initial implementation is based on Ada83 with extensions, but the extensions are fully compatible with Ada95, which will become the supported language in the future, as market forces dictate.

T-SMART is also important within non-critical applications with tight memory or execution time requirements, since the Ada runtime system is compact, efficient and time-bounded.

The addition of a restricted form of tasking and protected objects into an Ada executive which has achieved auditing to DO-178B level is valuable input to those tasked with the evolving definition of Ada95 Annex H. The recommendation based on experience with T-SMART is that a similar subset extension would be highly desirable to meet the concurrency requirements of safety-critical and hard real time applications.

6 References

[ADA83]   Reference Manual for the Ada Programming Language, ANSI/MIL-STD 1815 A, January 1983.

[ADA95]   Ada95 Reference Manual, International Standard ANSI/ISO/IEC-8652:1995, January 1995.

[AUD91]   Audsley N.C., Burns A., Richardson M.F., Tindell K., Wellings A.J., Hard Real-Time Scheduling: The Deadline Monotonic Approach, Proceedings of the 8th IEEE Workshop on Real-Time Operating Systems and Software, Pergamon, May 1991.

[BCAG91]   BCAG Digital Avionics Ada Standard, Boeing Commercial Airplane Group, Doc: D6-53339 Rev A, 1991.

[CSMART96] Safety Critical Sotware Handbook, Aonix, Burlington, 1996.

[DO-178B]   DO-178B Software Considerations in Airborne Systems and Equipment Certification,   RTCA   Inc,   Washington   D.C   1992

            [Also European Joint Standard EUROCAE ED-12B, December 1992]

[GOOD88]   Goodenough J.B., Sha L. The Priority Ceiling Protocol : A Method for Minimizing the Blocking of High Priority Ada Tasks, Proceedings of the 2nd International Workshop on Real-Time Ada Issues, and in Ada Letters 8,7, Autumn 1988.

[KLEIN93]   Klein M.H., Ralya T., Pollak W., Obenza R., Gonzalez-Harbour M. A Practitioner's Handbook for Real-Time Analysis : Guide to Rate Monotonic Analysis for Real-Time Systems, Kluwer Academic Publishers, 1993

[LEH90]   Lehoczky J.P. Fixed Priority Scheduling of Period Task Sets with Arbitrary Deadlines Proceedings of the IEEE Real-Time Systems Symposium, IEEE Computer Society Press, 1990.

[LIU73]   Liu C.L. Layland J.W. Scheduling Algorithms for Multi-Programming in a Hard real-Time Environment, Journal of the ACM 20,1 January 1973

[PSS91]   ESA Software Engineering Standards Issue 2, PSS-05-0, European Space Agency, February 1991

[SHA90]   Sha L., Rajkumar R., Lehoczky J.P., *Priority Inheritance Protocols: An Approach to Real-Time Synchronization* IEEE Transacions on Computers 39,9, September 1990

[SPRUNT89] Sprunt B., Lehoczky J.P., Sha L. *Scheduling Sporadic and Aperiodic Events in a Hard Real-Time System,* CMU/SEI-89-TR-11, Software Engineering Institute, Carnegie Mellon University, 1989

[TIND92]   Tindell K.W., Burns A., Wellings A.J. *Mode Changes in Priority Pre-Emptively Scheduled Systems,* Proceedings of the IEEE Real-Time Systems Symposium, IEEE Computer Society Press, 1992

On Programming Atomic Actions in Ada 95

A. Romanovsky,
University of Newcastle upon Tyne, UK

S.E. Mitchell and A.J. Wellings
University of York, UK

Abstract. This paper describes the development of two kinds of atomic action schemes for Ada 95. We start by discussing the basic features required of an atomic action scheme and what choices, e.g. between synchronous and asynchronous actions, are appropriate for Ada 95. We then present two implementations of actions; first using Ada 95 packages to create asynchronous actions and secondly, as sets of tasks for synchronous actions. For each action type, we present code fragments illustrating their development and use. Finally, we discuss some related issues (exception resolution, action nesting, state restoration, software re-use and extension, preventing information smuggling, distributed execution) which have been addressed in our work and show some of the problems encountered (the deserter problem, using different sorts of interparticipant communications and resources).

1 Introduction

1.1 The Basic Requirements of Atomic Actions

Atomic actions (AAs) can be used as a mechanism for structuring complex concurrent systems and for achieving system fault tolerance. The first proposal in this direction was the conversation concept [8], which was later extended to the atomic action concept [7]. Subsequently, important steps were made in [2], where general rules for building atomic actions were outlined. The AA characteristics are summarised in [1]:

- Well-defined boundaries: each action has a start, end and a side boundary.

- Indivisibility: no information exchange between participants and the outside world.

- Nesting: AAs can be nested but they may not overlap. The permissible overlapping and nesting situations are illustrated in Figure 1.

- Concurrency - it should be possible to execute different AAs concurrently.

- Recovery: AAs form the basis of damage confinement within a system and allow recovery procedures to be programmed.

The most important characteristic of actions is the handling of errors. If an error occurs within an action, all participants take part in the action recovery, and if the participants are not able to recover then the action is completed, marked as 'failed', and recovery initiated in the containing action. When several errors (exceptions) are concurrently raised in an action, an *exception resolution scheme* is required which uses a resolution procedure to resolve concurrent exceptions, find the *generalized exception*, and call the appropriate handler in all action participants. The resolution process may use the concept of an exception tree (which is often more appropriate than exception priorities) to resolve exceptions. The tree includes all exceptions associated with the action and imposes a partial ordering on them in such a way that the handler for a higher exception is capable of handling any lower level exception. Abortion handlers for nested actions may be needed for some applications and backward and/or forward error recovery can be used.

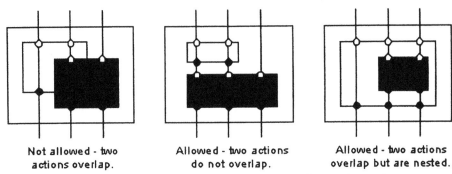

| Not allowed - two actions overlap. | Allowed - two actions do not overlap. | Allowed - two actions overlap but are nested. |

Fig. 1. Illustration of allowed nesting of atomic actions

1.2   Appropriate Atomic Action Schemes for Ada 95

One of the problems faced by researchers in fault tolerance is the big gap between conceptual language proposals and their use in real applications. This gap occurs because there is little chance that new languages which incorporate the features proposed actually being developed and used, and a possible solution is therefore to employ sets of programming conventions within standard languages. Moreover, this makes it possible to experiment with new conceptual proposals quickly.

Ada 95 [5] has no language level support for AAs, but initial work has shown that it is powerful enough to allow the AA paradigm to be implemented [1, 12, 13]. The aims of our current work (within the context of the DeVa Project [3]) are:

•   To produce a set of carefully chosen and checked rules/conventions specifying how to design Ada applications using AA concepts, and how to structure applications from atomic actions,

•   To maintain the separation of concerns between system layering, on the one hand, and hiding system software from application programmers who use it to design systems, on the other hand. This is achieved by hiding (as many as possible) implementation details from the application programmer,

•   To make the approach as object-oriented as possible.

The intention here is to make the application programmer's job easier (and so less error prone), which has led to the following goals for the research described in this paper:

•   To maximise the re-use of actions and to hide implementation structure by embedding as much as possible of control structure within a support package with a well-defined interface,

•   To make "client side" action packages (i.e. action users) as simple as possible,

•   To allow the extension of an action via inheritance.

Several AA schemes have been proposed for Ada 83 (e.g. [4, 12]). Our analysis shows that the new features introduced in Ada 95 ease the implementation and use of AAs. The use of object-oriented programming makes it possible to design reusable and extendable AA schemes; the improved concurrency features, namely protected objects and asynchronous transfer of control (ATC), simplify action control (in Ada 83 it was impossible to design an asynchronous scheme); and finally, the use of the Distributed Annex [5] allows distributed AA schemes to implement.

1.3   Using Atomic Actions for System Structuring

Various atomic action schemes have been designed (see [9] for a comprehensive survey). They are intended for different applications and languages, differ in how participants enter actions and exchange information, allow backward and/or forward error recovery, etc.

There are two potential approaches to designing systems consisting of actions:

•   Actions have internal tasks (e.g. concurrency is hidden from the outside world in [12], where tasks are forked when an action starts and jointed when it finishes) and the system is executed by processing actions in some order.

•   The system consists of a set of tasks which participate in actions. This approach can be realised in several ways, for example, in [10] the synchronisation agents required to implement AAs are encapsulated in a package and a procedural interface is provided to end/recover actions. The scheme described in Section 2 extends this approach by encapsulating the user code, too.

We believe that the second approach with actions programmed/represented as tagged abstract data types (as in [1, 13]) provides for better encapsulation, in much the same way as a monitor provides better encapsulation for mutual exclusion than a semaphore, and should therefore be preferred. Such an approach also permits the development of libraries of atomic actions, the extension of actions through inheritance, re-use, etc.

1.4   Synchronous and Asynchronous Schemes in Ada 95

As well as there being two different mechanisms for structuring a system with actions, one can classify atomic actions into two distinct kinds depending on how action participants are involved in recovery:

•   *Synchronous* - Each participant in an action has to either rendezvous at the action end or to find an error and inform other participants of the exception; it is only after each participant has completed that it enters a phase where it is ready to accept information about the state of other participants.

•   *Asynchronous* - In contrast to synchronous schemes, asynchronous approaches do not use a "wait" but instead use some language feature to interrupt all participants when one of them has found an error. Consequently there is no 'wasted time' while participants that have found an error wait for others to complete their computation before the action can itself be completed.

Error recovery and exception resolution are much easier to provide in synchronous systems because each participant is in a consistent state, ready for recovery, when handlers are called. As a consequence, there is no need to program the termination of nested actions because they either will have completed successfully or have had any errors dealt with by the nested action's handler. Obviously, there is a risk that deadlock can arise in these systems, but we believe that cautious programming with an intensive error detection makes it possible to avoid this problem and simplify subsequent recovery. Some additional programming rules can increase the efficiency of synchronous schemes and decrease the amount of time wasted (e.g. time-outs; assertions;

checking invariants, pre- and post-conditions; etc.). This can allow an early detection of either the error or the abnormal behaviour of the participant which has raised an exception and is waiting for the other participants.

Asynchronous schemes avoid many of the above problems but have been little used because the required language feature (e.g. ATC) is not readily available in many languages and systems. Even when available, the costs can be very high; for example, many implementations of ATC in Ada 95 use the two thread model with the termination and re-creation of a thread [1] resulting in high overheads. Moreover, they usually have complex semantics, are more difficult to analyse and understand, and it is harder to prove programs which use these features. To try and make the implementation less expensive, restrictions are often imposed on the facilities that can be used in a program segment that can be interrupted asynchronously. Finally, programming nested action abortion is a difficult problem because, first, this action is supposed to be indivisible and invisible for the containing action and, secondly, it can have its own faults and nested actions.

Which approach is appropriate depends largely on the application, on the errors which are to be detected, on the failure assumptions, etc. Thus any generalised scheme should allow programmers to choose the most suitable approach.

2   Atomic Actions as Packages

[1, 13] described the development of a set of asynchronous AA schemes, and ongoing work at both the Universities of Newcastle and York has continued to improve on this work. Within these schemes, actions are Ada packages and participants enter them by calling interface procedures. Actions can use both forward and backward error recovery. This section presents a brief introduction to the current state of the implementation.

The execution of the AA is controlled by a protected object `Action_Controller` that uses ATC to interrupt the execution of participants in the event of an error. A tagged type `Action_T` includes the controller as a component. Derived packages can be written which will implement atomic actions for particular systems. In these packages all action participants are represented as procedures called by external tasks. Actions can also be parameterised on the number of participants. The Ada code for the protected object is encapsulated within an `Atomic_Support` package:

```
1   with Ada.Exceptions; use Ada.Exceptions;
2   package Atomic_Action_Support is
3     type Action_T(At_Least : Positive) is tagged
4                                   limited private;
5     type Vote_T is (Commit, Aborted);
6     generic
7       with procedure Work;
8       with function Error_Handler(E: Exception_Id)
9                                           return Vote_T;
10      procedure Action_Component(A: access Action_T'Class);
11
12    Atomic_Action_Failure : exception;
13  private
14    protected type Action_Controller(At_Least : Positive) is
15      entry Wait_Abort(E: out Exception_Id);
16      entry Done(Vote: Vote_T; Result: out Vote_T);
```

```
17      procedure Signal_Abort(E: Exception_Id);
18    private
19      entry Entered(E: out Exception_Id);
20      entry Wait(Vote: Vote_T; Result: out Vote_T);
21      entry Done_Cleanup(Vote: Vote_T; Result: out Vote_T);
22      -- ...
23    end Action_Controller;
24
25    type Action_T(At_Least : Positive) is tagged limited
26      record
27        C : Action_Controller(At_Least);
28      end record;
29  end Atomic_Action_Support;
```

The body of this package which controls the execution of all action participants wrapped into a standard template in procedure Action_Component is as follows:

```
1   package body Atomic_Action_Support is
2     protected body Action_Controller is separate;
3
4     procedure Action_Component(W: Work; EH: Error_Handler;
5                                 A: access Action_T'Class) is
6       X : Exception_Id;
7       Decision : Vote_t;
8     begin
9       select
10        A.C.Wait_Abort(X);
11        Raise_Exception(X);
12      then abort
13        begin
14          W;
15          A.C.Done(Commit, Decision);
16        exception
17          when E: others =>
18            A.C.Signal_Abort(Exception_Identity(E));
19        end;
20      end select;
21    exception
22      when E: others =>
23        Decision := EH(Exception_Identity(E));
24        A.C.Done_Cleanup(Decision, Decision);
25        if Decision = Aborted then
26          raise Atomic_Action_Failure;
27        end if;
28    end Action_Component;
29  end Atomic_Action_Support;
```

In line 9, the select statement signifies the start of the ATC block. At this point, the run-time system detects that it must wait on the event specified in line 10 (an entry in the Action_Controller) but in the meantime begins to execute from line 14. If the event is triggered (by an exception occurring in another component) before the then abort branch completes then execution is halted and line 11 executed. If an exception is raised by procedure W (i.e. the procedure encapsulating the work for the action participant) then the exception handler in line 16 is invoked which uses an entry on the Action_Controller to signal all components that an error has occurred which will cause ATC to propagate to each component. The exception handler in lines 21-27 is used after the completion of the component to decide whether or not to commit or abort the action.

When an action is to be used within a program it is declared within a package which uses the support described above. An example specification of an atomic action Action with two participants is given below:

```
1   with Atomic_Action_Support; use Atomic_Action_Support;
2   package Action is
3     type My_Action_T is tagged limited private;
4     procedure Participant_1(A: access My_Action_T);
5     procedure Participant_2(A: access My_Action_T);
6     Action_Failure: exception;
7   private
8     type My_Action_T is tagged record
9       C: Action_T(2);
10    end;
11  end Action;
```

Lines 3 and 8-10 create a new private type, My_Action_T, derived from an existing type supplied from package Atomic_Action_Support and constrained to contain two components. Since this type is private, its internals cannot be accessed from outside the package Action; also, because the unconstrained base type is declared as abstract in package Atomic_Action_Support, one must first derive a new type before an instance can be declared. The package also declares a new exception (line 6) which is used to propagate failure by the support package - this relives the client of having to "with" the support package. The package body is declared as follows:

```
1   with Ada.Exceptions; use Ada.Exceptions;
2   package body Action is
3
4   procedure Participant_1(A: access My_Action_T) is
5     procedure My_Work is
6     begin
7       -- perform work ...;
8     end My_Work;
9
10    function My_Error_Handler(E: Exception_Id) return
11                                                  Vote_T is
12    begin
13      -- handle error ...
14      return Commit;
15    end My_Error_Handler;
16
17    procedure A1 is new Action_Component(My_Work,
18                                         My_Error_Handler);
19    begin
20      A1(A.C'Access);
21    exception
22      when Atomic_Action_Failure => raise Action_Failure;
23  end Participant_1;
24
25  procedure Participant_2(A: access My_Action_T) is
26    -- as before for Participant_1
27  end Action;
```

The new `My_Action_T` type can be subsequently used by clients as follows:

```
1   with Action; use Action;
2
3   A1 : My_Action_T;
4
5   task Client_1;
6   task Client_2;
7
8   task body Client_1 is
9      -- ...
10     Participant_1(A1'Access);
11  exception
12     when Action_Failure =>  -- ...
13  end;
14
15  task body Client_2 is
16     -- ...
17     Participant_2(A1'Access);
18     -- ...
19  end;
```

At first sight it would seem simpler to declare action A1 in global scope and to incorporate the code for components directly in the tasks. However, the use of a package promotes the reuse of the components as well as prevents possible *information smuggling* [6] - the escape of the internal details of the action prior to the commit/abort decision.

Further details of this scheme and more examples of its use can be found in [13].

3   Atomic Actions as Sets of Tasks

Two synchronous schemes which use forward error recovery with concurrent exception resolution have been designed [10, 11]. In the first, one of the participating tasks (the head process) synchronises the rest of them at the action exit. When all tasks have reached it, this process either resolves the exceptions raised and propagates the resolved exception via nested rendezvous, or lets the tasks leave the action. The second scheme [10] uses a "resolving" protected object to synchronise the participant exits, to resolve all exceptions and to raise the resolved exception in all participants. The parameterised protected type `SR_Object` can be implemented as follows. It has two entries `Finish` (called from each action participant) and `Wait_All` (which is private). The identities of the raised exception(s) are collected in a list kept by `SR_Object`. The procedure `Resolution` uses this list and a resolution tree to find the resolved exception which is assigned to variable `Resolved`. Note that if `Resolved` is equal to `Null_Id` (all participants have raised exception `No_Exception`), no exception is raised and the action completes successfully. An important detail is that an additional exception, `No_Exception`, should be declared and raised when a participant completes the action successfully. This scheme treats predefined exceptions and the programmer's exceptions in the same way. An instance of type `SR_Object` is created for each action. The specification of this type is as follows:

```
1   protected type SR_Object(Participants_Number: Positive) is
2      entry Finish(E: in Exception_Id := Null_Id);
3   private
```

```
 4    entry Wait_All(E: in Exception_Id := Null_Id);
 5    procedure Resolution;
 6    Finished : Integer :=0;
 7    Results : Results_T; -- list of all exceptions raised
 8    Resolved : Exception_Id := Null_Id;
 9    Let_Go: Boolean := False;
10 end SR_Object;
```

The Resolution procedure is called from the body of Finish when all participants have completed execution, and the resolved exception is then propagated to all
of them. The body of this object is much simpler than the body of the action controller intended for the asynchronous scheme:

```
 1 protected body SR_Object is
 2    procedure Resolution is ...;
 3
 4    entry Finish(E: in Exception_Id := Null_Id) when True is
 5    begin
 6      Finished:=Finished+1;
 7      -- add E to Results
 8      if Finished = Participants_Number then
 9        Resolution; Let_Go:=True;
10      end if;
11      requeue Wait_All;
12    end Finish;
13
14    entry Wait_All(E: in Exception_Id := Null_Id) when Let_Go is
15    begin
16      if Wait_All'Count=0 then
17        Let_Go := False; Finished :=0;
18      end if;
19      Raise_Exception (Resolved);
20    end Wait_All;
21 end SR_Object;
```

When an action participant executes the exception context, it is only allowed to raise
an exception of this action. The signalling of the failure exception can be done in
handlers. Within this scheme, re-raising exceptions (found in many exception
schemes) is understood as raising the failure exception of the containing action, which
is a uniform signal of the nested action failure.

4   Comparison

Both kinds of schemes have a number of common features, the most significant one
is that all of them are centralised in the sense that there is a single action controller
[1, 13], a resolving and synchronising object [10] or a resolving head process [11].
This limits their scope for distribution and consequent ability to cope with network
failures. However, one can distribute actions so that each node within an action is
assigned a nested action which restricts the load placed on central services. Another
realistic approach is to replicate the partition containing the action controller.

A synchronous scheme, as presented here, has the disadvantage that it is not extendable since the actions are not Ada 95 packages with internal tagged type. However, in
a multi-processing environment, asynchronous schemes also suffer because of the lack

of exception resolution leaving them susceptible to an incorrect handling of concurrently raised exceptions.

The analysis of asynchronous schemes shows that it is impossible not to lose some of the exceptions which are raised concurrently when Ada 95's ATC is used as the only means to implement an asynchronous scheme.

The two kinds of schemes are complementary since they are suited to different application areas. For example, an asynchronous scheme such as in [13] would be better for real time systems whereas distributed systems would require a scheme with exception resolution to handle exceptions raised concurrently.

5 Related Issues

5.1 Information Smuggling

Information smuggling was first defined in [6] for the conversation scheme [8] and occurs when a task participating in a conversation either obtains information from or leaks information to a task not participating in the conversation. Generally speaking, information smuggling is difficult to prevent without explicit language support. One approach we hope to explore for Ada 95 is a set of rules which could be defined to enforce the required restriction on the components operating as AAs. For example, if action components are encapsulated in a package then only pure packages may be "with'ed" in the package. Also, only access parameters pointing to constants should be allowed in the parameters of these package procedures.

5.2 Use of an Asynchronous Scheme: Type Extension

A very important characteristic of the schemes in [13] is extendability, for which Ada 95 offers a comprehensive set of mechanisms. We have explored ways of extending the Action_T type. Generally speaking, a derived type My_Action_T can be created from the parent type by:

• Combining any new participant procedures with the parent package or overriding the parent's participant procedures,

• Adding new components (which may be action states, say, local objects) for new and overridden participants to work with,

• Making the number of participants concrete.

A chain of derivations can be used to extend, step by step, the original Action_T type. It is important to note that:

• Participant procedures can be kept 'abstract' (virtual) in this inheritance chain as long as is required (but obviously the type remains abstract and so cannot be used to create objects); the same is true for the Action_T type itself.

• The number of participants is a parameter of all types derived from Action_T, so, it is just of type Positive (no restriction) in the basic Action_T type. It can be either made concrete in the derived action type with a known number of participants or left unchanged.

Ada 95 imposes minor restrictions on this:

• If the parameter (number of participants) is made concrete it cannot be changed in the derived types;

• One cannot rename the parent participant procedure without overriding it with the same name and renaming it (in the same type definition);

• One has to know how many participants are in the action to make it non-abstract (this can be known only if all elements of the derivation chain are known, which is basically an engineering issue).

5.3 Nested Actions

Only properly nested atomic actions are allowed. Nested actions are programmed by introducing an object of the action to be nested in the body of the nesting action. Consider, for example, a new action which wishes to use package Action as part of its implementation. Suppose this action has three participants; i.e.

```
1   with Atomic_Action_Support; use Atomic_Action_Support;
2   package New_Action is
3     type My_Action_T is tagged  limited private;
4     procedure My_Action_1(A: access My_Action_T);
5     procedure My_Action_2(A: access My_Action_T);
6     procedure My_Action_3(A: access My_Action_T);
7     Action_Failure : exception;
8   private
9     type My_Action_T is tagged limited
10    record
11      aliased Action_T(3);
12    end record;
13  end New_Action;
```

Now suppose that My_Action_1 and My_Action_2 use the Action package as part of its implementation. The body of this package would be:

```
1   with Ada.Exceptions; use Ada.Exceptions;
2   with Action; use Action;
3   package body New_Action is
4     Nested_Action: aliased Action.My_Action_T;
5     procedure My_Action_1(A: access My_Action_T) is
6     procedure My_Work is
7     begin
8       -- ...
9       Action.My_Action_1(Nested_Action'access);
10      -- ...
11    exception
12      when Atomic_Action_Failure =>
13        -- nested action has failed
14        raise;
15    end My_Work;
16
17    function My_Error_Handler(E: Exception_Id) return
18                                          Vote_T is ...;
19
20    procedure My_Action_1 is new Action_Component(My_Work,
21                                        My_Error_Handler);
22    begin
23      A1(A.C'access);
```

```
24    end My_Action_1;
25    -- similarly for My_Action_2
26    -- My_Action_3 does not use the Nested_Action
27  end New_Action;
```

With the synchronous model, no further consideration is necessary as no attempt is made by My_Action_3 to abort its action until all participants are ready. However, in the asynchronous model, extra facilities are needed to ensure that the nested action is not aborted without error recovery being undertaken [13].

To facilitate recovery in the inner action, it is necessary to use another Ada 95 facility called Controlled types. Objects of a controlled type can have (amongst other things) finalisation routines defined. Hence, each Action_Component procedure has the following extra components:

```
1  type Abort_Recovery(N: access Action_T) is new
2              Finalization.Limited_Controlled with null record;
3  procedure Finalize(Ar: in out Abort_Recovery);
```

Here the finalisation action is to signal to the action controller that the action is to be aborted. A variable of Abort_Recovery is now introduced into the Action_Component:

```
1  procedure Action_Component(A: access Action_T'Class) is
2    Ar : Abort_Recovery(A);
3    -- ...
4  begin
5    -- ...
```

When the action is aborted, the Ar controlled variable goes out of scope. However, before this can happen, the finalisation procedure is called. Note that some small modifications to the controller type are required as the Finalize routine is called *every* time the variable goes out of scope irrespective of whether the action was aborted or not!

6   Discussion and Future Work

In [4] the authors discussed why Ada 83 was not sufficient for programming AAs. Whilst we agree, to a limited degree, with this view (thus, neither Ada 83 nor Ada 95 support the prevention of information smuggling), we believe that one should not wait for the standard language to include AAs. Moreover, although Ada 95 does not solve all the problems mentioned, it does allow us to program actions in a simple and re-usable way whilst hiding the implementation details in the support units.

A potential problem with both synchronous and asynchronous schemes is their susceptibility to failure if a participant stops and thus never arrives at the end of the action. One possible approach to avoiding this is to implement a timeout (using either ATC or timed entry calls) based on the worst case execution time of each participant and thus other (waiting) participants or an action controller can detect the situation when a failure has occurred.

Further research will be required to address the problems mentioned in the paper as well as a number of outstanding issues. State restoration features for different kinds of inter-participant communication and of local data will need be designed to support backward error recovery and provide the atomicity semantics. More investigation and experiment is necessary to provide distributed atomic actions, though a general outline of the schemes was given in [10, 13]. Also, research is required to help programmers to solve (or to avoid) the deserter process problem [6].

We believe that a synchronous scheme could be programmed on the basis of the schemes described (with SR_Object playing the role of the action controller): actions will be presented as tagged types with methods playing the roles of action participants, which would allow for extendability, reuse, encapsulation and exception resolution.

This paper has presented two practical and usable kinds of AA schemes written in Ada 95. With these schemes, it is possible to create systems of actions with a minimal application programmer code. The use of Ada 95 features has improved confidence in the non-interference firewalls between actions and also promoted extendability of actions through type extension. The work is still in development but nevertheless forms a solid and usable implementation of actions in Ada 95.

Acknowledgements. This research is supported by DeVa, ESPRIT Basic Project No. 20072. We would especially like to thank the members of the DeVa project who have commented on initial versions of this paper - A. Burns at York University, J.-C. Fabre, T. Pérennou, D. Powell and Y. Crouzet at LAAS and R. Stroud at Newcastle University.

References

[1] A. Burns and A. Wellings, Ada95: An Effective Concurrent Programming Language, in: Proc. Ada Euro 96, Switzerland, 1996, 58-77.
[2] R.H. Campbell and B. Randell, Error Recovery in Asynchronous Systems, IEEE Transactions on Software Engineering SE-12, 8 (1986) 811-826.
[3] DeVa Project Programme and Description, Design for Validation, Proposal Document (http://www.newcastle.research.ec.org/deva/index.html, 1995).
[4] S.T. Gregory and J.C. Knight, On the provision of Backward Error Recovery in production programming languages, in: Proc. FTCS-19, USA, 1989, 506-511.
[5] Information technology - Programming languages - Ada. Language and Standard Libraries. ISO/IEC 8652:1995(E), Intermetrics, Inc., 1995.
[6] K.H. Kim, Approaches to Mechanization of the Conversation Scheme Based on Monitors, IEEE Transactions on Software Engineering SE-8, 3 (1982) 189-197.
[7] P.A. Lee and T. Anderson, Fault Tolerance: Principles and Practice (Springer-Verlag, Wien - New York, 1990).
[8] B. Randell, System Structure for Software Fault Tolerance, IEEE Transactions on Software Engineering SE-1, 2 (1975) 220-232.
[9] B. Randell and J. Xu, The Evolution of the Recovery Block Concept, in M.R. Lyu, eds., *Software Fault Tolerance* (J. Wiley, 1994) 1-22.
[10] A. Romanovsky, Atomic actions based on distributed/concurrent exception resolution, TR 560, Comp. Dept., University of Newcastle upon Tyne, 1996.
[11] A. Romanovsky, Practical exception handling and resolution in concurrent programs, TR 545, Comp. Dept., University of Newcastle upon Tyne, 1996.
[12] A. Romanovsky and L. Strigini, Backward error recovery via conversations in Ada, Software Engineering Journal 10, 8 (1995) 219-232.
[13] A.J. Wellings and A. Burns, Implementing Atomic Actions in Ada95, TR YCS-263, Department of Computer Science, University of York, 1996.

Static Analysis and Diversity in the Software Development Process - Experiences with the Use of SPARK

J Phil Thornley

British Aerospace Military Aircraft
W376C, Warton Aerodrome
Warton, Preston PR4 1AX

phone: +44 1772 855705   fax: +44 1772 855216
email: phil.thornley@bae.co.uk

Abstract: This paper discusses the need for diversity in any development process used for high integrity software and describes some ways in which differing levels of diversity can be created. A summary of the SPARK language is given and experience with the use of SPARK in creating the highest level of diversity for safety critical software is described. Current best practice for the use of SPARK is then described as well as potential future developments in its use.

1.   Introduction - The Need for Diversity

A safety critical software component of a system is one where failure of that component on its own creates a hazard that could result in an accident causing death or serious injury to one or more people or other unacceptable consequences such as major financial loss, widespread environmental damage, etc [1, 2].

The utility of trying to measure or predict failure rates for software components is the subject of much debate [3]. Irrespective of how software reliability is measured, it is unquestionably directly related to the quality and integrity of the development process used to create the software [2].

Each step in the software development process is known to be unreliable in some way (it is either a manual activity or performed by a non-trustworthy tool). Furthermore neither extensive testing [4] nor long periods of failure-free operation [5] can supply the required confidence that safety critical software will always operate as required. Formal methods are not yet proven to be cost-effective for large-scale software (although the prospects for the future are improving) so the confidence required must come from the development process used in spite of the inherent unreliability of each step. The only way that the process can deliver this confidence is for it to contain a sufficient number of diverse activities.

This paper describes different ways of introducing diversity and reports on experience with the use of static analysis to provide increasing levels of diversity. The following sections cover this as follows.
-     Part 2 describes the general topic of diversity in the software development process. The work reported in this paper has used SPARK [6] as the basis for static analysis.

- Part 3 briefly describes the main features of both the language and the Examiner, which is the primary tool supporting the language.
- Part 4 reports on the evolution of the process for using SPARK within British Aerospace Military Aircraft so that increasing diversity is achieved.
- Part 5 describes the potential for further developments in the use of both the current and the future versions of SPARK.

2. Diversity in the Safety Critical Software Development Process

2.1 Overall Process Definition

The highest possible level of confidence is needed for safety critical software components, and to create this confidence the development process should show (at least) the following characteristics:-

- a credible overall development with:
  - a realistically sized development task
  - experienced and reliable staff
  - well-understood methods
  - reliable tools with known and stable fault lists

- error and fault avoidance strategies in the process, for example:
  - simple design of control and data structures
  - use of a 'safe' language subset
  - strict upper limits on code complexity
  - strict configuration management and change control

- diverse verification and validation (V&V) activities such as:
  - rigorous code inspection
  - strict application of dynamic test coverage requirements
  - independence of V&V process from development process
  - various forms of static analysis of the source and object code:
    - control flow, data flow and information flow analysis
    - subset conformance
    - object code verification
    - run-time system safety analysis
    - stack and timing analysis

Most of the features listed are more rigorous versions of the same features of the normal software development process. The major addition is the use of static analysis of the source and object code. Much of the confidence in safety critical software comes from the diversity that these activities introduce to the V&V process.

2.2 Static Analysis in Verification and Validation

Static analysis is the term used for any method that analyses the properties of a program without executing it; such methods may be manual or automatic. Verification applies to each phase and confirms that the work of the phase has been performed correctly. Validation confirms that the products of the software development remain consistent with the overall requirement.

The diversity introduced by static analysis has three basic forms which are (in increasing order of diversity):-

1. activities that repeat checks on aspects of the software using a different method for performing the check,

2. activities that check aspects of the software that are not otherwise checked at all, or only checked indirectly,

3. activities that require additional statements about the software (written as code annotations) that can be checked against the implementation.

Examples of the first form are stack analysis and timing analysis. Both of these use a very simple, one-dimensional model of the execution environment (memory space and time respectively) and analyse the demands placed on that model by the software. This can be contrasted with the use of dynamic execution and measurement of the actual software - the use of models removes the effect of the instrumentation otherwise necessary and can produce worst-case figures of higher accuracy. Thus, for timing analysis, tools are now available that analyse the loadable image and calculate worst case execution times of code segments. By using these timings, backed up by a small number of measurements of actual execution, it is possible to produce a reliable prediction of the maximum processor load that could be presented by the application.

Other examples are object code inspection and run-time system safety audit, where direct manual inspection of the assembler level code is performed in parallel to execution based testing of the code.

The second form of diversity is shown by tools that inspect the code for constructs that may indicate errors. Some of these tools measure aspects of the code, such as complexity, where experience has shown that values of a metric beyond some limit indicate that a unit of code should be modified to be readily comprehended by both author and reader. Alternatively they look for particular constructs that are often symptoms of errors either in the code or in the understanding of the code by the author. These include:-

statements that read the value of uninitialised variables,
ineffective statements,
unreachable code, etc.

The third of these types of diversity comes from the introduction of an additional development activity, running in parallel with the design and coding of the software, to create statements about the code that can be cross-checked with the code. An example is the annotations required and checks performed by the SPARK Examiner.

As the diversity in these activities increases, so the confidence in the software development process resulting from them increases.

Note that, since there is no 'diversity' metric, the description above is informal (and based solely on the author's experience). If process diversity is used to justify a claim for confidence in software then the developer should ensure that the process produces reliable metrics that either support the claim or indicate aspects of the software that need further attention.

3. The SPARK Language and the SPARK Examiner

3.1 The Need for a Language Subset

The need to restrict the features of Ada 83 used in safety critical software has come from recognition that Ada is a very large language (with some features that make formal reasoning about program behaviour either very difficult or impossible) and from recognition that the language definition is neither entirely clear nor logically consistent [6, 7].

Several subset definitions have been produced for Ada 83 [6, 8, 9] and for Ada 95 [10, 11]. Furthermore the Annex H Rapporteur Group (a subgroup of WG9) is currently working on the production of a Guidance document that will recommend avoidance of some of the features of Ada 95 in high integrity applications.

3.2 The SPARK Language

The SPARK language is defined in [6] and comprises a subset of Ada 83 and mandatory annotations. The Ada 83 subset can be summarised as follows [12].

- it includes packages, private types, functions returning structured values and the library system
- the following parts of the language are omitted:
  tasks, exceptions, generic units, access types
  use clauses, type aliasing, anonymous types
  goto statements
  declare statements
  default values in record declarations and default subprogram parameters
- overloading is avoided as far as possible
- all constraints are statically determinable

The annotations are written as structured Ada 83 comments so SPARK source can be processed by any Ada 83 compiler. Annotations are required for each package (specification and body) and each subprogram declaration as follows:-

- Package annotations define a (possibly abstract) view of the state data of the package.
- Subprogram annotations define
  a) the data items that are accessed globally
  b) the dependency relationships between the data items imported and exported by the subprogram.

The dependency relationships are a partial restatement of the software specification and design, and provide an independent view of the code that can be verified against the code.

Code written in the SPARK language can be analysed by the SPARK Examiner, which performs an analysis of the source text, and reports on:-

subset conformance,

control flow errors,

data flow errors and anomalies,

information flow errors.

3.3 Example

The following code is an implementation in SPARK of a stack as an abstract state machine. All SPARK annotations are preceded by --#.

```
package Integer_Stack
--# own State;
--# initializes State;
is

    procedure Push (The_Value : in      Integer);
    --# global  State;
    --# derives State from State, The_Value;

    procedure Pop  (The_Value :      out Integer);
    --# global  State;
    --# derives State, The_Value from State;

    function Is_Empty return Boolean;
    --# global  State;

    function Is_Full  return Boolean;
    --# global  State;

end Integer_Stack;
```

The 'own' annotation lists the package own variables, which define the abstract view of package state. The 'initializes' annotation states which of the own variables are initialized within the package.

The 'global' annotation following each procedure declaration provides a complete list of all own variables that the code of the procedure will access. A procedure can only access the data defined in its global annotation and its formal parameters. The 'derives' annotation on each procedure is its dependency relationship - the code for each procedure must match exactly the dependency relationship for that procedure.

The 'global' annotation following each function declaration similarly limits access to the global data listed. In this case access is read-only as SPARK functions cannot have side effects. There is no 'derives' annotation for a function as it is required to derive the function result from all the imported data (global and formal parameters).

Every subprogram must define (in its 'global' annotation) all own variables in all packages that are accessed by the subprogram, and (in its 'derives' annotation) the dependency relationship for all exported data. For example, any procedure calling Integer_Stack.Push (above) must include Integer_Stack.State in its global annotation and a suitable completion for:

```
derives Integer_Stack.State from Integer_Stack.State, ...
```

In the package body the annotations refine the abstract view in the specification into a concrete view in terms of the actual package data.

```
package body Integer_Stack
--# own State is Stack, Pointer;
is

   Stack_Size : constant Integer := 1024;
   subtype Stack_Index is Integer range 1 .. Stack_Size;
   type Stack_Vector is array (Stack_Index) of Integer;
   Stack : Stack_Vector;

   subtype Pointer_Range is Integer range 0 .. Stack_Size;
   Pointer : Pointer_Range;

   procedure Push (The_Value : in      Integer)
   --# global  Stack, Pointer;
   --# derives Stack   from Stack, Pointer, The_Value
   --#      &   Pointer from Pointer;
   is
   begin
      Pointer         := Pointer + 1;
      Stack (Pointer) := The_Value;
   end Push;

   procedure Pop  (The_Value :      out Integer)
   --# global  Stack, Pointer;
   --# derives Pointer   from Pointer
   --#      &   The_Value from Stack, Pointer;
   is
   begin
      The_Value := Stack (Pointer);
      Pointer   := Pointer - 1;
   end Pop;

   function Is_Empty return Boolean
   --# global Pointer;
   is
   begin
      return Pointer = 0;
   end Is_Empty;

   function Is_Full  return Boolean
   --# global Pointer;
   is
   begin
      return Pointer = Stack_Size;
   end Is_Full;
begin -- package initialization
   Pointer := 0;
   Stack   := Stack_Vector'(Stack_Index => 0);
end Integer_Stack;
```

The 'own' annotation defines how the variables declared within the body map onto the own variables in the specification. Each procedure and function in the body has refined 'global' and 'derives' annotations. By using refinement in this way, an abstract view in the specification is combined with a precise definition in the body.

Changes can be made to the structure of the internal package data or the package operations with, often, no change to the specification and hence to the annotations of client packages.

4. Use of SPARK at BAe Military Aircraft

4.1 Experience in the Use of SPARK

Within BAe Military Aircraft the use of SPARK has evolved in the direction of increasing independence of the annotations from the code.

The maximum gain in confidence is achieved when the annotations are defined from the specification during the software design, and are influenced as little as possible by the actual code (ie by maximising the diversity between the code production and annotation production steps). We have found that it is not possible in practice to separate the annotations completely from the code as implementation decisions have an effect on the dependency relationships defined in the annotations.

At the time of the earliest development, the Examiner tool and the annotations were unfamiliar to the development team and there was a natural tendency to get on with the design and coding task and leave until later the writing of the annotations. This tendency was reinforced by the lack of support in the software design tool for code annotations which, as a result, were mainly written after completion of the code. Using SPARK in this way had two significant effects.

- Changes to configured code were required to correct syntax and semantic errors (where the code did not conform to the subset).

- Changes to the annotations were made based on the flow errors reported by the Examiner (in effect the basic assumption was that the code was already correct and the task was to make the annotations agree with it).

Whilst there is clear benefit from this exercise, it was felt that more could be achieved. The next significant software development was a major upgrade of this software, and since many of the final annotations were already written, it would have been inappropriate to require the development of the annotations to start again from the revised specification. The following changes were therefore made to the development process.

- The annotations were revised at the same time as the changes were made to the code and they were submitted to the Examiner prior to code inspection.

- During the code inspection for each package, one of the reviewers inspected the annotations against the specification, design and code to ensure that every annotation was traceable to and justified by either a specification, design or implementation requirement. This check concentrated on the package internals.

- As groups of related packages were completed, an independent reviewer repeated the inspection of the annotations and checked the consistency and correctness of the annotations which defined the data flows between packages.

Furthermore:-

- The code was not tested (ie not executed) prior to inspection.

- As changes occurred to configured code during development, any changes to the annotations that were required were justified against the changes to the software.

This process ensured that all annotations (whether reused, amended or added) had a justified purpose. All defects found at the inspection were recorded and the source code was brought under change control immediately after it passed code inspection. All defects subsequently discovered by testing were easily identified, as the resulting changes required further code inspections, so the numbers of defects was a reliable measure of the effectiveness of the coding and inspection processes. For this development the number and types of errors found during inspection and testing gave a high level of confidence that the testing had found all the remaining defects.

More recently another safety critical software development has been going through design where the process in use allows an easier inclusion of the SPARK annotations in the design documentation. This has shown the value of being able to comment on them, make changes to the design at the earliest possible stage, and, as a result, improve both the software and the annotations. The process has therefore evolved from developing code in Ada and then getting it to 'jump through the SPARK hoop' to designing software in the SPARK language.

4.2 Future Use of SPARK

As a result of this experience, the current view of best practice in the use of SPARK for a newly written package is as follows[1].

1. During the preliminary design the package specification is produced. This will contain the annotations that define the package own variables and the dependency relationships of the imports and exports of the visible operations in terms of the own variables and formal parameters manipulated by each operation. The package specification is formally inspected and brought under both configuration and change control.

2. During the detailed design the initial package body is produced. The actual package data is defined along with the refinement annotations that link the own variables with this data. The annotations for the visible operations are rewritten in terms of the package data and formal parameters. The Ada declaration of each internal operation is produced. This version of the package body is formally inspected and brought under both configuration and change control.

3. During coding the annotations for the internal operations are produced at the same time as the code.

---

[1] This section is concerned only with the future use of the SPARK facilities already discussed. The SPARK toolset provides further forms of analysis which can be used for further diverse activities in the development process.

4. When all the package code and annotations are complete the package is checked by the Examiner. The code inspection looks at:
   a) the code for all the operations
   b) the annotations produced for all internal operations
   c) any changes that have become necessary to the previously approved package body or package specification
   d) the Examiner report

Although the annotations for the internal operations could be produced at the second rather that the third step above, this is not considered to be cost-effective. Even those engineers who have considerable experience in the use of SPARK find it difficult to express their detailed understanding of a group of operations in terms of the dependency relationships, furthermore coding decisions can introduce implementation dependencies into them. To define them before writing the code would therefore be of limited value. This is not felt to be a significant issue as the annotations produced for the internal operations must conform with the annotations previously defined for the visible operations (or have any changes in the visible operations justified at the code inspection).

With this process the defect rate for errors found at inspection and in the subsequent test phases provides a reasonable basis for establishing the level of confidence in the software that can be justified by the process.

One of the beneficial side-effects of producing the annotations as early as possible during software design is the resulting preference of the designer/coder for those implementation choices that minimise the increase in the number of annotations - so the number of dependencies introduced by the implementation decisions tends to be kept low. Although there is no formal connection, it is anticipated that this will reduce the scope for incorrect code to pass the SPARK Examiner checks.

5. Future Developments in the Use of SPARK

5.1 Annotations as a Guide to Unit Testing

Unit testing can be simplified by further developments in the way that SPARK is used. These methods were not widely used during the developments reported on above.

The dependency relationships can be used in the definition of the unit test cases. Since, in general, each exported variable depends only on a subset of the imported variables, full coverage of the algorithm can be defined from these subsets, rather than from the full set of imports. If the size of the 'biggest' subset can be reduced then the number of unit test cases required can also be reduced without loss of confidence in the effectiveness of the test cases.

SPARK annotations can be used when an operation has imported variables whose values are only relevant in some cases. By defining internal subprograms to isolate these variables from the code where their values are irrelevant, testing of this code need not be repeated with different values of the irrelevant imports. In this way the contributions of the Examiner (control over visibility of variables) and of the unit tests (proof of correct outputs for a given set of inputs) are combined to produce a cost-effective and reliable process.

For example, an operation could have the following truth table (where each import has two possible values and "-" indicates "don't care").

```
Import_A  |   A   |   A    |   A    | not_A | not_A | not_A |
Import_B1 |   B   | not_B  | not_B  |   -   |   -   |   -   |
Import_C1 |   -   |   C    | not_C  |   -   |   -   |   -   |
Import_B2 |   -   |   -    |   -    |   B   | not_B | not_B |
Import_C2 |   -   |   -    |   -    |   -   |   C   | not_C |
=============================================================
Export_X  |  Up   | Right  |  Left  | Down  | Left  | Right |
```

If this is coded in a single piece of code in the 'obvious' way then complete testing will require tests with all 32 possible combinations of the values of the five inputs in order to prove conclusively that there is no incorrect reference to one or more wrong imports in the code. However if the operation is coded as shown below then only eight test cases are required:

```
Import_A = A     with all four cases for Import_B1 and Import_C1
Import_A = not_A with all four cases for Import_B2 and Import_C2


procedure Example_Truth_Table (Import_A  : in      A_Type;
                               Import_B1 : in      B_Type;
                               Import_C1 : in      C_Type;
                               Import_B2 : in      B_Type;
                               Import_C2 : in      C_Type;
                               Export_X  :     out X_Type)
--# derives Export_X from Import_A, Import_B1, Import_C1,
--#                                 Import_B2, Import_C2;

is
   procedure B1_C1
   --# global Import_B1, Import_C1, Export_X;
   --# derives Export_X from Import_B1, Import_C1;
   is
      ...
   end B1_C1;

   procedure B2_C2
   --# global Import_B2, Import_C2, Export_X;
   --# derives Export_X from Import_B2, Import_C2;
   is
      ...
   end B2_C2;

begin -- main body of Example_Truth_Table
   if Import_A = A then
      B1_C1;
   else -- Import_A = not_A
      B2_C2;
   end if;
end Example_Truth_Table;
```

With this structure it would be extremely difficult to write incorrect code that passes the Examiner checks and the eight unit test cases.

5.2 SPARK and Automatic Code Generation

All of the preceding discussion is concerned with manually produced code. In considering the possibility of SPARK code being wholly or partly generated by a tool then a number of issues arise.

1. There is an unacceptably high risk of common cause failure if the annotations are generated by the same tool as the Ada (unless the tool is formally proven to be correct) and it is likely that SPARK annotations will continue to be manually produced.

2. Since the annotations must be embedded in the Ada, the annotations will need to be added each time the package is regenerated. If the method for doing this could cause an error then inspection of the output will be required each time it is performed.

An approach that avoids most of the problems of mixing automatically generated Ada and manually written annotations is to use code generation mainly for the individual operations of a package and to define them as separates. All the annotations are in the package specification and body and these will only need to be regenerated when there is a change to the specification of an operation (and it may be acceptable to make such changes manually once the initial version of the package has been generated).

5.3 SPARK 95

The definition of SPARK 95 is given in [10]. Of the major developments in Ada only the hierarchical library structure has been added to this version of SPARK.

There has however been a significant addition to the options for using SPARK - if the requirement for full information flow analysis is dropped then there is no need to produce the 'derives' annotations. By moding the 'global' annotations (as 'in', 'out' or 'in out') full control and data flow analysis is possible along with the checks on subset conformance. This will give a reasonable level of assurance for a moderate amount of effort and makes more options available for mixing levels of analysis within a single system: either by segregating a system into subsystems which have different integrity requirements or by fully annotating only the lower levels of a calling hierarchy.

References

[1] Defence Standard 00-55, The Procurement of Safety Related Software in Defence Equipment, Issue 2

[2] Defence Standard 00-56, Safety Management Requirements for Defence Systems, Issue 2

[3] IEEE SESC Software Safety Planning Group, Action Plan, 15 October 1996

[4] Ricky W Butler and George B Finelli, The Infeasibility of Experimental Quantification of Life-Critical Software Reliability
Proceedings of the ACM SIGSOFT'91 Conference on Software for Critical Systems, December 1991

[5] Bev Littlewood and Lorenzo Strigini, Validation of Ultrahigh Dependability for Software-Based Systems, Communications of the ACM, Volume 36, No 11

[6] SPARK - The SPADE Ada Kernel Edition 3.2, October 1996
available from Praxis Critical Systems

[7] A Study of High Integrity Ada: Language Review,
Study for UK MoD, Document Reference SLS31c/73-1-D, 9 July 1992

[8] A Study of High Integrity Ada: Analysis of Ada Programs,
Study for UK MoD, Document Reference SLS31c/73-2-D, 30 April 1993

[9] Jacques Brygier and Marc Richard-Foy, Certification of Ada Real Time Executives for Safety Critical Applications
Proceedings of Ada-Europe '93, Michel Gauthier (Ed), Springer-Verlag 1993

[10] John Barnes (with Praxis Critical Systems), High Integrity Ada: The SPARK Approach, Addison Wesley Longman 1997

[11] Mark Saaltink and Steve Michell, Ada 95 Trustworthiness Study: Analysis of Ada 95 for Critical Systems
ORA Canada Technical Report, TR-96-5499-03a, January 1997

[12] Bernard Carré, Jon Garnsworth and William Marsh, SPARK - A Safety-Related Ada Subset
Proceedings of the 1992 Ada UK International Conference, October 1992, 'Ada in Transition', WJ Taylor (Ed), IOS Press 1992

Techniques for Testing Ada 95

S. R. Waterman
IPL, Eveleigh House,
Grove Street, Bath, BA1 5LR, UK
simonrw@iplbath.com

10th January 1997

Abstract

The Ada language is widely accepted as the language of choice for the implementation of safety related systems, and as a result much effort has been put into the identification of successful techniques for its testing. In this paper we discuss the impact of the new Ada standard upon the testability of safety related systems, and describe techniques which can be utilised to improve the likelihood of achieving testing success.

Keywords : Ada 95, Testing, Controlled Types, Protected Objects, Hierarchical Libraries

1. Introduction

The Ada language is often chosen for the implementation of safety related systems because it encourages good software engineering practices. Unfortunately, some of these practices make efficient testing difficult. As a consequence many techniques have been developed which, when applied at the design stage, can improve the testability of Ada software. These techniques remain useful when testing Ada 95 due to the similarity between Ada 95 and the previous Ada standard. In this paper we discuss the impact of Ada 95 upon the testability of safety related systems, and describe techniques which can be utilised to improve the likelihood of achieving testing success. In particular we concentrate on unit and small scale integration testing, as these are the areas likely to be affected by use of the new language features. Throughout this paper our aim is to emphasise design for testability as the primary means of achieving testing success.

In this paper we focus our attention upon three new features of the Ada language: Protected Objects, Hierarchical Libraries and Controlled Types. We begin by considering the effect that the hierarchical library has on the testing process and find that it provides the single most significant increase in testability of all Ada 95 language features. We then consider protected objects because we expect them to be one of the first features of Ada 95 to be widely accepted in safety related applications. Finally we consider the significance of using controlled types and discuss the problems that they cause during testing.

2. Testing Techniques

In this section we discuss each of our chosen Ada 95 language features in turn. We begin our discussions with a brief précis of each feature which is intended as a refresher for readers who are already familiar with Ada 95. Those with no Ada 95 experience should supplement this with a good Ada 95 textbook, for example Barnes [5].

2.1 Hierarchical Libraries

There are several drawbacks to the package model of Ada 83, which become apparent when programming large or complex systems. For example it is often desirable to use multiple library packages to model a complex abstraction, either for ease of implementation, or so that different aspects of the user interface can be encapsulated separately. In Ada 83 the only way to achieve this implementation is to put the details of the abstraction into the visible part of a package, thereby breaking the encapsulation. The alternative 'safe' approach results in a single monolithic package which is more difficult to use and to maintain.

A more common problem, which almost all Ada engineers have encountered at some time, is the inability to extend a package without recompiling all of its clients. This results in long and unnecessary periods of recompilation.

In Ada 95 these problems have been solved by the introduction of a hierarchical structure to the package model. In this revised model, child units can be declared which have visibility of the private part of their parent package. The simple example below is based upon that in Barnes [5] and illustrates the typical use of a child unit:

```
package Complex is
    type Complex is private;
    function "+"(X, Y : Complex) return Complex;
    function Real(C : Complex) return Float;
    function Imaginary(C : Complex) return Float;
    ...
private
    ...  -- Private type implementing Complex
end Complex;

package Complex.Polar is
    function R(C : Complex) return Float;
    function Theta(C : Complex) return Float;
    ...
end Complex.Polar;
```

In the example Complex.Polar is a child package of Complex, and as a result the operations R and Theta can be implemented efficiently using knowledge of the internal representation of the Complex type.

As the name implies it is not only packages which can be child units, in fact a child unit can also be a subprogram, generic or generic instantiation.

Using Hierarchical Library Units to Increase Testability

A problem which is present to some degree at all levels of testing is how to gain access to the information hidden inside a package. The traditional way of obtaining this access is to make use of the test point technique as described by Liddiard [4]. In the simplest form of this technique, a procedure, which is known as the test point, is inserted into the package under test. This procedure serves no purpose in the normal implementation of the package and is usually given a null implementation. During testing the null implementation is replaced with test code which consequently has access to the information hidden inside the package. Unfortunately this approach suffers from two drawbacks: it is intrusive, and it is difficult to use in all but the simplest of configurations.

Hierarchical libraries provide the Ada 95 tester with an alternative to the test point approach, as noted by Barbey [7]. Unlike test points the use of a child unit is completely non-intrusive and is extremely flexible. The example below illustrates how a child subprogram can be used to perform an isolation test of one operation of a simple stack abstraction :

```
package Integer_Stack is
    type Stack(Size : Natural) is limited private;
    procedure Push(S : access Stack;
                   E : in Integer);
    function  Pop (S : access Stack) return Integer;
private
    type Stack_Array is array (Natural range <>) of Integer;
    type Stack(Size : Natural) is record
        Depth : Natural := 0;
        Data  : Stack_Array(1 .. Size);
    end record;
end Integer_Stack;

-- Test implemented as a child subprogram
procedure Integer_Stack.Test is
    S : aliased Stack(10);   -- Declare a 10 element stack.
begin
    Push(S'access, 20);      -- Push is under test.
    Check(S.Depth,   1);     -- Checking operations provided by
    Check(S.Data(1), 20);    -- a test harness verify that the
                             -- Push operation was successful.
end Integer_Stack.Test;
```

Under many circumstances child units are a suitable replacement for test points. However, we cannot eliminate test points entirely. Although child units give access to the private part of a package, the content of the package body remains hidden. In situations where there is information in the body that is required during testing we must again rely upon the test point technique.

Careful consideration of the requirements of testing during the design phase makes it possible to minimise the need for test points by simply reorganising the implementation of an abstraction. The simplest technique is to move declarations from the body of a package into the private part of its specification, but this technique should be treated with caution for several reasons:

- Declarations that are promoted to the private part of a package are visible to both test and non-test children alike. This is often considered an advantage because it is difficult to know in advance whether an abstraction will need to be extended in the future, and if so which aspects of the implementation will be needed.
- A compile time dependency is introduced between the implementation of an abstraction and its clients. The independence of implementation and interface is one of the great strengths of the Ada package model and the introduction of new dependencies is something which we try to minimise.
- Many object-oriented mappings, for example [8] and [9], assign special significance to the private part of a package and consequently there may be conflicting constraints upon the placement of some declarations.

The addition of extra compile-time dependencies may be acceptable for a very stable abstraction, but as a general purpose technique this approach is inadequate. Fortunately there is a powerful alternative which provides full visibility to the implementation of an abstraction while actively reducing compile time dependencies. This technique relies upon the use of *private* child units which are discussed below.

While public child units are used to extend the interface of an abstraction, private child units can be used to decompose the implementation of an abstraction without exposing any additional functionality to its clients. To enable this, the visibility of a private child unit differs from that of a public child in two ways. A private child unit is totally private to its parent package. It is only accessible to its siblings, and even then only to their bodies; and the visible part of a private child has access to its parent's private part. The first rule is required to prevent a private child exporting any private information from its parent by, for example, using a rename.

Consider an alternative implementation of the simple stack shown above. In this example the test requires access to the package body data to verify that the Push operation was successful.

```
package Integer_Stack is
    procedure Push(E : in Integer);
    function  Pop return Integer;
end Integer_Stack;

package body Integer_Stack is
    type Stack_Type is array
            (Natural range 1 .. 100) of Integer;
    Stack_Data  : Stack_Type;
    Stack_Depth : Natural := 0;

    procedure Push(E : in Integer) is separate;
    function  Pop return Integer is separate;
end Integer_Stack;
```

One way of gaining visibility of the internals of this stack is to move the hidden data and type declarations into the private part of the package. However if the stack is changed, for example to increase its size, all of its clients must be recompiled. A better solution is to move the declarations into a private child package as shown below. This introduces no extra compilation dependencies yet renders the stack completely open to inspection during testing.

```
private package Integer_Stack.Impl is
    type Stack_Type is array
            (Natural range 1 .. 100) of Integer;
    Stack_Data  : Stack_Type;
    Stack_Depth : Natural;
end Integer_Stack.Impl;

with Integer_Stack.Impl;
package body Integer_Stack is
    procedure Push(E : in Integer) is separate;
    function  Pop return Integer is separate;
end Integer_Stack;
```

In this scenario the test for the stack abstraction is implemented as a public child of Integer_Stack, giving it unrestricted access to the declarations in the specification of the private child:

```
with Integer_Stack.Impl;
use  Integer_Stack.Impl;
procedure Integer_Stack.Test is
begin
    Push(10);
    Check(Stack_Data(1), 10);
    Check(Stack_Depth, 1);
end Integer_Stack.Test;
```

Abstractions that are designed in this way, using a private child package to declare package body data, are not only easier to test but are also more easily extended. Section 4.1.6 of the Ada 95 Style Guide [6] recommends this technique and also goes further, recommending that entire sub-systems are implemented using private child packages.

Besides their usefulness as a replacement for test points, hierarchical library units can also improve the testability of a system in other ways. In particular, there are many operations which are specific to testing that would benefit from increased visibility of an abstraction. A good candidate for this type of operation is a "check" procedure which can be used during testing to verify that an object has a particular value. Increased visibility of the internals of an abstraction allows this procedure to take advantage of the full view of a type to give improved diagnostics when the check fails. The great benefit of using child units to implement these utilities is that they can be made available during testing and removed when no longer needed, without affecting any other packages.

The example below illustrates the use of a child package to provide testing-specific operations for the Complex type. The Is_Valid operation can be used to ascertain that a Complex object satisfies its invariants, and may be implemented using the new Ada 95 Valid attribute.

```
package Complex.Test_Utilities is
    procedure Check(X, Y : in Complex);
    function  Is_Valid(X : Complex) return Boolean;
end Complex.Test_Utilities;
```

Careful consideration must be given before adding testing utilities to a package because they introduce an unwanted dependency between the test and the implementation details of the abstraction. This becomes a problem if the utilities are added on a per-test basis because any change to the representation of the abstraction requires them all to be updated. To avoid this the utilities should be considered part of the design of the abstraction, and a few general purpose operations should be added rather than many test specific ones. As a general rule the dependencies of a test should be a subset of the dependencies of the software under test. This ensures that the test will only need modification when the software under test changes.

The Impact of the Hierarchical Library Upon Testing

We have shown that hierarchical library units are a valuable tool when implementing unit and integration level tests, because they allow us an unrestricted view of the private part of a package. Private child units also provide us with a simple idiom for structuring the body of a package so that declarations that are needed during testing are readily available.

In this section we consider the testing issues that arise when hierarchical library units are used, not for testing per se, but to improve the properties of a design.

As mentioned previously public child units can be used to partition different aspects of an abstraction, or to extend an existing abstraction with new functionality. We expect the latter to become common in Ada 95 due to the increased use of object-oriented techniques and the emphasis that they place upon programming by extension. In both of these cases the techniques that we have described in the previous section are sufficient to gain access to all of the information that is needed during testing. The example below illustrates the typical use of a child package to segregate operations that are only of interest to a limited number of clients:

```
package Message is              -- The core message abstraction
    type Message is private;
    procedure Send_Message(M : in Message);
    ...                         -- Other operations
private
    type Message is ...;
end Message;
package Message.Tracking is -- Operations to track a message
    procedure Find_Message(M : in Message);
    ...                         -- Other operations
private
    ...
end Message.Tracking;
```

There are several ways in which this pair of packages can be tested. The first alternative is to write a combined test for both sets of operations, using a child package of Message.Tracking to gain visibility of both private parts. The obvious problem with this approach is that we lose the independence between the core abstraction and the tracking extensions; although we can use the message abstraction on its own we cannot test it without the tracking extensions. A better approach is to implement a stand-alone test for the core abstraction and then to test the tracking operations separately.

During testing it is important to remember that the operations of a child package have privileged access to the internals of their parent package. As a result it is possible for a child operation to break some of the existing operations of the parent package which were considered adequately tested. This means that an adequate test for the child package, as identified by Harrold [10], must re-test all of the operations of the core abstraction which may have broken. Without careful analysis it is difficult to tell which operations will need to be re-tested in the light of the new package.

Private child units will often be used to structure the implementation of a complex abstraction as a sub-system of packages. For example the Message abstraction shown above may be implemented using a queue of incoming and outgoing messages. The fact that the abstraction is implemented using a queue is of no significance to its clients, and so a private child package is used to hide the details. The private descendants used in implementing a sub-system should be subject to the same tests as other units in the system, and in practice private child units introduce no extra difficulty for the test engineer. The queue package from the Message sub-system is shown below, together with a child subprogram used to test it:

```
private package Message.Queue is
    procedure Push(M : in Message);
    function  Pop return Message;
```

```
   . . .
end Message.Queue;
procedure Message.Queue.Test is
begin
    Push(...);
    Check(...);
end Message.Queue.Test;
```

Note that this child subprogram can be made the main subprogram of the test even though it is a private descendant of the `Message` package.

There is at least one other motivation for the implementation of a design using a set of hierarchical library units and that is to avoid polluting the library name-space. The structure of the Ada 95 predefined library hierarchy is in part motivated by this. The use of hierarchical library units for this purpose does not introduce any new testing considerations.

Recommendations

- Use a public child unit instead of a test point to gain visibility of the internals of an abstraction.

- Declare data and types that are local to the implementation of an abstraction in a private child instead of the package body. This makes the declarations available during testing, and also to extensions.

- At design time use a child package to implement utilities that will be useful during testing, e.g. check functions.

- Perform an integration test of the operations of a child unit with those of its parent. This ensures that the child unit has not abused its privileged visibility and detrimentally affected the operations of its parent.

- Avoid extending an abstraction using a child package when the visibility of a normal client will suffice. This will avoid unnecessary re-testing of the parent abstraction.

2.2   Protected Objects

Protected objects were added to Ada 95 to provide a passive and data oriented means of synchronising access to shared data. These objects can be considered similar to packages or tasks in that they are divided into a distinct specification and body. The specification of the protected object encapsulates the data that is being shared, and defines the interface used to access the data. The body of the protected object provides its implementation.

The interface to a protected object is defined by its protected operations, either procedures, functions or entries, which the language guarantees will have exclusive access to the object's data.

The example below uses the familiar concept of a quantity, or counting semaphore to illustrate the typical use of protected objects. For a detailed discussion of the implementation of semaphores and other building blocks using protected objects see [1].

```
protected Semaphore is
    procedure Signal;     -- V operation
    entry Wait;           -- P operation
    function Available return Boolean;
private
    Number_Allocated : Integer := 0;
```

end Semaphore;

Protected procedures and entries have read and write access to the shared data and consequently require exclusive access to the object. Protected functions have read-only access and therefore more than one function can be active simultaneously.

Testing Protected Objects

The Ada 95 Style Guide [6] recommends that the time spent inside protected operations is kept short so that the protected object is locked for as little time as possible. If this guideline is followed, the amount of code involved in the implementation of the protected object will be small. As a result the overhead of isolation testing each protected operation is unacceptably high, and we therefore recommend that the protected object as a whole is considered for isolation testing. Further motivation for testing at this level is the difficulty of isolating protected operations from each other without changing the protected object. The usual means of obtaining this independence is to use separate compilation, but for reasons of efficiency Ada 95 does not allow protected operations to be declared separate.

A problem encountered when testing protected objects, as with any software that encapsulates state, is that there will often be areas of functionality that are difficult to exercise in a test environment. In order to make this functionality testable it is useful to have access to the shared data inside the protected object so that we can manipulate it directly. This can be realised by adding operations to the object's interface which access each protected data item. This allows the protected object to be conveniently set into any state that is required during testing.

It is interesting to note that neither of the techniques described in section 2.1 can be used to improve the testability of protected objects: the child unit approach is ruled out because protected objects cannot have children; and the test point technique is not practical because of the lack of separate compilation.

The example below shows the semaphore example modified for testing:

```
protected Semaphore is
    -- Normal Interface
    procedure Signal;
    entry Wait;
    function  Available return Boolean;

    -- Testing Interface
    procedure Test_Set_Number(N : in Integer);
    function  Test_Get_Number return Integer;
private
    Number_Allocated : Integer := 0;
end Semaphore;
```

The problem with adding testing operations to the protected object is that there is nothing to distinguish them from the object's normal interface. This distinction is important because the testing interface must not be used by any normal clients of the object. One solution to this problem is to encapsulate the protected object inside the private part of a package. This allows the normal interface to be exported from the package while the testing interface remains hidden inside the private part.

The example below shows the semaphore example modified to add a hidden testing interface:

```
package Semaphore is
    procedure Signal;
    procedure Wait;
    function Available return Boolean;
private
    protected Semaphore is
        -- Normal Interface
        procedure Signal;
        entry Wait;
        function Available return Boolean;

        -- Testing Interface
        procedure Test_Set_Number(N : in Integer);
        function  Test_Get_Number return Integer;
    private
        Number_Allocated : Integer := 0;
    end Semaphore;
end Semaphore;
```

To utilise the testing interface all tests are written inside a child unit of the Semaphore package, from where they have visibility to both the normal and testing interfaces:

```
procedure Semaphore.Test is
begin
    ...
    -- Test code at this point has access to both the testing
    -- and normal object interfaces
    ...
end Semaphore.Test;
```

The disadvantage of this structure is that all children of the Semaphore package have access to the testing operations of the protected object. An alternative encapsulation strategy is to declare the protected object inside the body of a package and use the test point technique [4] to give test code visibility to the testing operations. Testing is performed by replacing the normally null implementation of the test point with test code which can then freely utilise the testing operations.

```
package body Semaphore is
    protected Semaphore is
        -- Normal Interface
        procedure Signal;
        entry Wait;
        function Available return Boolean;

        -- Testing Interface
        procedure Test_Set_Number(N : in Integer);
        function  Test_Get_Number return Integer;
    private
        Number_Allocated : Integer := 0;
    end Semaphore;

    protected body Semaphore is separate;
    procedure Signal is separate;
    procedure Wait is separate;
    function Available return Boolean is separate;
```

```
        -- Testing Interface
        procedure Test_Point is separate;
    end Semaphore;
```

It is important to note that there are circumstances in which a protected entry must be called directly, not via an interface subprogram. A good example of this is a protected entry which is the target of a timed or conditional entry call, or the trigger of an asynchronous transfer of control.

Testing Clients of Protected Objects

Protected objects can have a negative impact on the testability of parts of a system that use them unless care is taken to ensure that they can be sufficiently de-coupled from the rest of the system. When the client of a protected object is subject to isolation testing all calls to the protected operations must be simulated. This would normally be achieved by writing "stubs" for the called operations using a suitable test harness [11]. The efficient use of this technique relies upon the simulated operations being declared separate. As mentioned above, Ada 95 does not allow protected operations to be declared separate, so during testing the protected body as a whole must be simulated.

An attractive alternative is available if the protected object is encapsulated inside a package as described above. In this situation it is the interface subprograms of the package which, when declared separate, are simulated, rather than the protected operations themselves.

Recommendations

- Consider testing protected objects as a whole rather than isolation testing each operation.
- Define testing operations for each protected object, to allow direct manipulation of the object's state.
- If testing operations are added, shield them from the user by defining a testing interface.
- Consider using a testing interface to de-couple the protected object from its clients during isolation testing.
- Alternatively, declare the body of the protected object separate to allow it to be simulated.

2.3   Controlled Types

Regardless of how well an abstraction is designed and implemented, if it is not used correctly then it will not work. Probably the most common misuses of an abstraction are incorrect initialisation and inadequate clean up when it object goes out of scope. The Ada language exacerbates this problem by allowing a scope to be left in many different ways, for example by the propagation of an exception, an abort, a return statement, or an asynchronous transfer of control.

In Ada 95 the designer of an abstraction can ensure that these operations happen correctly under all circumstances by using Controlled Types. A controlled type is created by derivation from one of the predefined types in package Ada.Finalization, and from this type it inherits either two or three of the following subprograms:

- Initialize, which is called to provide default initialisation of a new object;
- Finalize, which is called to clean up an object when it is no longer needed;

- Adjust, which is called during assignment to modify Ada's default bit-wise copy. Note that adjustment is only available for non-limited types.

The default implementation of these subprograms can be overridden by the derived type, and is automatically called by the Ada runtime system when an object of the type is created, deleted or assigned.

The example below, which is taken from the Ada 95 Rationale [3], illustrates the use of a controlled type for the safe management of a resource:

```
package Handle is
    type Handle(Resource : access My_Resource)
            is limited private;
    ...     -- Operations on the Handle abstraction
private
    type Handle is new Ada.Finalization.Limited_Controlled
            with null record;
    procedure Initialize(H : in out Handle);
    procedure Finalize  (H : in out Handle);
end Handle;
package body Handle is
    procedure Initialize(H : in out Handle) is
    begin
        Lock(H.Resource);
    end Initialize;
    procedure Finalize(H : in out Handle) is
    begin
        Unlock(H.Resource);
    end Finalize;
...
end Handle;
```

In this example the creation of a Handle object causes the Initialize procedure to be called, which in turn locks the specified resource. When the object goes out of scope, no matter how the scope is left, the Finalize procedure guarantees that the resource is unlocked.

The Impact of Controlled Types Upon Testing

It is expected that many abstractions will take advantage of the benefits of controlled types to provide a cleaner, more reliable interface. When a controlled type is used for this purpose it is considered an implementation detail of the abstraction and its use is hidden from the abstraction's clients. This is of course advantageous because the abstraction can then be re-written to add or remove the controlled type without changing the remainder of the system. It is unfortunate then that the use of a controlled type often emerges during testing and must be considered part of the abstraction's interface. To understand why this happens consider the way in which the simple abstraction shown below, which is built using the Handle abstraction, might be tested :

```
package Resource_Wrapper is
    type Resource_Wrapper is limited private;
    procedure Operation1(R : in Resource_Wrapper);
    ...
private
    The_Resource : aliased My_Resource;
```

```
type Resource_Wrapper is record
    H : Handle(The_Resource'access);
    ...
end record;
end Resource_Wrapper;
```

Assuming that the isolation testing strategy is used to test this abstraction, all calls to subprograms that are not part of the software under test must be simulated. This causes a problem because the controlled operations are implicitly called during the test whenever a Resource_Wrapper object is created or deleted. Like the other operations the controlled operations can be simulated, but doing so introduces a dependency between the test and the implementation of the abstraction. For example the test for Resource_Wrapper must change if the Handle abstraction is rewritten to avoid the use of controlled types. In practice the problem is made worse if the software under test is implemented using several different abstractions, all of which use controlled types. In this situation the test transitively depends upon the implementation of all of the abstractions.

The simulation of controlled operations and the dependency that this introduces can be avoided by using the operation's real implementation during testing. However, the integrity of the test can only be guaranteed if the controlled operations have already been thoroughly tested. A large part of the system may be involved in the verification of the controlled types, particularly when they have a non-trivial implementation, and many of the benefits of isolation testing are lost.

A solution to this problem is to provide a null implementation of the controlled operations during testing. This enables the test to remain independent of the controlled nature of the abstraction because the offending operations need not be simulated. In addition the implementation of each null operation is trivial and therefore does not need to be tested before it is used. It is important to note that this strategy will only work if the encapsulation provided by an abstraction is complete, in other words the software under test must not directly depend upon the actions of the controlled operations. The elided example below helps illustrate this point :

```
type T is new Ada.Finalization.Controlled with record
    X : Integer;
end record;
procedure Initialize(O : in out T) is
begin
    O.X := 1;  -- During testing this is replaced by null.
end Initialize;
function F return Integer is   -- Software under test.
    Object : T;                -- Null Initialize called.
begin
    return Object.X + 1; -- X has not been initialised.
end F;
```

A controlled abstraction, like any other abstraction, must at some point be tested. During testing the controlled operations are considered part of the software under test and are not simulated. However, the subprograms that are called by the controlled operations are simulated and this may cause difficulties.

The number of calls made to controlled operations will often be large; every time a controlled object is created, deleted or assigned a call is made. This places a significant burden upon the tester who must specify the order of these calls. In some situations it may also be difficult to identify the precise order in which the calls occur. This is due to the implementation permissions granted by the ARM for non-limited controlled types. A good example of the use of such permission is in the elimination of temporary objects during the assignment of controlled types.

In practice these problems only occur when a controlled operation results in a call to a subprogram that is outside the software under test. Fortunately most of the common uses of controlled types will not cause this problem.

Recommendations

- Do not simulate calls to controlled operations during testing; simulating these calls introduces a dependency between the test and the use of the controlled type.
- During testing, provide a null implementation of any controlled operations that are not part of the software under test. These operations can then safely be called as part of the test.
- Be aware that difficulties may arise when testing a controlled abstraction. In particular remember that the implementation permissions granted by the ARM may result in platform specific tests.

3. Summary and Conclusions

In this paper we have presented several techniques that can be used to improve the testability of software written in Ada 95. In particular we have focused our attention upon three new features of the Ada language: the hierarchical library, protected objects, and controlled types. We have shown that the hierarchical library has the greatest impact upon the testing process because it provides a convenient method of accessing the information hidden inside an abstraction. The lack of visibility of this information was a significant obstacle to achieving testability when using Ada 83. We have also shown that the full benefits of the hierarchical library can only be realised if testing is considered at an early stage in the development process.

We followed our discussion of the hierarchical library by considering some of the difficulties encountered when testing software that uses protected objects; the effects of controlled types were also considered. Again, the techniques that we recommend emphasise that early consideration of the testing process is essential if testing is to be both thorough and efficient.

4. References

[1] A. Burns and A. Wellings, "Concurrency in Ada", Cambridge University Press, 1995.

[2] Intermetrics Inc., "Annotated Ada 95 Reference Manual", International Standard ANSI/ISO/IEC-8652(E):1995, January 1995.

[3] Intermetrics Inc., "Ada 95 Rationale", Department of Defense Ada Joint Program Office, 1995.

[4] J. Liddiard, "Achieving Testability when Using Ada Packaging and Data Hiding Methods", Ada User, 14(1), March 1993.

[5] J. Barnes, "Programming in Ada 95", Addison-Wesley Publishers Ltd., 1996.

[6] "Ada 95 Quality and Style: Guidelines for Professional Programmers", Department of Defense Ada Joint Program Office, 1995.

[7] S. Barbey, "Testing Ada 95 Object-Oriented Programs", Springer, Lecture Notes in Computer Science vol. 1031, Marcel Toussaint (Ed.)

[8] S. Barbey, "Ada 95 as Implementation Language for Object-Oriented Designs", Ada Europe News issue 23, April 1996.

[9] J. Jørgensen and R. Ellis, "A Comparison of the Object Oriented Features of Ada 95 and C++", Ada UK.

[10] M. Harrold and J. McGregor, "Incremental Testing of Object-Oriented Class Structures", International Conference on Software Engineering, May 1992, ACM Inc.

[11] I. Gilchrist and J. Liddiard, "A General Purpose Ada Test Harness", Ada User issue 13, 1992.

[12] IPL Technical Paper, "Why Bother to Unit Test ?", IPL Information Processing Limited, August 1996.

Author Index

Lecture Notes in Computer Science

For information about Vols. 1–1169

please contact your bookseller or Springer-Verlag